PRAISE FOR
Surrendering to Motherhood

"Without a doubt, the significant role of a mother has no substitute and is the highest and most notable of positions. These pages follow the author's remarkable journey into motherhood as she travels from doubt and confusion into understanding and acceptance and finds that what is most personal is most general. A profound, moving odyssey!"

—Dr. Stephen R. Covey, author of
The 7 Habits of Highly Successful People

"At the heart of Krasnow's book is the quintessential question all of us struggle with: Am I the best mother I can possibly be? . . . That struggle revolves around the balance between work and family."

—*The Boston Globe*

"As Krasnow sees it, running a household is 'the core element of feminism: power, independence, and freedom.'"

—*Frontlines*

"To be sure, the tug-of-war between parenthood and career is the central angst among Krasnow's generation of women. And in *Surrender*, Krasnow discovers she can't win without letting go of one side of the rope."

—*The Detroit News*

PRAISE FOR
Surrendering to Marriage

"This story is pure oxygen."

—*Newsweek*

"Krasnow shows us that our daily lives are in fact blessed places where we can, if we try, find our true happiness. . . . a bracing book that gives comfort."

—*O, The Oprah Magazine*

"One book, *The Rules for Marriage*, will get a lot of attention. But the other, *Surrendering to Marriage*, is the one to read."

—*Time*

"*Surrendering to Marriage* is contrary to the 'yes, dear' approach touted in the similarly titled *The Surrendered Wife*."

—*U.S. News & World Report*

"Iris Krasnow provides an inside look into a venerable institution. This is valuable because few people openly discuss the personal aspects of their partnership."

—*The Washington Post*

"Reading this book will show how important true bipartisanship is."

—Sam Donaldson, *ABC News*

PRAISE FOR
Surrendering to Yourself

"In *Surrendering to Yourself*, Iris Krasnow says that now is the time to live your dreams, and she teaches us how to listen to our gut instincts and find the true passion of our souls."

—*Parade*

"Krasnow examines several important issues for women—work vs. family responsibilities; relationships with elderly parents; time to oneself; etc. Her writing is appealing; the transitions between the anecdotes from other people and her own experiences are seamless."

—*Publishers Weekly*

"To some people, the word 'surrendering' might mean giving up, relinquishing power, waving the white flag of defeat. To author Iris Krasnow, 'surrender' means just the opposite—'It means surrendering to who you truly are, your most powerful, honest soul-deep self,' she says."

—*The Dallas Morning News*

LINDA MCCARTHY

IRIS KRASNOW is the author of the *New York Times* bestseller *Surrendering to Marriage*, as well as *Surrendering to Motherhood, Surrendering to Yourself*, and *I am My Mother's Daughter*. A longtime journalism professor at American University, she has appeared on numerous national shows, ranging from *Oprah* and *Good Morning America* to *Today* and *All Things Considered*. Iris lives in Maryland with her husband and four sons.

www.iriskrasnow.com

THE
SECRET LIVES
OF WIVES

*Women Share
What It Really Takes
to Stay Married*

Iris Krasnow

GOTHAM BOOKS

GOTHAM BOOKS
Published by Penguin Group (USA) Inc.
375 Hudson Street, New York, New York 10014, U.S.A.

Penguin Group (Canada), 90 Eglinton Avenue East, Suite 700, Toronto,
Ontario M4P 2Y3, Canada (a division of Pearson Penguin Canada Inc.); Penguin Books Ltd,
80 Strand, London WC2R 0RL, England; Penguin Ireland, 25 St Stephen's Green, Dublin 2,
Ireland (a division of Penguin Books Ltd); Penguin Group (Australia), 250
Camberwell Road, Camberwell, Victoria 3124, Australia (a division of Pearson Australia
Group Pty Ltd); Penguin Books India Pvt Ltd, 11 Community Centre, Panchsheel Park, New
Delhi–110 017, India; Penguin Group (NZ), 67 Apollo Drive, Rosedale, Auckland 0632,
New Zealand (a division of Pearson New Zealand Ltd); Penguin Books (South
Africa) (Pty) Ltd, 24 Sturdee Avenue, Rosebank, Johannesburg 2196, South Africa

Penguin Books Ltd, Registered Offices: 80 Strand, London WC2R 0RL, England

Published by Gotham Books, a member of Penguin Group (USA) Inc.

Previously published as a Gotham Books hardcover

First trade paperback printing, October 2012

10 9 8 7 6 5 4 3 2 1

Gotham Books and the skyscraper logo are trademarks of Penguin Group (USA) Inc.

The Library of Congress has cataloged the hardcover edition of this book as follows:
Krasnow, Iris.
The secret lives of wives: women share what it really takes to stay married / Iris Krasnow.
p. cm.
ISBN 978-1-59240-680-7 (hc)   978-1-59240-739-2 (pbk)
1. Wives—Psychology.   2. Married people—Psychology.   3. Marriage.   I. Title.
HQ759.K723 2011
306.872'309051—dc22
2011009403

Printed in the United States of America
Set in Bembo Standard • Designed by BTDNYC

ALWAYS LEARNING   PEARSON

To my husband, Chuck

Smart. Sexy. Reliable. Resilient.

Contents

Prologue

I AM SETTLING INTO my seat on a Southwest flight en route from Cleveland to Baltimore, and as I'm buckling up I notice that Dennis Kucinich is in the row in front of me. The Democratic congressman and 2008 presidential candidate from Ohio, if you can't picture him, is short, in his mid-sixties, and has large ears and an elfin face. It is five minutes from takeoff and just as the flight attendant is about to begin her air-mask spiel, a six-foot latecomer with waist-length red hair and tight jeans comes racing on board, puts one long leg over the armrest, and cozies up so close to Kucinich she is practically sitting on top of him. This is not hyperbole: She is one of the most beautiful women I have ever seen. And she looks like a college student.

She kisses his ear, his cheek, then they start making out. They radiate the heat of teenagers in the backseat of a car. I break the "cell phone off" rule and text my friend Max: "Need NOW. Google Dennis Kucinich and tell me if he's married and if yes, how long." God love Max: In less than a minute, before we start our *whoosh* down the runway, she reports that these incongruous lovebirds are thirty-one years apart and have been married for six years, Elizabeth Harper is his third wife, and he is her first husband. (I then turned my phone off, for any FAA official reading this.) Back in my office, I did some more digging on her official website, on which is posted a thorough article titled "How Kucinich Found Love," by Evelyn Theiss, that ran just after they wed, in the October 30, 2005, edition of Cleveland's *The Plain Dealer*.

I discovered that Harper is an activist from the English village of North Ockendon who grew up in a cottage where Pea Lane meets Dennis Lane. She saw this as a sign that the politician, always the shortest boy in his class, was meant to be with her, always the tallest girl in the class. She met Kucinich when she visited his office on Capitol Hill on behalf of her job with the Chicago-based American Monetary Institute.

Harper said that she knew within "eight minutes" of their first encounter that Kucinich would be her husband, and that she "loves everything" about the man known for championing humanitarian crusades. Having traveled to India at the age of eighteen to work with Mother Teresa's charity, she immediately noticed the bust of Gandhi on Kucinich's shelf, another sign of a soul mate.

A few months later, they were dancing at their wedding reception in the rotunda of Cleveland City Hall. The groom was fifty-eight, and the bride, who has a pierced tongue, was twenty-seven. Elizabeth shoos off naysayers of the May-December match with this explanation to *The Plain Dealer* reporter Theiss: "And it's not like I'm some ditsy young thing and he's an old fogey. He has the wisdom of an ancient and the energy of youth."

Theiss got the first story, fresh off the blush of the nuptials. I would love to interview Elizabeth Harper Kucinich in ten or thirty years, when she has lived with her mate as long as the rest of the women portrayed in *The Secret Lives of Wives*. These are wives who have accrued lots of ancient wisdom about what can feel like ancient marriages. Not many of them would lope down an airplane aisle and start nuzzling and necking with their husbands, oblivious to the crowd, lost in lip-locks.

Let's just say that the majority of my subjects, many of whom have been married longer than Mrs. Kucinich has been alive, have a bit less romantic spring to their steps. Yet, with each passing year, they have more grounding intelligence about matters of the heart.

They have shown me through example that the fleeting intoxication of new love, if we're lucky, leads to something deeper and better—a permanent attachment.

I wish Mr. and Mrs. Kucinich that luck, and most importantly, grit and the ability to surrender in paving the way toward a forever marriage. Voices in this book will help show them the way.

I've only been a wife for twenty-three years, a newcomer compared to the Golden Anniversary girls you are about to meet. But we vintage wives of a certain age know that while steamy moments of intimacy do stoke the fires of marriage—lots of us do still make out with our husbands—it's stamina at the level of soul that makes for a lasting relationship.

I have learned so many valuable lessons and secrets on how to stay married during this two-year research project on love, hate, and carrying on. One thing I know for sure that is personified in the congressman from Ohio and his English fair maiden is that what draws a couple together is a spiritual mystery that only the two of them can understand. Yet what keeps a husband and wife together is not so mysterious.

There are some very basic survival strategies that definitely inflate our odds of staying on this side of the divorce rate that hits about 43 percent of first-time American marriages. Frankly, that's why I wrote this book: I'm a midlife wife facing an empty nest looking for answers on how to accomplish what can feel like the impossible dream: maintaining passion, commitment, and my sanity with one person, in one house, for the rest of my life. The biggest takeaway for me is the importance of sustaining a strong sense of an evolving self apart from the relationship.

I consistently make the point throughout this book that there is no gold standard for marriage, that each couple can write their own rules that match their individual levels of acceptance and intolerance—and that it's really no one else's damn business. In fact, many of my sources opt to remain anonymous, and in those cases, a pseudonym of their choice has been given; there is no surname, and identifying details have been changed. Sources who spoke freely on the record are quoted with their real first and last names.

Whether an identity is shielded or not, the substance of all the oral histories is true to the bone and based on lengthy interviews that took several hours, and in most cases, several days. Any similarities to names or stories of persons portrayed in the oral histories to persons not interviewed are coincidental.

Terry and Pat Attridge epitomize the hard reality of a long marriage apart from the fantasy haze of new romance. Both children of Irish immigrants and raised Catholic in Brooklyn, they have been sweethearts since college and married for fifty-eight years. Pat, a retired school teacher, and Terry, a retired federal magistrate judge, are still standing strong after weathering some of the worst blows any couple should ever endure.

Three months after they got engaged, Pat was drafted to fight in the Korean War. He was deployed in February 1953 and severely injured within four months by mortar fire that tore up half his face, resulting in the loss of sight in his right eye and hearing in his right ear. At a time when a bride should be her most expectant and blissful, Terry was at the bedside of a fiancé with disfiguring wounds, healing from multiple reconstructive surgeries.

"This may sound like a lopsided reaction, but when Pat went to Korea, I was really afraid he was going to get killed," says Terry, eighty-one, a perky woman dressed in a navy jogging suit with turquoise piping. Her eyes are bright blue and her hair is champagne blond. "So even though his injuries were very serious, I wasn't overwhelmed with sorrow because I thought 'he's alive, he's coming home.'" In between treatments at Walter Reed Army Medical Center, Terry and Pat got married.

"I had a lot of loss all at once," Terry adds softly. "I lost my dad and my mother and my brother very close to each other. We lost one of our grandchildren, and I lost a breast to cancer. I am someone who is able to deal with challenges well. Because instead I focus on what we have!"

Terry rises and shows me a large photograph on the entry hall wall of what she calls "Attridge Nation"—their four children, who spawned eleven grandchildren, all of whom have Attridge Nation bumper stickers on their cars.

"I know we've been through a lot but I got off easy compared to what other people have gone through," she says. "Truthfully, you live long enough, bad things eventually happen to us all. I've been able to handle just about everything because I know my husband is there for me, and I am there for him.

"You ride the waves together."

As she walks me to my car, Pat, a vigorous eighty-two-year-old with some facial paralysis, is on his knees planting heather in their garden. Terry holds my hands tightly and tells me that she hopes I stay married as long as she did so I can experience my own "grandmother joys." She witnessed the first marriage of a grandchild in the summer of 2010: "It was the happiest day of my life," Terry says, choking back tears. "Neither of us ever expected to live this long to see this; we were so proud of this dynasty we created. As a couple we have been so fortunate, to have one long life with the same person. I can still look at my old Pat and see the boy from Brooklyn.

"When things got tough I always believed that something good was around the corner. I was brought up to believe in my faith and that marriage was forever, and so I stuck it out. And the reward is that after making it this far I get to be Queen of Attridge Nation!"

I pull up in my driveway, and in the approach to our house I walk by the thirty-two-foot leyland cypress trees my husband and I planted as saplings when our four sons were toddlers. Our children, ages seventeen through twenty-one, now stand six feet to six feet five, and they've lived in the same house with the same parents for nearly their entire lives. As they venture out and start their own tribes I will be the queen waiting for them to come home again, so I can fuss over Anthony Nation, in our old house, in our old marriage, amid the towering trees.

As I write these last words in this book on long marriages,

many regions in our world are rippled with chaos and instability, from earthquakes, tsunamis, or multiple wars. I am grateful that this husband and wife have been able to provide a safe and stable harbor for our children and for each other.

What a relief.

THE
SECRET LIVES
OF WIVES

I

Who Needs Marriage?

"Marriage is the crucial engine of the
American dream."

—BRAD WILCOX, DIRECTOR OF THE
NATIONAL MARRIAGE PROJECT

"WHO NEEDS MARRIAGE?" screams a scary headline in two-inch red letters on the cover of a recent *Time* magazine. I do! And so do most of you. Close to 90 percent of Americans will get married at some point in their lifetimes. Despite a (still high) divorce rate among first marriages that has dipped to 43 percent from the 50 percent figure that held steady from the late 1960s through the late 1990s, the daughters and granddaughters of feminists who fought against male tyranny and archaic institutions like matrimony are still saying "I do" in big dresses in front of big crowds, harboring big dreams of children and lasting love.

I was one of those brides in white silk shantung and a floaty train, surrounded by 180 guests. And at the age of fifty-six, with a twenty-three-year-old marriage and four grown sons, I still love marriage—that is, when I don't loathe it. Marriage is difficult and mysterious and essential.

While surrogacy and sperm donation can produce an instant family without a partner or pomp, joining with another, officially and ceremoniously, remains a much sought after milestone in the human growth cycle. A wedding is one day of magic, a day of ultimate faith.

The wedding industry accounts for more than $40 billion a year, with knockoffs of Kate Middleton's lima bean–size sapphire making up a good chunk of that fortune. We witnessed the ill fate of that gem that once graced Princess Diana's slender hand, and the tattering of her union in the wake of London's 1981 royal wedding. Yet we still set our alarms for 3 A.M. so we could catch the nuptials (fifty times over) of her lookalike son on TV, and drool over another majestic spectacle that showcased the vows between two resplendent young people at Westminster Abbey.

I am hopeful and curious to see in twenty-five years the state of Queen Kate and King William, who entered into marriage as realists in their late twenties with no fairy dust in their eyes. Throughout the course of a three-decade journalism career covering family relationships, during which I wrote the bestseller *Surrendering to Marriage*, I have consistently been aware of a simmering malaise in the lives of many long-married wives. Now I'm one of them, and I hear their laments with a more sympathetic ear. Surrendering, as in yielding to an ideal stronger than your own selfish desires, is still the key to marriage. This book picks up where my first marriage book leaves off, taking aging wives into more abysses that demand surrendering, such as raising teenagers and dealing with sick husbands and an urgent desire to make later life a period of unprecedented growth and adventures.

I went to the wedding last weekend of Elizabeth North from Maryland to Joaquin Cedeno from Costa Rica. During the ceremony, the Unitarian minister John Crestwell thundered to one hundred family and friends assembled, with the rhythmic resonance of Martin Luther King Jr.: "How sweet it is that there is love in this world. How thankful we all are that these two have found each other. How grateful we are to life for giving us these precious moments. May we all be reminded that when we desire bliss, there will sometimes be trouble and despair. May we all be reminded that our greatest sorrows prepare us for our greatest joys. And may all of us be reminded that love endures all. Blessed be this man and this woman. Let it be so. Amen."

Amen, and let it be—we were all praying just that at the ceremony in a boathouse on a river, that this couple will be in the 57 percent who push through the inevitable trouble by the sheer force of their love. I've been to maybe sixty-five weddings in my life, and at each one, I cry a little longer. I know the eggshell-thin line that separates bliss from despair in marriage. I know what it means to say "I love you" at breakfast and mutter "I can't stand you" at dinner.

Yet, each wedding we witness fills us with joy and light, lifting us up from any gloom in our ordinary lives and from the dark global news. And despite the staggering rate of divorce most of us grew up with, marriage in America is more revered, more cherished, and more central to our culture than in most other countries. Despite its shaky recent history, we stubbornly cling to the belief that marriage is a pathway to a better life.

"A good marriage is something that the majority of people value very much," says Millie Bratten, the editor in chief of *Brides* magazine. "Most people want to be committed to somebody who has your back in life, because life is tough. It throws curves at you. The fundamental desire to be connected to someone else who has like values, who can navigate those highs and lows with you, and will grow up and grow old with you remains very strong. What has changed over time is that people now know that a good marriage takes constant work.

"The editorials in *Brides* magazine have evolved to reflect that change," continues Bratten, who has been married twenty-three years. "Now we have more stories on how to have a healthy marriage, how to fight fair, and how to realistically tackle the issues of building a life together. Many couples today have lived through the difficulties of seeing their parents divorce, and they know firsthand that breaking up doesn't necessarily solve every problem, or guarantee that the future will be richer and better. Our readers have seen both sides and they're rooting for a marriage that will last. Our goal is to give them the skills to help make that happen."

Another shift in wedding trends is that those optimists who are still dazzled by the prospect of wedding marches by Pachelbel and the fantasy of eternal love are college-educated, more financially secure, and older than generations past. According to the Condé Nast 2009 American Wedding Study, the average age of a first-time bride today is 27.6 years old, her groom is 29.5, and they are "affluent." Depression-era bride Thelma Post, featured in the last chapter, recalls that her husband, Ted, who became a successful TV and film director, "owned one handkerchief" at the time of their wedding seventy years ago in Brooklyn. Today, according to the Condé Nast survey, the average combined household income of an engaged couple is $80,400—not a bad figure for two kids starting out in their careers.

The results from two groundbreaking longitudinal studies on marriage, one a collaboration between the Pew Research Center and *Time* reported in the magazine's November 29, 2010, cover story, and another by the National Marriage Project at the University of Virginia, share one important conclusion: Highly educated, more successful Americans are increasingly enjoying stable and intact marriages. Simultaneously the middle class and lower-income groups in our country are ditching the idea of matrimony in growing numbers, thus the title "When Marriage Disappears: The Retreat from Marriage in Middle America" given to the extensive National Marriage Project study released in December 2010. Conclusions from this research come from the analysis of data from some forty thousand Americans, married and unmarried, collected over the course of thirty years.

Here is more on the changing face of American marriage from my interview with Brad Wilcox, director of the National Marriage Project. He addresses the steady evolution of lasting marriages as a "passage for the privileged," as out-of-wedlock children, divorce, and family instability are on the rise for the middle class that was once what he calls "the backbone of the American family."

BRAD

Not only does marriage serve the welfare of adults and children in general, but marriage is a crucial engine of the American dream in American life. Marriage is a source of security and stability in our families and in our nation's communities. We see from our research that couples who stay married tend to be more successful. And as they accrue more assets, they provide the foundation for their children to be more likely to graduate from high school, graduate from college, and go out into the world and be gainfully employed.

We also know from our studies that neighborhoods with a high number of married couples are more secure and safe. So although marriage is a private relationship, in reality when marriages are strong, the larger public benefits. We are seeing a shift happening among college-educated Americans in attitudes and behaviors about marriage. The point we make in our report is that middle-class Americans were doing pretty well in terms of staying married, but now divorce has crept up the social ladder into the middle class. So really marriage is becoming the preserve of the well educated and the privileged. Today if you're looking for one group that is able to hold onto the ideal of stable and intact marriage, it's the college-educated crowd.

Most Americans do aspire to happily-ever-after in a relationship. The new twist today is that our culture is increasingly tolerant of exceptions to the marital norm, which include divorce, cohabitation, and having children outside of marriage. Our growing tolerance to those exceptions is in fact a major reason we are seeing fewer and fewer Americans get and stay married outside of educated circles. Still, more than 85 percent of Americans will get married in their lifetimes, and those who get divorced are more than twice as likely to divorce again. The good news is that there is growing recognition among many Americans that divorce poses a real threat to their own social and economic welfare and even more to the welfare of their children.

Most divorces take place in the first eight years of marriage, and most divorces are initiated by women. It's not the seven-year itch; it's eight years. Couples who get past their eighth anniversary are much more likely to make their marriage last. If you could give some advice to these women who are in their late thirties and forties and entering midlife, tell them to be patient. This is when marriage can get hard; they have young children, and the wives often feel that their husbands aren't really emotionally plugged into the marriage. So the wives become disillusioned.

My message to women really of all ages is if they care for their children and families they should find a way to make their marriage work. What we are seeing among couples who stay together through difficult periods is that they will see their marriages become happy again within five years of the trouble. Men become more expressive and mellow out with age. These wives who are initiating divorce for really no good reason other than general dissatisfaction have to realize marriage is not only better for the children, it's better for them.

Who needs marriage? Women do, of this I'm convinced. While many wives now earn fat salaries and buy their own Jaguars and beach houses and pricey anti-aging procedures, no one can buy longevity and peace of mind.

Or can we?

A landmark study out of Brigham Young University conducted by Julianne Holt Lunstad and Timothy Smith analyzed data from 148 previously published longitudinal studies that measure frequency of human interaction and its impact on health. The conclusion of their research made headlines around the world: Being connected to a tight web of family and friends can substantially cut your chances of death by 50 percent on average, by lowering blood pressure and decreasing the risk of heart diseases. (Conversely, poor relationships, such as a bad marriage, have all sorts of negative physical and emotional side effects.)

Smith, the chair of the Department of Counseling Psychology at Brigham Young, told me that while the benefits of friendship in their findings made the splashiest news, the importance of lasting marriages was the real story and was only peripherally covered: "Our research has received substantial media attention, but I have been disappointed that the coverage typically emphasizes the positive value of friendships, with only sporadic mention of marriage or family," Smith started out. "Although friends can be helpful, strong and stable marriages promote most aspects of well-being. Lasting marriage and family relationships contribute more than any other factor to perceptions of social support among adults.

"The social, spiritual, and emotional well-being associated with close marital relationships far outweigh the fact of increased life span," Smith continues. "People typically care more about quality of life than its duration, but it is certainly nice to know that stable marriages indirectly help to maintain physical health.

"Humans are innately social. We are wired for connectivity. People who are involved with others live longer, regardless of their initial age or health status. A strong marriage provides not only consistent and meaningful social interactions for most humans but it also provides a supportive context for living a healthy life."

Indeed, committed spouses inflate the quality and quantity of life spans by simply taking care of each other, pushing one another to diet, exercise, and get regular medical checkups. We also hold our partners accountable for quitting bad habits, such as binge drinking, gambling, and smoking.

There have been numerous scientific studies on the effects of oxytocin, called "the bonding hormone," on a human's impulse to relax, which lowers stress. Oxytocin is released with a gesture as simple as fingers brushed across someone's cheek or an embrace.

According to studies conducted by researchers from the University of North Carolina at Chapel Hill, even hugging twice a day is directly related to lowering blood pressure and the reduction of heart disease. If you live with someone, you are probably touching often and oxytocin is steadily flowing, cutting your risk for other stress-related diseases such as stroke and clinical depression.

That's only the physical side. Marriage is also good for your soul—if you're not living with an ass, that is. Obviously an abusive relationship is unhealthy on all fronts, and it should be severed as quickly as possible. The wives in this book aren't in perfect relationships, but as they settle into what is often derisively called an "old married couple" phase, they report that a lengthy marriage does provide an anchor from which to fly in a multitude of directions that nourish self-esteem and personal growth.

Marriage does not give you a guarantee of happily-ever-after, but it gives you the foundation of family from which to shape a life that is interestingly-ever-after. Besides, it's really great to have someone readily available with whom to have sex, the best relaxer of all.

I am speaking not as a spiritual leader or a psychologist; I'm a veteran wife and journalist who has written about women's most intimate relationships for the past thirty years. And here's the straight truth: After riding the wave of the experimental baby boom, which created free love and open marriage and the divorce epidemic, many of us older marrieds relish this institution that has allowed us to stop climbing and to finally put our feet up and rest at a safe and comfortable plateau.

Dating means you have to Spanx every body part, then still suck in your gut and constantly be on your best behavior. Marriage means that you can become unhinged and soften at the belly, and that someone is there waiting for you when you come home. Just that alone, knowing that there is a mate you can count on in a world of chaos, makes marriage worth it to me. Predictability is the sexiest quality you could ever get in a spouse, and young women take note! The scoundrels who leave you breathlessly waiting or never show up may fill you with fierce longing, but they make lousy partners in the long haul.

One of my funniest friends, Texan Jimmy Krause, who has been married twenty-six years, gives this toast at weddings: "Marriage is like a hot bath. Once you get into it and get used to it, it's not so hot anymore." We all laugh and murmur between us about those ardent studs who stood us up yet we still loved obsessively. But the real secret is that we don't miss the wildness, the loneliness, or the bad boys who didn't love us back. A woman's desire for one partner who is loyal and committed is ancient and nonretractable, no matter how self-sustaining we've become post-feminism.

The wives in this book prove to us in countless ways that you can have an extraordinary life within the framework of an ordinary, even mediocre, marriage. And the embers of familiarity feel better with each passing year, as the frequent brawls that erupted over wailing infants and teenagers who miss their curfews smooth out into seasons of aging that do feel like a warm bath, not too hot and not too cold.

This is a survival guide for those of us at a gear shift in our marriages; we've survived the eight-year mark, and the fifteen-year mark, and are inching toward a twenty-five-year anniversary and beyond. We are resigned to the fact that a husband can be annoying, cloying, even boring. We also know that he is our partner in a sad, happy, and complicated history that took years of work and flinging a dish here or there to achieve.

He gave us children. He gave us the freedom to relax.

Yes, marry the right husband and you get an improved life. It could be argued here that living together without the legal bond could also provide these benefits. But I believe making a commitment allows us to worry less and relax even more, which in turn has a positive impact on biochemistry and emotional equilibrium. I have heard seemingly blissful unmarrieds like Goldie Hawn claim that the absence of an official document is perhaps more romantic because you are making the choice each day to stay together. With four kids and a consuming career, I have enough tough choices to make every day without this toughest of choices lingering in my crowded brain.

I love this aging marriage of mine—that is, when I don't detest it. I'll tell you what I love most; it's the tiniest of things, really. One freezing February morning I stepped out of the shower and there were no towels on the rack. I grabbed Chuck's red bathrobe, which I got him for his fortieth birthday—fifteen years ago. He is six feet two and it covered all of me; the thick polyester fabric that is pilling with time wrapped around me almost twice and fell past my toes. It smelled like his Old Spice aftershave. And it reminded me again that even with our nasty spells, it's always nice to have a man's robe in my bathroom and a husband in my house who scares off the obese raccoons that hover around our bird feeder.

I am here to coax any woman with newlywed panic or midlife malaise, of which I've had both, to hang in there. As Brad Wilcox of the National Marriage Project points out, the trouble comes, and if you're patient, the trouble goes. I know this from rolling with my own rocky phases with husband number one, and from a far-flung sisterhood of resilient older wives, who have much to teach us all. During the last two years, I traveled the country talking to more than two hundred women who have managed to stay married from fifteen to seventy years. They represent all economic brackets and are not all college educated. Their common denominator is that they all want to stay married, and so far they are succeeding. My research is centered around heterosexual relationships and how to fight fairly and lose humbly in the minor skirmishes and full-out wars that arise between the sexes. Knowing when to surrender remains one of my most trusty marriage-saving tricks.

This book is a compilation of our strategies and secrets that will well serve any woman who is hungry for marital commitment and reinvention. Many of my sources are outrageous older wives who like their martinis dirty, travel with their girlfriends, are in touch with college boyfriends, and still hold hands with their husbands.

They are women who have it both ways: a committed marriage and adventures in uncharted territory.

You should be able to find a theme similar to yours in at least one of these stories. My chorus of American wives is a blend of cultures and backgrounds: They are black, white, and a Bengali Muslim in an arranged marriage. They are Orthodox Jews, Catholics, and evangelical Christians. They are country club wives without jobs married to very rich hedge fund managers and wealthy advertising executives married to carpenters. They are attorneys and schoolteachers. They range from age forty through their nineties, an eclectic cast bound by their shared traits of audacity and tenacity. Their stories, racy and real, convince me that the only absolute truth about marriage is that no one knows what's going on in an intimate relationship except the two people in it.

In this book, I part the curtain to show you what *does* go on.

Some sources have endured challenges far more severe than the generic complaints of husbands who snore too loudly or watch too many sports. Shelley recalls the fallout after finding out her best girlfriend had been sleeping with her husband for more than a year. She dumped the girlfriend, and her marriage is better than ever. Marian Garrigan explains how the death of her twenty-six-year-old daughter from a canoe accident in Alaska, an unspeakable loss that statistically destroys couples, fortified her own marriage. There's Marilyn Charwat, a seventy-seven-year-old marriage and sex therapist in Florida who prescribes an orgasm a day for every woman and even suggests her choice for best vibrator: the Silver Bullet.

Karen's athletic and robust hippie husband, Arnold, took care of her for thirty-four years of marriage; now it's her turn as he endures debilitating chemotherapy for a recurrence of lung cancer.

Most of my wives do not have life-and-death dramas to share. They have typical complaints of everyday grating, the sense of yearning for more soulful communication, and mourning the death of romance. They speak of being repulsed by the same old, same old guy. Gretchen, age eighty-nine, says she cringes every morning when she wakes up and looks across her pillow at the "crinkled old man" she's been married to for sixty-five years. "He should have had a face-lift like me," she says. "Would have been much easier on my eyes." Tactics vary from wife to wife, yet there is a unifying core principle to avoiding divorce in *The Secret Lives of Wives*: to create a marriage that operates on many tracks, integrating friendships with both sexes, work we are passionate about, and new experiences and skills that keep us growing at every age.

In 2011, as I write these words, there is no gold standard of what a marriage should be and no perfect marriage toward which to aspire. No one even has to get married in a society that accepts live-in love and poses numerous other options for childbearing, with zygotes and wombs marketed on the Internet. More than five million unmarried couples live together in the United States, nearly eight times as many as in 1970. Those of us who followed the mainstream and went for the big crowd and the big dress are realizing, as we inch toward silver and golden anniversaries, that it is individual ingenuity and not pack mentality that fuels a marriage in the long run.

For some older wives, playing mahjong with the girls may be all the added oomph they need. Others may crave a spot of mischief. Who are we to judge? It's their marriage, not ours. A stolen kiss can go a long way, and a secret is different than a lie. Many women who have managed to stay married have done so because of their secrets, tiny ones and huge ones, theirs alone.

"It is absolutely okay to have a secret life; it's not even a question, if you're not hurting anyone," says therapist Charwat, who is based in Boca Raton, a mecca for adventurous older wives. "We all have secret lives; they don't have to be as dramatic as stealing or sleeping with a neighbor. I can't think of any one person who is self-revelatory about everything.

"How many women are spending money their husbands don't know about? How many people lie about their age and their weight? The whole point of getting dressed up and made up is you are hiding or enhancing the secret parts of yourself you don't want others to see. It's the same with intimate relationships; there are parts you would never reveal to anybody, not even your closest friends.

"But here's the key about relationships; you have to be totally honest with yourself about what is going on, and most people are not. You have to be brave enough to completely reveal all your fears and feelings to yourself so you can thoroughly understand who you are in this relationship. Too many of us are living in false dream worlds in marriage."

My goal is to shatter false dream worlds by airing the voices of real women willing to reveal all. They are adamant that their secrets and separate passions have helped them build lengthy marriages or have helped them endure empty marriages.

You will read about a happily married septuagenarian who goes to lunch with her college boyfriend every couple of months, and they end their date with petting sessions in his 1974 red Mercedes. She is joined on these pages by a Seattle country club wife and her sixty-year-old husband who are "relatively monogamous swingers" with a couple they met at a Hedonism resort fourteen years ago. The four of them make love in the same bed, "an incredible turn-on," says this crisp wife dressed in a pink and green Lilly Pulitzer sundress who could be cast in a movie as the president of the Junior League.

Hers is not a marriage I would want, but again, it's her husband, not mine. Their secret is kept from their friends and their children, but they call their marriage "honest and healthy" because there are no cover-ups about adultery. What is clear from my research is that modern marriage can look dozens of different ways, and this releases all of us to write our own rules. There is no textbook definition that captures this unprecedented era when women in their late eighties constitute the fastest growing segment of the aging population, and marriages are lasting longer than most people used to live.

With this extended forecast, we are going to need all the help we can get, and I am here to share what other vintage wives have done to stay married and stay sane. Often we figure out what we are capable of doing only after we hear what others have done. My goal is to inspire all wives to be authentic and bold, and to have more fun.

The *Time*/Pew Research Center study reinforces past research documenting that the Americans who claim to be the happiest are married men. Of course they are happy—they have multitasking women behind them, the gender that is wired to be everything to everybody. As for their wives, we know that the love of good men certainly adds to happiness, but that's only a piece of what it takes to feel hopeful and worthy, qualities that are essential to avoiding divorce.

Unlike generations past, females are increasingly outearning males in the workforce, so a disgruntled wife can ditch a dismal marriage, uninhibited by financial constraints, or a woman can choose to avoid marriage altogether. Yet matrimony is the trophy the majority of us Americans still aspire to win. Many children of the divorce revolution are callused from the marital splits in their own families and from the abundance of quickie marriages among their pop culture heroes. They know that "to have and to hold forever" is often a delusional fantasy that is over before the last wedding gift is unwrapped. According to the *Time*/Pew poll, 44 percent of Americans under thirty "believe that marriage is headed for extinction." Yet 95 percent of the cynics in that age bracket indicated they still want to get married.

And so it goes. We hate the myth of marriage and we love the myth of marriage, and we will likely keep doing it, even if we never get it right. As a feature writer for United Press International during the 1980s, I got to interview many stalwart widows and wives, from Yoko Ono to Queen Noor of Jordan. I always posed this question: How do you make your marriage go the distance? These were sturdy women who entered the institution of marriage in the harsh limelight created by their husbands' stature, enlarging the difficulty substantially. I figured they'd have hard-earned tips to offer for our generation of baby boomers coming of age with the divorce epidemic. Her Majesty Queen Noor spoke at length about emotional camaraderie, and Yoko was more about spiritual connectiveness.

"John and I had such an intense relationship. When we met, we knew that we knew," Yoko told me three years after John Lennon's death. "By connecting with John I became anchored. And I think the reverse works, too. Now that he's out there, the spirit, by connecting with his root, which is us, he's probably anchored and will live forever with us."

Barbara Bush's response was characteristically terse and practical. When I asked the former First Lady to reveal her formula for marital longevity, she said, "Pick the right husband in the first place"—and she left it at that. At the time I was a bride of not quite two years and hungry for advice from this white-haired grandmother who had quit Smith College at the age of nineteen to marry a skinny boyfriend named George. After hearing her appraisal, I thought, *Great. I've got an easy road ahead. I picked the right guy!*

Four children and twenty-three years later, I know it takes far more than a wise initial choice. You can pick the right guy and still feel like you are in the wrong life. If Mrs. Bush and I were close friends, I am sure we would have excavated a few more layers of truth about extended matrimony and the grind of going the distance with one mate in one house, until one of you dies. I would ask her how she kept her head high and her family strong amid rumors of her husband's infidelity. I would ask her how the hell she didn't pitch a frying pan at him when she was doing all the childcare and he was never home. (Perhaps she did.)

Here's what older wives who know each other well are talking about: In order to keep the promise "'til death do us part" without killing someone first, a woman must have work and hobbies she loves, extramarital adventures, and a wine cellar.

I'm not talking about opening up your marriage. I'm talking about opening up your whole life. Heed these hard-earned lessons from wives like me who may bitch about our husbands but are determined to stay on this side of the fence, working it out in relationships that are lasting longer than ever. With modern vigilance about fitness and diet, and dramatic medical inroads, growing numbers of women who dodge cancer, stroke, and heart disease can expect to celebrate ninetieth birthdays and golden anniversaries. With that seemingly endless marathon in mind, *The Secret Lives of Wives* will serve as a much-needed window into how other mature wives are managing to reach the finish line.

As a younger journalist, I did a feature article on women turning fifty with gusto and bravado for *The Washington Post*. One woman said the following, and it is the battle cry of this book, for all of us graying wives with teenage hearts: "My kids are leaving home, and I need more than just marriage and my job. I want passion, change, surprises. I want more fun."

When I started my first marriage book, I was in my early forties and our children were small. I am now in my mid-fifties and tethered to my original husband. It is shocking and satisfying. I have made it this far because I keep taking my own advice from *Surrendering to Marriage*, and that is: I don't expect my husband to make me happy; I know I must do that for myself. I have passion, change, surprises, and lots of fun on my own, and so do the dozens of other gutsy wives who serve up their secrets in the pages to come.

Hanging onto the soul of self while navigating a long marriage is crucial. I know this as much as any other woman in transition. As an empty nest looms in two short years, it's time to figure out the next step: I am the mother of four males, one age twenty-one, one nineteen, and seventeen-year-old twins. They are young men with stubble, not silky-faced toddlers, strapping sons who quickly wipe off my lipstick kisses and have girlfriends who leave their own lips red. Without the cushion of our four children between us, how do I make my own marriage survive with one thin husband in a large and empty house?

The choice to stay married is fortified by some of the divorcées I interviewed who told me, "If I knew then what I know now, I'd still be with my ex-husband."

Nora Ephron teaches us all that divorce is hardly a clean get-away. In her new book, *I Remember Nothing,* Ephron describes the pain of sharing children with a man (journalist Carl Bernstein) she is no longer married to: "I have been married to my third husband for more than 20 years now. But when you've had children with someone you're divorced from, divorce defines everything: It's the lurking fact, a slice of anger in the pie of your brain."

I came of age during the Me Decade that blew apart the staid 1950s model of marriage. Free love and women's liberation made it socially acceptable to have sex with whomever, whenever. My generation watched the eight-year-itch turn into a two-year or two-month itch, as friends disposed of marriages as if they were tossing out baby wipes. I find myself now more inspired by my mother and women of her generation who vowed "I do, and I will" and really meant what they said. They treasured their marriages as if they were sacred antiques, staying on board through the worst of times because the D-word was still an embarrassing taboo and they took the word *commitment* at its face value, as a promise.

We all have something to learn from those fifties housewives who pushed through the rage of being treated as second-class citizens, smart women who were banned from careers like law and medicine because that was a "man's work." So they vacuumed and they cooked and they herded screaming children, waiting for their men to return from their big, important jobs.

Obviously we don't want subordination, but we should be bolstered by the stamina of our ancestors who made their marriages work until death split them up. They were admirable matriarchs who ran households but could have run countries, yet they stuck it out through boredom and desperation, just like they said they would do on their wedding days. Hardened by the Depression, they knew life was painful and required patience and perseverance, and that you couldn't bolt whenever you felt discontent or you'd forever be on the run.

We all know people who keep marrying again and again, seeking to find the happiness that always seems to be eluding them.

At some point they realize their source of unhappiness is themselves.

When you're always searching, you're never finding.

Feminist pioneer Germaine Greer compared marriage to being in shackles in jail, a belief that was shared by my 1970s college crowd. Her book *The Female Eunuch* helped articulate the gripes that ignited the women's liberation movement of the sixties. One illustrious quote from this feminist bible sneeringly likens love to being "in pain, in shock, in trouble." In contrast, I have come to realize that marriage, if it runs on multiple tracks, actually gives a woman the freedom to become whoever she wants to be. To accomplish this goal of being married and liberated, you need the following: guts, grown children, work you are passionate about, girlfriends who like to travel, your old boyfriend's e-mail, and a confident, flexible husband. *The Secret Lives of Wives* reflects this spirit of release and reinvention, born out of an urgency to create a blueprint not only for myself but for all women who are asking the same questions about how to sail through the stormy seasons of marriage and come out alive.

The first secret is to work on yourself. I know this firsthand, because at the dawn of my own marriage, with four kids in Huggies, I nearly jumped the fence in search of greener grass.

II
Then and Now

"Even in your fifties and sixties you can still be
duking it out, and there is probably some degree of
duking it out until the day you die."
—FLORENCE WIEDEMANN

I T IS FEBRUARY 1994, and I am in my living room cluttered
with three high chairs, two baby walkers, and a hanging baby
swing. I am wearing a gray bathrobe streaked like a Jackson
Pollock canvas with poop, milk, and smashed organic peas. At the
age of thirty-nine, I have everything I ever wanted, more than I
ever dreamed possible—too much, actually.

I am married to a chiseled architect named Charles Edward
Anthony III. I call him Chuckles. We have four children. We own
a beautiful shingled house that Chuck designed and built most of
with his hands. I have ascended in my journalism career. I am the
woman who has it all. On this cold morning at 7:23 A.M., all of it
is pulverizing me, leaving my emotions splayed like the crusty
pieces of fried egg still stuck on my husband's plate.

I made my husband's breakfast, and I will clean up after him.
He just finished drinking a cup of coffee I prepared and reading
The Washington Post that I fetched. At breakfast a few weeks ago, I
hurled one of those crusty plates at Chuck while he sat dining, like
a placid prince, lost in news he considers monumental—a write-up
of the Redskins' loss. The flowered pottery plate from Santa Fe

that he never liked missed his beard by two inches and nicked his Neo-Colonial armoire that I never liked.

The plate survived, without even a chip.

At this incomparable moment in my female growth cycle, I am a wife of five years and the mother of four sons: Theo, age three, Isaac, age two, and six-month-old twins, Jack and Zane. Once sharp and taut, my mind and body are doughy. I recently left my job as a reporter at United Press International to stay home with this squirmy puppy pack, three of whom are still in diapers and breastfeeding.

My career meant lots of travel and interviews with cool people, including Annie Leibovitz, Ginger Rogers, Billy Graham, Ted Kennedy, Elie Wiesel, and Mr. Rogers. I wore silk shirts and tight jeans and alligator cowboy boots. In those adrenaline-laced years spent in the heat of daily journalism, when people asked me "How are you?" I used to retort with this smug one-liner: "I am hot, happening, and alive!"

On this dark morning in an excrement-streaked robe, I am dull and fat. I am wincing at the incandescent memory of sitting with Queen Noor in her parlor at her palace in Amman. We sipped orange juice from silver goblets and nibbled on sugar-dusted almonds, talking about everything from the best boutiques in London to her disdain for Yasser Arafat, who was meeting in the next room with her husband, His Majesty King Hussein.

I am now sprawled on a filthy brown carpet surrounded by boys shrieking along to Raffi's "I want to eat, eat, eat apples and bananas . . ." Their diapers look like water balloons. Some of the white foam filling is dripping down Jack's and Zane's legs. My flannel nightgown is unbuttoned, and most of one breast is exposed. My darling husband, cleanly shaven, spruced up in a crisp pink shirt and a bolo tie and a leather bomber jacket is coming toward me whistling. He is whistling! I am hormonal and crazed and he is whistling a happy tune.

He heads for the door, eager to escape to his clean, child-free Dupont Circle office, then glances over his shoulder at the crumpled housewife he courted when she was hot, happening, and alive. "Bye honey, I'll be home at six. Oh . . ." He pats his chest, smirks, and adds in a whisper, "Button up. Your boob is showing."

Oh *really?* My boob is showing? You jerk. What if I told you while you are whistling in your pristine architect's office three miles away that my breast is usually exposed because I am breast-feeding three of your four children most of every day. Oh, and by the way, I only have two boobs, not three, so it's busy, busy time for Mommy while Daddy is away at his important work.

"I despise my husband! I despise my husband!" This sentiment became a pounding mantra as I flashed back again to Iris without a husband and with pluck.

With Chuck out the door I reached for a new item I had just ordered from an infant product catalog. In that parcel from Texas was something advertised as a "hands-free twins breast-feeding pillow." The picture in the catalog showed a radiant, relaxed mom waving with both hands as two serene infants rested on a ruffly gingham pillow belted to her chest. Discombobulated by my own three guzzlers, who fed one at a time and required two hands, I just had to have my own hands-free mother's little helper. Now what to do with that free hand?

I strapped on the pillow, secured the twins to my chest, supported them with one hand, and with the other started to vacuum. Radiant and relaxed for about forty-seven seconds, I suddenly caught an image of myself in the mirror—and then started to bawl.

Who was this lunatic walking around with two babies and a Hoover? At that moment of new motherhood and new marriage, I was struck with this epiphany: "I'm leaving Chuck. I'm doing everything around the house. Who needs him? I'm getting a divorce!"

Maniacally elated with fresh purpose and direction, I buttoned up, threw a coat on over my bathrobe, buckled the boys in four car seats, started up our 1994 teal blue Suburban, stuck Raffi in the tape deck, and circled the block three times so they would all fall asleep.

Hands shaking, I prepared myself to tell my mother that I wanted out of my marriage. My mom was always the first person to hear my news, good or bad. This urgent dispatch was not easy to share. No one in my close family had ever gotten divorced. Not that my relatives were all happily married—they were just still married. As Raffi droned, "I want to eat, eat, eat" and tiny heads lolled into morning naps, I reached for my mobile phone, which in the early 1990s was a foot-high contraption screwed to the front seat console. My Polish-born mother, whose accent got thicker as she aged, answered my "Hi, Mom" greeting like she always did: "Helllo dahling, how ahhhrrr you?" I breathed in, and quickly answered, "Mom, I've got bad news."

"What's wrong? Ahrrr you seeek?"

"No Mom, I'm not sick. I'm just not happy. I'm leaving Chuck," I told her, starting to whimper.

Without a gasp or a pause, she replied, "Achhhh, don't vorry dahling. I don't give a damn. I never liked him anyways."

Well, I never did leave Chuck, and my mom backpedaled over the years, saying she really did love him all along; she just didn't think he was "loud enough" for me. She was right. Yet, since that whacked-out hormonal meltdown caught between two selves—the svelte correspondent in silk and the slovenly mom in a dirty bathrobe—I've not again been seriously on the brink of divorce. I am like many aging wives, content for two days, sulking four days, frequently perched on the flimsy line that separates love from hate from a fistfight.

As I've chronicled family relationships over the years, I have learned from other young mothers that marriage wars in the early years generally stem from physical exhaustion. Most eruptions in an old marriage spring from emotional exhaustion. I remember when I was a child and I would stop playing with a friend for a while. My mom would ask, "What happened to Kathy?" I'd shrug and say plainly, "I'm sick of her." Well, we get sick of each other as grown-ups, too.

Chuck grimaces like he's been stabbed if I spear food off his plate. Lots of couples eat off each other's plates, I tell him. He says, "Go marry someone else." I tell him, "I wish I could." He tells me, "Go. Your next husband will do something worse." I tell him that not sharing his food reminds me that he is also stingy about sharing other parts of himself, that while I spout vein-throbbing paragraphs about my day, he responds with a few words, in a monotone, without looking up from the TV.

With that, he suddenly looks up from ESPN, spears a chunk of barbequed chicken off his plate, and dangles it in front of my lips. "See, I'm *sharing* myself," he says, flashing his little boy grin that unfailingly melts my heart. And so it goes in a long marriage: The squabbles never change; the chafing and laughter goes round and round. The urges to flee are smothered by layers of history, making an exit nearly impossible.

Sixteen years after I told my mom I was leaving Chuck, I soldier on because of the sweet and unexpected sentiments, at odd moments, of gratitude and of lust. I am grateful that Chuck is still here, that I am still here, that despite habits and quirks that are like fingernails on a chalkboard there remains a soul-deep commitment. The scrambled hausfrau that was me in the mid-1990s seems like a stranger who lived a century ago. The noise of boys is waning. Who will I be when I'm not Mommy anymore? I know that I can't be just a wife.

I am in love with my imperfect husband. He is reliable and craggy and kind. He gave me four perfect sons, with his long legs and my wide-set eyes and my father's twisted sense of humor. I intend to stay married. Marriage is at my center, yet marriage is amorphous, not enough to fuel me and fill me. Thankfully, I have wise older mentors.

I am sitting in my kitchen with my neighbor, Gail, who just celebrated her forty-third wedding anniversary. We are drinking J. Lohr cabernet, my house brand. On this day that the news broke about the split between Al and Tipper Gore, we are discussing what every wife with some decades of marriage under her belt is talking about: How did *this* happen? Is *this* the next boomer trend?

You marry, have children, those children have children, then you get the hell out of there and have your own fun. Why now? Was Tipper in love? Was Al in love? Was Al intolerably inflated with the notion that he was the savior of the entire planet? Was Tipper withering in that shadow? Is one of them gay?

I'm feeling a twinge of envy at the vision of the Gores, two people who get to re-create themselves at midlife and become different people for the next twenty-five years or so. Healthy, attractive, and rich, they will have their pick of new relationships that offer, at least early on, nothing but promise. They are released from the shackles of shared baggage and liberated from what to them must have felt like leaden layers of time. I know the weight of that lead suitcase and the blackness of sparring. I know that the light of reconciliation can take days or years to break through.

"I'm a little jealous," I admit to Gail. "Tipper gets a fresh start."

"Don't be," says Gail, who has been a wife twenty years longer than I have. "New men become old men. Best to just stick with the first one. You can still reinvent yourself within a marriage, more so when the kids leave home. Wait it out."

Gail is married to an oncologist who is often on call, and their two children are adults. With that freedom she has been able to spend her summers in Italy, studying art and painting and generating her own income. (Her story is fleshed out in the next chapter on the benefits of separate summers.) At seventy, Gail is lithe from yoga five times a week, and she displays her art in galleries around the world. While she has had only one husband, she has managed to flex many sides of her spirit and her potential.

We women of a certain age know that sustained contentment must spring from our own self-exploration and a plethora of friendships, not solely from our husbands. We are the generation that had defiant feminist guides and gurus showing us the way. This passage in the 1973 edition of *Our Bodies, Ourselves,* a handbook of my college sisterhood, was the first indication that our marriages could be anything we wanted them to be: "A woman is always expected to put this relationship (marriage) before everyone and everything else in her life. We want to open the definition of marriage and we want to explore intimate relationships in addition to marriage, intimate relationships instead of marriage and intimate relationships with ourselves."

This relationship with ourselves grows more important with each passing year.

Mary, age fifty-three, is a travel agent who is married to the owner of a national chain of retail stores. While her husband is enmeshed in a business made volatile by the recession, Mary is rarely hand-wringing at home. She is in places like Morocco and Norway, researching affordable hotels and tours for her clientele, who are mostly what she calls "middle-income, middle-aged women on girlfriend getaways." She recently sent me a text message that read: "I'm on a horseback ride in Agadir with a 32-year-old innkeeper. Glad you are not here."

Mary is seated in her Philadelphia kitchen. The late afternoon sun highlights her high cheekbones and her spiky gray hair. She wears a silver hamsa, the hand of peace from the Middle East, around her long neck and a black skirt threaded with squiggles of turquoise silk from Mumbai. Her three children are long out of the house, and her husband is in Hong Kong on a shopping trip for his stores. She will meet him in Hong Kong for a few days, then go off solo to Switzerland to research ski resorts. Reared in a middle-class family, Mary's schoolteacher mother instilled in her daughter that "a woman should always make her own money and not depend on a man." Mary further describes how separate journeys enhance self-fulfillment and marital balance.

"My international life in the travel trade is on parallel tracks with my husband's international life, but most of the time we definitely aren't taking the same ride," she begins. "We are close enough to see what the other person is up to, and I know his train is moving alongside mine. But if my track would merge over to his, then I become a passenger on his train, and I would be hanging on to him for the ride.

"I've been his passenger in the early years of our marriage.

When I'm hanging on to a man who owns a big business and is obsessed by that world, it feels like I'm hanging on for dear life. When I get back on my own rail, I'm my own person, hanging on to me. I love this man, but I don't need this man for survival, and that's very reaffirming for me."

Mary's self-worth and momentum come from within, excellent qualities for marital survival. She knows what her husband can deliver and doesn't expect anything else. I, too, know what to expect of my husband and what to expect from myself. Lowered expectations in marriage can definitely lead to long-term marital happiness. I wouldn't have raved about multi-tracked marriage as a newlywed or even on our fifteenth anniversary. With gray hair and a diminishing nest, I am less fearful of anyone else judging what goes on behind my closed doors. I take ownership of this simple truth: Having lots of experiences and lots of relationships is holding my one marriage together.

I know the miracle cure of spending summers apart, something my husband and I have done for the past eight years. As the lone female in a house of five men and two male cats, I know the salvation of exuberant girlfriends who will never refuse a glass of wine, and who never fail to empathize with my whines. I know that you can't change a husband; you can only change yourself. The research concludes—and I, too, have found—that contentment and acceptance of marital imperfections do rest just on the other side of the first eight years. Those early years for us often aped the 1974 rematch between Joe Frazier and Muhammad Ali at Madison Square Garden. My advice to you if you want to stay married is to surround yourself with people like Gail, wives who have been at it longer, who have toughed it out, and who are actually more at peace now than they've ever been.

Another of my hero-wives is Jungian psychologist Florence Wiedemann, who has been married for sixty-four years. This statuesque octogenarian who wears flowing Japanese tunics and has a Buddhist sensibility has been the go-to relationship guru for the past forty years in her hometown of Dallas. My old friend and guide whom everyone calls Flo describes a tranquility we can all look forward to if we play our own marriages right.

FLO

The stages of a marriage go something like this: The wedding brings on crazy and delusional joy. Then come the babies and years and years of fighting for equanimity. In your forties, that can be the hardest part of a marriage— that certainly was true for us. I wanted to be right, and I wanted to win. Then in the later years, you are calm because you both have achieved equality and you each know your own power.

Even in your fifties and sixties you can still be duk-ing it out, and there is probably some degree of duking it out until the day you die. But at my age, you have got-ten to a place where you really love your partner again. Because after a long life together, you cherish the history you have created. You know how to resolve conflict. You have let go of feelings of hurt and betrayal. In the last lap of a marriage, you are really getting close to being merged and whole as one. If you make it as long as we have, you end up lovingly and joyfully joined. It takes a lifetime to get to this wonderful place. We have three grown sons and nine grandchildren, and we have lived in the same house for sixty years.

Fred and I may have a fight every three months but it lasts about three minutes. In a good marriage you have to learn how to fight well and honestly and briefly. After sixty-four years together, we are very aware of how much we love each other and how much we are going to miss each other. He's had cancer; I walk with a cane. The Buddhists say you have to think about your own death every single day. It makes you more humble to know this day is all there is, so be joyful and grateful, and enjoy it. We really have a lot of wisdom now, about ourselves and about each other. The happy golden years are real for us now.

We are not climbing to get anywhere; we are here, in this very peaceful time we fought hard to achieve. Over time in a marriage, your two circles that have been totally separate will start to overlap. You get to this wonderful place at the end of a marriage where you are like rocks in a rushing river that have been banged up against each other so many times that you are now smooth and soft around the edges, as you rest side by side.

I lived in Dallas during the 1980s, working as the fashion writer for the now defunct *Dallas Times Herald*. Whenever a problem arose in the tumultuous romantic lives of my band of journalists, all in our early twenties, we'd say to each other, "Go with the Flo." Her psychotherapy practice was filled with the lovelorn from our newspaper. Three decades later, I still call Flo with questions about the nature of long love, and, as usual, she is right.

Flo is exemplary of what research on long marriages suggests: Older couples who maintain good communication skills experience less discord and greater marital satisfaction than do younger couples. They have learned how to defuse their conflicts quickly, partially because they are worn with age, like stones in the river, and also because they are deeply appreciative of this moment and the limited time they have left.

Despite the yo-yo of emotions that comes with marriage, I am more settled in my role as wife than I've ever been. With older children and a self-sufficient spouse, I am able to resurrect passions and dreams that were overshadowed by parental responsibility. Marital bliss *is* possible, if each partner is blissful apart from the other.

Husbands die, children leave home, people we love get cancer. As the gender with extended life expectancy, wives usually end up alone. To survive the inevitable seasons of loss, mature women need immense soul power and strength, so that when our worlds fall apart we have the rock of ourselves to fall back onto. When I interviewed a seventy-eight-year-old woman in San Francisco who has been married for fifty-five years to a man with chronic heart disease, she told me: "I will feel like half a person when my husband dies." No wife should feel like half a self when her marriage ends. That said, we should fully cherish what we have while we have it, even when he pisses us off.

Today at breakfast, I study my husband at the kitchen table, drinking coffee I made and reading *The Washington Post* that I fetched. (Some things never change.) I am telling Chuck, with elaborate hand gestures, that my baby fig tree is dying, expecting some advice on where to move it, or even an "I'm sorry, honey." But he is not looking up from the hockey scores.

Granted, this is not a topic of cataclysmic proportion. I'm not asking him to opine on whether U.S. troops should stay in Afghanistan. But I am *trying* to engage my husband. I try all the time. I am tired of trying. I am sick of this, sick of him. He is nodding and not looking at me and obviously not listening as he says, "I don't know, what do you think?"

What do I think? I think I'll call Todd, my verbose and gorgeous gay hairdresser, a man who knows that giving a woman your full-on attention is way to keep her coming back for more.

Years ago, in our four-under-five parenthood phase, my frustration during these detached breakfast scenarios would amp into rage. I would scream and stomp and perhaps throw a little something for theatrics. As a vintage wife of twenty-three years, I am softer and less reactive; the storm passes quickly these days. The swift change of winds can come from the most subtle of gestures or glances. This morning, after thinking Chuck is an ass for thirty-two seconds, I look at the wrinkles around his blue-green eyes and the sprigs of gray in his curly hair, the length of his legs in worn blue jeans, and I want to have sex, right now. We are a quarter of a century older than the day we met, but damn, he still looks good to me. We made this home together; I am home when we are

together. Our sons are the perfect composite of our imperfect relationship.

I fear and I hope we are like Flo and Fred, attached for life.

So there's the rub. As hellish and horrific as long marriages
can become, if the urge to jump your partner still jolts you into
conjugal action once a week, once a month, or, as some wives
reveal, even once every six months—you have a solid chance of
staying with husband number one. In fact, most men and women
who are still married to their first partners at the age of forty-five
will likely be married to them until one of them dies. The prospect
of forever can send many a midlife wife imagining thirty or forty
more years of *him* into a panic attack.

Are you tempted to bolt *now*, after only a decade or two of
marital un-bliss? Do you have fantasies of replacing your older,
aloof model for a poetic and chatty younger boyfriend? What
would it take to bring you to your breaking point? I am sure there
is a valuable lesson for all of us if we knew what really happened in
Tipper and Al's marriage—but alas, no one will ever know, and
perhaps by the time you're reading this they will have found their
way back together.

I ask Chuck if he thinks we'll leave each other after forty
years, bracing myself for him to spill some pent-up angst. But the
only spilling he wants to focus on at this moment is Wolf Blitzer
projecting the economic impact of the BP oil deluge on the Gulf
states. Eyes affixed on Wolf, Chuck responds: "Haven't we already
been married for forty years?"

Indeed, it seems like four hundred years.

Amidst the glut of op-ed pieces and gossip column snippets
speculating on why the Gores, and *not* the Clintons, were the
political marriage that combusted, Deirdre Bair's piece in *The New
York Times* titled "The 40-Year Itch" was the controversial stand-
out. Bair, author of the book *Calling It Quits: Late-Life Divorce and
Starting Over*, wrote in the *Times* essay that appeared June 3, 2010:
"For my book, I interviewed 126 men and 184 women who

divorced after being married 20 to 60-plus years. And what surprised me most was the courage they showed as they left the supposed security of marriage. To them, divorce meant not failure and shame, but opportunity. . . . No matter how comfortably situated they are, how lovely their home and successful their children, they divorce because they cannot go on living in the same old rut with the same old person.

"Men and women I interviewed insisted they did not divorce foolishly or impulsively," Bair added. "Most of them mentioned 'freedom.'"

Letters to the editor arrived in a deluge and for the most part voiced outrage. How dare Bair condone the demise of four decades of marriage as an "opportunity"? How dare she champion the selfish notion of "freedom"? What about keeping your *commitment* to remain a couple, a vow made before family and God? Readers also scolded Bair for failing to mention that divorce is debilitating for families.

"Bair is wrong," wrote a man from Dayton, Ohio. "Divorce is a failure. It makes people feel disposable. It is no fun for kids or grandkids."

I wonder if this man, who has obviously been bruised by the collapse of a marriage, has to now alternate attendance at family dinners with his ex, so that a grandma and grandpa who can't stand each other don't have to confront each other's new lovers.

Genette, age sixty-three, is on a self-imposed every-other-year schedule with her own grandchildren's birthdays. She refuses to meet her urologist ex-husband's new wife, whom he married eight years ago. Wife number two was his patient; she is half his age, and their affair went on for the last five years of Genette's thirty-five-year marriage. Would *you* want to hang out with this woman?

I took Genette out for dinner recently, and no one, man or woman, should ever have to feel her raw pain. At the age of fifty-eight, she was blindsided when what she thought was "a good marriage, not great, but stable," imploded.

GENETTE

It came out of nowhere. Suddenly we are going along in a steady marriage and I find out he's been having an affair with this young woman for many years. I did everything I could to keep the marriage together because that's how I was brought up, as a devout Christian. My parents were married for more than fifty years, and that was the example of a marriage I believed we would have. Sure there was trouble at times, raising three kids close in age, but my belief was you don't bail; you kept working it through.

I had a plan for my life, and it was to be a wife and a mother and a grandmother. And all of a sudden I was alone. I had never been alone in my life; I went straight from college into my marriage. It was horrible, crushing, absolutely devastating when my husband moved out of the home where we raised our children. It was like my life had been completely ripped apart. For almost a year I couldn't sleep in my bed, the bed where we had slept together as husband and wife for thirty-five years. I slept on the couch. I dreaded going home after work because each time I walked into that front door the emptiness hit me like a ton of bricks. For the longest time I felt like my life was over. You are not supposed to be starting menopause and losing the foundation of your family life at the same time. In my extended family, you grow old together.

After a lot of sadness, my life is full and joyful now; my kids don't leave me alone, and I've got five grandchildren who often have Grandma as a babysitter. My kids are still really mad at their father for doing this to us, still, after eight years. So I am the one who gets to spend most holidays with the family. But we will never be able to be a whole family again, celebrating birthdays and Christmas together. Something seems like it is always missing from our dinner table. We could have made it; it's not like the marriage was abusive or awful. I believed he was my partner for life, and I would have done anything to work things out.

Genette's tears about the splintering of family traditions doused any trace of jealousy I initially felt over the Gores' potential for rebirth and blank slates and new sex. They, too, will take turns missing family gatherings unless they have the most amicable divorce on record.

Deirdre Bair is right in her assessment that divorcing after a long marriage requires courage: courage to be alone, courage to figure out money matters, courage to co-parent with someone you loathe, courage to strip naked with someone new.

That last one requires unflinching bravery. I can't imagine unveiling a soft belly that has housed four pregnancies to a new partner who had nothing to do with destroying my once flat abs. When my husband asks me if my dress has shrunk, at least I can blame my maturing body on the incubation of his beloved children. I gained seventy pounds with the twins and lost all but sixty of it in seventeen years. Any barbs over my evolving physique—he weighs *less* than he did on our wedding day, damn him—end abruptly when we look at our sons and reminisce about the scenes at the hospital when they first arrived. During those huffy episodes when I'm wishing that Chuck would become the first architect to spend six months in space, I can melt quickly by picturing the cold night in 1995 when he first held our twins, Jack and Zane, one tiny baby in each of his large hands. That indelible vision fills me with so much hope about our old marriage, even on the worst of days.

I'm thinking of the sliced-up family portrait of the Gores and their own four children. Though Mom and Dad are divorcing, they are all attached for life. No document will change that fate. I am drawn to the *New York Times* letters to the editor again and find one of the only supportive voices of acting on the late-life itch. It comes from a seventy-three-year-old surgeon in Princeton, New Jersey, who is cool in his appraisal of elder-divorce, a transition he recently experienced himself. As he writes, "After many coffees and lunches with septuagenarians in similar situations I have concluded that the most prevalent common denominator causing couples to break up at this stage of life is weariness at making the compromises that are inevitably part of living with another person." He adds this clincher: "I can now do what I want when I want to do it."

This husband released into freedom to start over as what he calls a "recycled single" likely has been married for fifty years or more. We hear you, Doc; many of us veteran spouses feel your pain. With new wrinkles and old woes, we know from living with our own mates for decades that the grind of the ordinary can whittle us down to nubs. Over time, lots of marriages aren't pretty. We snarl. We retreat. We forget to have sex. One or both of us gets fatter. One or both of us may meet someone thin and dewy and believe that new love will fix our lives. Then we remember that this life is already fixed in time, that we can leave our spouses but will always be joined by our history, whether we like it or not.

Perhaps if the Princeton doctor could read this book, he would pick up some advice from older wives who have figured out, in his words, "how to do what I want, when I want to do it" within a marriage. I do not know the Princeton doctor's unique circumstances or the extent of the compromises he had to make. Yet I do know this, from the dozens of recycled singles I interviewed age fifty and beyond: Even if your partner is the reason you're on Xanax, exhilaration over separation will be doused with uncontrollable flashbacks—flashbacks of the twentieth-anniversary trip to Tuscany, of the moment you hugged when your son scored the winning basket in the last twelve seconds of a championship game, of the time you grasped each other's hands as if you were clinging to buoys in a roaring ocean as a child lay ill in the hospital.

When our eldest, Theo, was thirteen months old he got a near-fatal case of croup and spent two weeks on a respirator. As he hovered near death, we held vigil in the intensive care ward, our hands clenched together, afraid to let go. Chuck saved me and I saved Chuck, and the force of our combined militancy with doctors saved Theo.

You can shake loose legally from a vintage marriage, but you will forever be entangled in a place so deep that even the best lawyer is incapable of performing a clean extraction. Some marriages definitely need to end, because of abuse or abandonment or serial adultery. Yet many marriages are terminated for the wrong reason: for the unreal expectation that another person can make you happy. Better to stick with the first flawed union if you can; the second could be worse. I'll take my familiar problems any day rather than be buried in bigger problems from a new love with children who won't speak to me. Talk to your single friends who are having intimacy on the fly with weird strangers who may have STDs. Your life will look great. More and more couples are willing to seek help when aging love goes awry, because they are realizing that staying married is better for them, better for the children, and better for their pets. There's much that is extraordinary about a life that is predictably ordinary.

While more Americans are delaying committing to one person due to many factors, from building careers to an understandable wariness of lasting love, those who have embraced marriage are working hard to stay there when problems arise. The business of couples counseling is enormous, as many divorce lawyers send clients to therapists first if they think the marriage can be saved. There are more than fifty thousand licensed marriage and family therapists in the United States, a fiftyfold increase since 1970, according to figures from the American Association for Marriage and Family Therapy. Despite our modern culture, which promotes instant gratification and short attention spans, the human instinct to want one partner to count on in this one hard life is ancient.

Marriage and family therapist Diane Sollee is an early pioneer of the marriage preservation movement and founder of the organization that runs Smart Marriages workshops in the United States and in the Mideast. She is one of the smartest and sharpest critics of divorce, having experienced her own in 1977 from her husband of sixteen years, the father of her three children. I have turned to Diane in much of my journalistic work on relationships. She is the woman who told me early in my marriage to think of my husband and children as a priceless tapestry that should never be torn apart.

DIANE

Marriage is a stitch in an intergenerational tapestry, a connection of emotional and financial and cultural resources between families and between generations. Break the stitch and the whole tapestry begins to unravel. Even in the best of divorces, children lose touch with some of their aunts and uncles, cousins, grandparents, great uncles, and great aunts. People make the mistake of thinking that you leave divorce court and come out the other side into the garden of perpetual bliss. The sense of freedom and relief is most often short-lived as you deal with someone else's baggage and your own baggage from breaking up a family.

Our research tells us that later life is a very happy stage of marriage if you can make it that far. Marriage is two people coming together who will always disagree, and it's my mission to teach people how to manage disagreements, big and small. You are going to disagree over lifestyle, parenting, sex, religion, everything. And as it turns out, you don't need to resolve all of these disagreements. You just need to manage them. You need, most of all, to understand each other's positions, and you need to allow each other to change, to become different people than the ones you married. Because the opposite of embracing change in a partnership is to divorce. Marriage earns you your citizenship papers into this club called adulthood. This whole idea that parents raise children—well, I believe children raise you into becoming grown-ups.

The anguish of divorce is for life. I got divorced thirty-four years ago and I am still frustrated that my kids and grandkids will be doing their summer trip with their father out West. We will never all be together again skiing or climbing mountains.

Divorce is tearing apart a tapestry woven by your ancestors. Your parents and great-great-grandparents and all the way back worked really hard to get you where you are today. This is a tapestry you want to hand off in one piece to the next generation. You received it from your parents and grandparents and you can pass it on to your children for them to build upon and pass on to their children.

I'll tell you one of the worst phrases of the feminist movement. I adore the work of Gloria Steinem but I hate her quote: "A woman needs a man like a fish needs a bicycle." That was such a damaging idea to give women, that they don't need men. What we should teach our daughters is to teach their men to get on that bicycle and take the children places then come home to them. We should teach our daughters to show their husbands, "I need you! The family needs you." We definitely don't want men to ride off on their damn bikes and have to live our lives alone. I'm sixty-eight years old and I've been in a good relationship with the same person now for twenty-four years. I can tell you definitely from the work that I do and from my own life that the happiest period of life comes when you stick it out.

I love Diane's imagery of marriage as blocks of history stitched together. Indeed, ours feels like an intricately crafted quilt: mottled patches pieced together through adoration and annoyances, mud slinging and lovemaking, babies and adolescents and emptying nests. The quilt lengthens with age, wearing out in spots like a baby blanket a ten-year-old still carries around. Chuck and I have seen each other through much sickness, the funerals of four parents, two high school graduations, and dozens of missed curfews.

Divorcing Chuck would be like unraveling my entire adult life, leaving shards of fabric and frayed threads and a torn self. This twenty-three-year-old marriage quilt, though thinning and flawed, keeps me warm. I know that even if we leave each other, unless we are lobotomized, we are still stuck with each other because we have the same memories.

I am sentimental about how far we've come. I am determined to stay in what can seem like a cage of wild animals. I've met enough graying singles maniacally surfing Internet dating sites to realize that the grass is seldom greener on the other side. Yet I am also a realist: I know that marriage is a pain, and that this green grass is often brown and dry. I know that marriage wasn't designed to make us happy; it was designed to make us grow up and accept that it's about us and not "all about me." I've had itches to leave every week, yet they pass and I remain a wife to husband number one because I know a secret: You don't get it all from one person in one place.

III
Separate Summers

"And this may be a revelation to many young, starry-
eyed brides: I knew instinctively from early on that
my husband was not going to be responsible for
my happiness."

—TECLA

I AM STAYING IN a cottage of bleached shingles in Leucadia, California, a block from the ocean—alone. The marine layer is socking in the coast with drizzle and a record-breaking run of cool temperatures for July. Prolonged mist has infused the bougainvilleas with intense color; neon pink and coral blossoms burst over the teak arbor and white stone gate. The palm trees are flawless fans of jade without the crusty curls that usually appear in summer. As I open the door to embrace the surreal afternoon, I am hit with perfumed air, a cleansing vapor of jasmine and rosemary.

If a fairy fluttered overhead, it would not be a surprise.

My husband is in our air-conditioned home of bleached shingles on the Severn River in Maryland. He is escaping a record-breaking run of one-hundred-degree-plus weather for July. The grass is brown, and the air is so foul it's difficult to breathe. "It's like being in hell," he tells me on the phone.

I feel guilty about being in heaven—for about twenty minutes. Bliss is cut short when the house trembles with a 5.3 magnitude earthquake felt throughout much of San Diego and Los

Angeles. There is no real damage other than stalled elevators in a few high-rises, and no injuries—just a piercing reminder that perfection is fleeting. I have spent a lot of time in California, having gone to college here and taken most of my writer's retreats and family vacations here. While East Coasters often pass off this land of lush beauty and relaxed people as la-la land, I find its inhabitants to be startlingly real. When you live in California, you are constantly reminded of the fragility of life. Your fairytale gardens, laden with bougainvilleas and fragrant with jasmine, can whirl into nightmarish flurries in a finger snap when earthquakes hit, which they do with increased frequency.

I appreciate California for its what-if mentality, which puts you in a perpetual state of wakefulness. Each rumble of the earth forces you to face your own death and savor every detail of your life.

At a distance, I am supremely grateful on this day for the gifts of health, husband, children, and solitude.

For the past decade of marriage, Chuck and I have spent most of the month of July apart. Many couples take separate vacations. We take separate summers. Throughout three decades as a writer unraveling women's most intimate relationships, I have found that many of the happiest wives need stretches of time away from their husbands, time alone in which to remember and celebrate who they are and the autonomy of their souls. The self of truth for a woman, the command central of the family, is often diluted by our compulsion to take care of everyone else. Separateness brings growth and renewal, and my solitary excursions make Chuck happy, too.

This summer Chuck is working seven days a week launching a rustic furniture company with an apprentice, our son Isaac. I am on the other coast working on this book, a painstaking process that requires self-absorption and an absence of distractions. Both of our professions demand periods of solitude to succeed, and we give that to each other: We know that when our work flourishes, we flourish as individuals, bringing more energy and luster—and money—to the marriage. When we come together again in August, we epitomize the cliché "absence makes the heart grow fonder." Our separate summers leave us hot to see each other, high on our personal accomplishments, and purged of the inevitable resentments that arise in the grind of the ordinary that long marriage becomes.

My other sons are relishing separate summers, too, in out-of-state programs tailored to their individual interests, in environmental science, in journalism, and in filmmaking. So I am not knotted with guilt that anyone is home clamoring for Mom. My recommendation of separate summers for spouses does not mean separate summer flings. It means that I and others have realized that the ticket to a long-term and fulfilling union is for each person to have time to pursue passions outside of their relationships and domestic duties. Marriage twines us together in many ways, yet we need our own turf on which to breathe, to explore, *to live*. I miss my husband when we are apart, yet these breaks bring a true knowledge that we as a couple are solidly right.

I'm not a psychologist trained in analysis, yet from the hundreds of stories that have been poured into my tape recorder, these are a few facts I can confirm: If your husband gives you space, you can trust him—and yourself—while you're apart, and if you want to have sex with him when you return, that's a love that can last.

For eight of our separate summers, I was a counselor at Raquette Lake Boys Camp in the Adirondacks, when our sons were of camper age. Chuck joined me for one summer as the director of woodworking, and one season of being "Wood Chuck," as the children called him, was enough for him. He was not smitten like his wife with the summer camp experience—the demanding kids, black bears shoving over garbage cans, huddling in down sleeping bags during frosty mountain nights, reveille played at seven A.M., heaps of starchy camp food.

I loved it all.

During summers on Raquette Lake, a group of us older counselors—one of them the septuagenarian waterfront director we call Splash—lived together in a cabin on the edge of the icy lake, facing West Mountain. While the campers slept, I took my walks at dawn through the hilly forest of birch and pine, with chipmunks and deer and squawking ducks as my only companions. Feeling the crunch of pine needles under my hiking boots, the morning sky a piercing blue, slapped by cold air, I was home.

On Raquette Lake, I am transported to Blue Lake at Camp Agawak, to the birch and pine forest of northern Wisconsin, another source of intense self-discovery where I spent ten summers of my youth. The woods inspired my passion for writing, beginning at the age of eight when I contributed to our weekly camp journal, the *Agalog*, the site of my first bylines. Nearly a half century later, lots of chapters in each of my books were born amid the languor of summer, deep in the woods. As I sit in a rickety Adirondack chair as a grown-up camper, toying with its peeling green paint and facing the burn of sunset over the mountains, my thoughts are pure and language flows freely. Solitude in summer is when I am inspired to believe that anything is possible.

In *A Room of One's Own*, Virginia Woolf's 1929 literary portrait of women writers and sexism, the author advises that "a woman must have money and a room of her own if she is to write . . ." Specifically, Woolf also suggests that the room should have a "lock on the door."

What a gift to write with a laptop on the lip of a lake, the horizon broad and beckoning, and not locked in. I inhale deeply during my last days at camp, absorbing the beauty and the solace to store for reserve fuel when it's lead-gray winter and I'm in a dark office, with writer's block and the noise of boys.

Leaving Raquette Lake, driving south on Highway 87 to our departing airport in Albany, I would talk to my sons about how the Adirondacks have long been a well of artistic inspiration. We would see the exits for the resort town of Lake George, and I would tell them about the summers during which Lake George was home to Georgia O'Keeffe and Alfred Stieglitz, and their beguiling love affair. As first his muse and then his wife, the

Wisconsin farm girl O'Keeffe painted some of her finest early works on the banks of Lake George, starting in the early 1900s. Her initial impressions of Lake George are described in Benita Eisler's astonishing biography of the couple, *O'Keeffe and Stieglitz: An American Romance*, in which she relays this O'Keeffe quote: "[Looking] out across the marshes, at the cattails, patches of water and birch trees shining white at the edge. In the darkness, it all looked just like I felt—wet and swampy and gloomy, very gloomy." That blackness of the soul that ignited some dark and gorgeous canvases became more of a spiritual obstruction to O'Keeffe than an inspiration. When Oaklawn, the Stieglitz family home, was sold in 1922, Alfred's servants, acolytes, and relatives shifted their base to a renovated nearby farmhouse dubbed "The Hill," which became an enclave for artists and writers such as Paul Strand and Waldo Frank. O'Keeffe eventually found the place and the people who swarmed there suffocating. Oaklawn was Steiglitz's place, not hers.

"Lake George is my blood, the trees and lake and hills and sky," Stieglitz effuses in Eisler's book. While he was on an Adirondack high, his wife was realizing there was room for only one grand ego on The Hill, where some of her most iconic landscapes and his most startling portraits were spawned. Although Stieglitz's series of nudes of O'Keeffe evoke a timeless sense of erotica, as she offers her long and full breasts to the camera, tweaking a nipple for effect, the fiery romance between two self-obsessed artists proved to be too feverish to be encased in one house. One separate summer spent by O'Keeffe in New Mexico led to a separate life altogether from her mercurial relationship. This led to a permanent departure from the thunderstorms and opaque marshes that were fluorescent beacons for Stieglitz in Lake George, and to her own place amid the pastel sunsets of Abiquiu, New Mexico, where she developed Ghost Ranch and settled for the rest of her life.

O'Keeffe needed distance in order to reclaim herself and her artistic center. When she died in 1986 at the age of ninety-eight, her ashes were scattered over Ghost Ranch, a country away from the buried ashes of the husband she loved vehemently yet needed to leave, a man she outlived by forty years.

Whatever you think of Georgia O'Keeffe, the sharp-tongued early feminist who slept with her husband's friends and their wives, ranch hands half her age and millionaires twice her age, her astounding legacy cannot be denied: Launched by Stieglitz, she bloomed into a fearless woman who could paint poetry into cattle skulls and sketch life into death, and who made more money than nearly any other artist in American history. On a hilltop in Abiquiu, thousands of miles from her husband's Hill in upstate New York, she was Miss O'Keeffe the painter, never Mrs. Stieglitz. (She would have been a Ms. but the term had yet to be coined.) Her intimate relationships were tortured and her poppies were derided as fluff by many art snobs. Yet the renegade force that was Georgia O'Keeffe was never snuffed out by heartbreak, critics, or the towering shadow of her husband's fame. O'Keeffe and Stieglitz remained together forever through their love letters, yet their legacies are distinctly individual.

Few women would construct a marriage like hers, yet I am thankful for O'Keeffe, and other undaunted female artists and writers, particularly the four-times-wed Erica Jong. Jong tells the truth about the chafes of togetherness and the time-outs that are necessary so you can breathe your own air and remember who you are. I know what Jong knows when she says in her essay "The Perfect Man": "We were soul mates at one period of our lives, but then our souls changed."

When my soul shifts, I split from my husband for a while and get some work done. When I return, my soul is replenished, replete, and open.

In the Leucadia cottage, or in an Adirondack chair on Raquette Lake, I am thankful for Simone de Beauvoir and Germaine Greer and other warrior women who made it possible for generations of women that followed to have peace about their choices: the choice to postpone marriage and childbearing and establish a career, the choice to have sex and not get pregnant, the choice to leave our spouses for a while so we can remember who the hell we are, the choice to be both strong and vulnerable and not be labeled as "manly" or "ballbreaking."

I want what Virginia Woolf wanted when she wrote to Leonard Woolf after he proposed: "I want everything—love, children, adventure, intimacy, work . . . a marriage that is a tremendous living thing, always alive. . . ." Alas, she never got it all—no one does, but we can come close.

Today, I am back in Annapolis from Leucadia, with seventy-eight new pages written and blood pressure that registers 110/70, a rejuvenated wife poised to resume her old life. On my California retreat, I took along several classics that highlight the struggle that never changes for women, of personal desires versus societal expectations. I became newly obsessed with Charlotte Brontë's nineteenth-century *Jane Eyre*, a book I hadn't picked up in thirty-three years.

Jane is an orphan who doggedly rises above a life of poverty and abuse, becoming a cultured and educated teacher. To evade the agony of loving an unavailable man, the craggy and rough Mr. Rochester, who already has a wife yet wants Jane desperately, she takes on the pseudonym Jane Elliott so that her suitor can't find her. Jane moves in with a family of cousins, including St. John, a dispassionate clergyman who yearns for Jane to become his wife, not out of a romantic tug but because he admires her work ethic. In the Victorian era, when romance was not a necessary precursor to marriage, the self-possessed Jane refuses to settle for an evangelist she finds dull and doesn't love, and who doesn't love her.

St. John's view of marriage was to form a business partnership as missionaries in India, with a proposal that went like this: "Jane, you are docile, diligent, disinterested, faithful, constant, and courageous; very gentle, and very heroic. . . . I can trust you unreservedly. As a conductress of Indian schools, and a helper amongst Indian women, your assistance will be to me invaluable."

"I scorn your idea of love," she hisses back. "I scorn the counterfeit sentiment you offer. . . ."

A year later, with Mr. Rochester now a widower, Jane, now worldly and rich after an inheritance from an uncle, hears her old love calling to her in the middle of the night, and she dashes toward him in his manor, a classic Victorian supernatural scene.

"Reader, I married him," Jane announces at the start of the last chapter, a happy ending for a fighter who followed her heart and not the mandates of society. We sense that although Jane has joined in matrimony, she will hold on to the original spirit she voiced in her refusal to become the wife of St. John, as she dispatched him to India without her: "I should still have my unblighted self to turn to, my natural unenslaved feelings with which to communicate in moments of loneliness. There would be recesses in my mind which could be only mine."

There should be parts of each person that are "only mine." That's why the term *soul mates* to me doesn't mean one soul but a dance of two souls, partners who each retain their unique essence and become all the more powerful when they meld. With images of souls dancing in my head, I get a breathless call from my neighbor Gail, with the news that a painting of hers has just been accepted in a highly competitive show of alumnae art at the Katzen Gallery of American University. I met Gail when my sons were all in diapers, and I used to envy her freedom as an artist with an empty nest who spent her summers solo, painting in Italy. Her physician husband, Stanley, head of a large oncology practice, can't spend long stretches of time away from the hospital and patients. On his vacations, his preference is to go hunting and fishing in Alaska with his male pals, on excursions led by the Watkins' son, Stanley Junior, a cardiologist in Anchorage.

I am now entering Gail's summit in the female growth cycle, with mature children, a seasoned marriage, and the ability to get on an airplane with one carry-on and no companions. I have known Gail for seventeen years, and I often tell her I want to be just like her when I grow up. This is a woman who is unblighted and unenslaved, a wife at age seventy who belongs to herself, yet has been married for more than four decades. While building her own international reputation as an artist, Gail has mothered two accomplished children—a scientist daughter and the cardiologist son—and erected an indestructible marriage, one of equality and respect and independence.

Gail is slim and wiry, a yoga devotee long before it became mainstream, with short brown hair streaked with red. Of Lebanese and Italian descent, she has large oval eyes that are almost black, and her skin is smooth and tanned. Looking out at her dock on the Severn River, we watch Stanley on his wooden fishing boat, *Miss Cleo*, unloading a catch of rockfish and perch. Gail smiles as if she can already taste the fresh fish when relaying her simple recipe for dinner: the filets dusted in panko crumbs and panfried in garlic-infused olive oil. Stanley's preoccupation with *Field & Stream* excursions and the endless needs of cancer patients used to cause Gail much loneliness. Today, she credits her busy husband, who spent much of their marriage on call or with a rifle or fishing rod in his hand, with releasing her to become a self-reliant artist who served on the faculty of St. John's College for twenty years.

GAIL

It took me a long, long time to become who I am today. When the children were small, I was so busy with their swim teams, lacrosse, basketball, and homework it didn't bother me as much that I was often left alone. As the kids turned into absent teenagers, the fact that my husband was often gone became a source of sadness for me. I would throw these little tantrums out of loneliness. When you are married to a doctor, you can expect the phone calls that say "I'm going to be late" or "We need to cancel our plans." Oncology, of course, is even more unpredictable. It is constant, and though I have enor-mous sympathy for his patients—many of whom over the years have been friends of mine with breast cancer—it did put a distance between us in our early years. I am very proud of Stan in his work. But a doctor's wife is generally not on the top of her husband's list; some days you don't even make the list.

I can't tell you how many times we had plans to go out to a cocktail reception and I'd be dressed up, waiting for him, in the kitchen. He'd arrive home two hours late and we'd show up for the last fifteen minutes of the party. After years and years of this, it's like Chinese water torture. It just pings at you and pings at you and finally, I started going to parties by myself. I would tell Stan, "Show up when you can, but I'm not waiting for you."

In the early years of our marriage, I was just too dependent on him and his schedule. He'd say, "I'll be home for dinner at six thirty," then show up at eight thirty. Since we both believed in family dinners, we'd all wait for him, hungry and upset. It was like being stood up for a date every night of my life. It didn't occur to me that I needed to create my own life and that could help ease my blaming him for my own unhappiness.

My early memories of meeting Stan, though, are very happy, and this history we have anchors our long marriage, no matter how displeased I may have gotten at times. I was trained as a nurse at Duke University, and worked for a while at the National Institutes of Health, in Bethesda. Stan was a doctor there, and he came by the nurse's station one night and asked if anyone knew how to cook soft-shell crabs. He was six feet four and had sparkly blue eyes and a beautiful smile, so I said, "Yes, I do." So our first date we ate crabs, and a year later we were married. Living in Maryland, home of the famous blue crabs, we have probably eaten crabs together thousands of times since that time.

In spite of an overwhelming schedule, Stan was a very good father to our kids. Although he didn't have time for swim meets after school like I did, he would take our son and daughter and their friends on weekend camping trips. Our kids know how to hunt and fish because of Stan, and to this day it is seldom that we eat any meat or fish that someone in our family didn't catch. We have enough moose, duck, venison, caribou, salmon, and halibut in the freezer to feed our neighbors for months.

I am fortunate to be with someone who has given us a wonderful lifestyle, and I know there isn't a lot to complain about. The biggest problem in our marriage was that I was always put in a position where I was waiting for Stan. This changed when the kids went to college, and it was a real turning point for me. We had a neighbor across the street, and she knew that I was alone a lot. She asked me to go to an ashram with her in California, a trip that would cost five thousand dollars for the week. Stan said, "No way am I paying that amount of money. Can't you find somewhere less expensive?"

I could have found somewhere cheaper, but I was drawn to this ashram; it was a time about twenty-five years ago when I began to get serious about yoga. Because of Stan's hesitation, I decided I needed to start making my own money. I went back to painting seriously, something I hadn't done in a big way since getting my master's in art in 1963. I started selling my work and teaching art classes. It felt good to become self-sufficient financially and be able to take any trip I wanted to take.

I grabbed back my independence, really grabbed back my whole self, when I got into painting again. I love my husband, and we have many things in common, including four grandchildren, my son's children, who live in Anchorage. We spend about three weeks a year in Alaska visiting them, and this is a very binding time for Stan and me. It makes up for all the time back home we spend apart.

I still tell Stan thank you for refusing to pay for the ashram trip. In order to stay married for a really long time, you have to be yourself, which I really wasn't in the early years. Then my work began to get recognized and I started getting commissions, and I became confident and strong. In retrospect, I was blaming my marriage for my feelings of emptiness when it really was me that was unfulfilled. In 1986, I got an appointment to be the artist-in-residence for the University of Georgia summer program based in Cortona, between Florence and Rome. For six weeks, I would paint in a studio on the top floor of a fourteenth-century palace, with a stunning view of the rooftops and countryside. I would look out over a patchwork of fields of crops and vineyards and sunflowers and corn. The sunflowers move their faces to the sun as the sun passes overhead, and that is an amazing sight to see.

I made friends with a lot of other artists in Italy, and I started spending several weeks each summer in Cortona, studying art and painting. The colors and landscape of Italy really formed what has become my signature of layering earth-colored paint, plaster, and comics to evoke antiquities melding with the twenty-first century. I was inspired by the cracked surfaces of the stucco walls, the pinks and ochres and umbers and siennas. Many of these walls have been here since the thirteenth century, and you stare at their surfaces and see ancient layers of paint and pieces of posters and imagine how many people over the centuries have stood there, just like you, awed by the countryside and the beauty of the buildings.

From my summers in Italy, I have become nearly fluent in the language and a different person, which has been a real surprise to have happened at midlife. Stan built me a studio adjacent to our home, and with no children living there anymore it meant I could continue painting for prolonged stretches of time during the year as well, with no interruptions. In order to do what I do, you need to literally shut out the world. You can't answer the phone. You can't check your e-mails. You have to be vigilant about claiming your solitude, and your friends and family need to learn to respect that.

I found my voice through those summers in Italy; my work really was transformed. I was trained in still lifes and figure painting, and my focus now is much more evocative of the passing of time. I am very aware now that I want to create works that are weathered, paintings that look like time has altered the surface like the walls of Cortona. I am an artist who deeply feels the passing of time, and the work is a metaphor for aging. I am certainly aware that time alters the human surface, too.

Being separated from Stan during the summer, I stopped being so grumpy about his round-the-clock schedule. I come back energized, full of new ideas. Those five weeks away form a scaffolding for the rest of my year, as the climate and hues of Italy guide my palette and imagination. I could never have done this when my children were young. Stan has come to Italy during the summer a few times, but he even admits that it "cramps my style." I spend long hours trying to translate for him so he can buy fishing tackle and get fishing permits when I should be painting. I feel responsible for his happiness there, and the charm of Italy for me is being responsible only for myself and getting my work done.

I am seldom now in a position where I am upset in my kitchen because I'm waiting for Stan. By having my own passions and my own income, I can get on with my own life; I don't have to ask anyone's permission to buy this or go there. It has made my marriage much healthier and has made me much happier. If he's not home and I want to go out for dinner with friends, I go. I am able to paint whenever I want. I do yoga every day. I take Italian classes. Because I was left alone so often in my marriage, I have had the time to invest in myself. Creative work revolves around loneliness, and I have grown to appreciate the lonely life. It's one of the perks of aging—you really do come to savor your own company.

I am proud of the evolution of me and our marriage. My husband is a steady man; he doesn't fly off the handle. I've seen him upset maybe a handful of times in more than forty years of marriage, and that is usually because he couldn't keep a young person from dying. He's a very, very good person for me. He looks like something out of an L. L. Bean catalog, and I'm a bohemian. He's the rudder in an artist's life.

We just happen to have very separate interests. Ten years ago he bought a farm about an hour away from Annapolis, on the Corsica River. He goes there most weekends to hunt, drive around on his tractor, plant crops, and fish. I think I've been there twice. It used to piss me off that whatever free time he did have away from the hospital he chose to be shooting deer rather than spending it with me. I am no longer upset; I am busier than I've ever been. When he comes home at dark with something for me to cook, I am happy to see him and happy I got so much done that day. We have pasta with a sauce made from tomatoes and basil from my garden and venison from his farm. I love how our relationship has unfolded, that we each have our own fulfilling orbits. But as a bride, I really thought marriage would be very different than how it turned out to be. I thought we'd be together all the time.

Some people probably look at us and think, "How could two so very different people stay married?" But we know our secret, and it is precisely our differences that has made this relationship last.

I'm sure my marriage arrangement also raises some eyebrows, and I don't care. It is my marriage, not anyone else's, and it works for us. Like Gail and Stan, we clearly do not restrict each other from doing what we want to do, or from taking our separate journeys. We recognize that I need his yang and he needs my yin, and thankfully we are not planted in the same profession. The journalists I have dated have been needy romances of the "can't eat, can't sleep" variety—volcanic and short-lived.

Chuck is a steady architect who doesn't need much else other than his own space. The summer of 2006 was Chuck's high point of what we called "self-actualization" in the 1970s.

This was the summer of God.

I was with the boys at Raquette Lake Camp, and Chuck, a lapsed Methodist, went to Israel with a group from our temple. He had just been hired to be the temple's architect, to design a new building after the roof caved in during a wicked snowstorm. He was eager to go to Jerusalem and other holy sites to observe the types of materials that were used and study the ancient structures. Well, that wasn't his only draw to Israel, as it turned out. Unbeknownst to me, for the entire year before the trip, when he was meeting with our rabbi to talk about design plans and costs for the synagogue he was also discussing what he needed to do to convert to Judaism.

I am Jewish and our kids are Jewish and we celebrated four bar mitzvahs. I asked Chuck only one time to convert—before our wedding—so he could please my Holocaust survivor mother. He said then that if he ever did convert, it would be because he felt Jewish, and not because anyone wanted him to be Jewish. I never pushed the subject again, yet over the course of our marriage Chuck attended synagogue with our family, developed a brisket addiction, and was captivated by the haunting music of Yom Kippur services. After years of immersion in Jewish traditions, he decided that he felt Jewish and that he wanted to be Jewish. Only he didn't tell me. Our rabbi, Ari Goldstein, ushered him through the gate.

One quiet morning in Jerusalem, while his family was at Raquette Lake Boys Camp, Chuck said his conversion prayers at the Western Wall, accompanied by Ari. No one else in their tour group of twenty-two knew of this side trip. Reunited at our first family dinner in eight weeks, Chuck cleared his throat, and with a beatific smile he announced he had something to say.

All eyes on him, he quietly told us: "This summer I became Jewish."

Jack, who was then eleven, said, "Dad, we thought you *were* Jewish." Along with his brothers, he then quickly resumed bashing away at the shells of their Maryland blue crabs, digging out the sweet meat. (We do not keep kosher.) As they shucked away and sucked on claws, I felt like I couldn't breathe, socked with confusion and disbelief. One of my best qualities is intuition, reading deep below the surface of people. Not a clue on this one! I thought Chuck was talking architecture with Rabbi Goldstein all these months they were meeting for dinner. He was *converting!* When the children left the table, I stared at Chuck and shrugged and said nothing.

We sat there for a long uncomfortable stretch of silence, then he responded with this: "I wanted this to be about me, not about you. I had to do this my own way." Friends were shocked that my husband would become *another religion* without informing his wife. I made excuses like, "Oh, you know, that's just Chuck. He's his own guy," while really thinking he was a self-centered recluse, that at the very least he could have invited me to the ceremony. Yet, after a few days my own shock dissipated and I came around to realizing that Chuck's conversion method of choice, to stand alone at the ancient wall of our people, was right. This change of faith was his own inward journey, not about an outward proclamation.

Yes, our separate summers bring about some sizable personal growth.

I actually believe that aloneness can enhance true intimacy with another because you get to know yourself better. Self-exploration leads to growth for you, and that renewal fuels growth for your marriage.

"Only by understanding that in its naturalness marriage is a spiritual state will we be able to answer the question of how we can be married and at the same time be our *selves,* personally fulfilled," write father and son psychiatrists Thomas Patrick Malone and Patrick Thomas Malone in their 1987 book *The Art of Intimacy,* a timeless classic. "Ideally, marriage should provide a nourishing medium within which each person can grow into his or her own personal fulfillment . . . ," they continue. "Far from being antithetical to your ability to find a *self,* a healthy marriage never jeopardizes your sense of identity as to who you really are. It enhances, enlivens, energizes, and renews until truly being oneself and in relation are indistinguishable."

The authors point out that the word *intimacy* throughout the ages has been referred to by other phrases, such as "the way," or "the source," or even "soul principle." Indeed, intimate knowledge of yourself is the way and the source of being able to further find yourself, the boomer quest, within the parameters of an intimate relationship.

I like to claim that I am my own soul mate, and that my marriage and family are the soul of my life, a concept I am discussing with Tecla Emerson Murphy, publisher of *Outlook by the Bay,* a magazine that focuses on the lifestyle of adults over fifty-five in the Chesapeake region. Standing nearly six feet tall, Murphy wears khakis and a navy turtleneck and is a woman you can easily picture hiking swiftly up a mountain. I am extolling the virtues of my separate summers as a recharge for my own longish marriage, and she is nodding knowingly as she relays that her own marriage has lasted forty-four years. "What's your survival secret?" I ask Tecla, mother of three, grandmother of eight. She answers with a droll smile: "My husband has been on the road half the time for those forty-four years."

Married to a Marine Corps officer, Tecla has lived the transient military life, moving with her family from Boston to Virginia to North Carolina, back to Massachusetts, and off to Michigan before finally settling in Maryland. The young family would frequently be plunked down in a new town, as her husband would leave for another city, or another country, dispatched to military duty or a government assignment. Calm but animated, she talked about a "solid marriage with frequent upheavals" that has not only been characterized by separate summers, but has been separate for months at a time.

TECLA

Our marriage has always been unsettled and mildly contentious. From day one, there was friction: He is an Irish Catholic, and I am German, English, and Protestant. We are both very independent, and we rarely agreed on anything. This type of long-distance marriage was good for both of us. We stuck with it and now appreciate each other more than ever.

After just eighteen months of marriage, which included a move from Virginia to North Carolina and the addition of baby number one, I was introduced to single parenthood. My husband was the recipient of an all-expense-paid thirteen-month tour of duty to Southeast Asia, compliments of the U.S. Marine Corps. After returning safely, he continued as a reservist with the Marines for almost thirty years. This required several days a month far away from home with additional duty during the summer and often at other times during the year. Also employed by a division of the U.S. Treasury Department, this man we all call Murph frequently was called out to travel to who knows where. (I never grilled him too closely.)

Our homes have included a tent and a one-bedroom house for a family of five without heat during a sub-zero New England winter. A move that we made to the Midwest was typical: He dropped us off in a small town in Michigan and pointed down the road and said, "The elementary school is that way and the middle school is just ten miles down the other way," and he left for the airport saying he'd be back in a couple of weeks. This was not unusual.

Over the years with the frequent separations, he was obviously missed. There's a companionship and an appreciation of another adult, even when it's a rocky relationship, when one is tied down with children. But it was nice to have my own space and not always have to share every thought and discuss each and every choice. Being independent, without a mate, makes day-to-day decisions easier. It eliminates the need to consult, negotiate, and acquiesce to another opinion. There is of course the problem of reentry, which every wife who has an absentee husband can identify with: As husband returns, wife is thinking, "Everything has run very smoothly in your absence. Why are you rocking the boat?" And his grumbly answer is invariably "Because I'm in charge." Pasting a smile on her good-wife face, she can barely be heard whispering to herself, "That's what you think." And so the conflict begins!

And this may be a revelation to many young, starry-eyed brides: I knew instinctively from early on that my husband was not going to be responsible for my happiness. My happiness depended on me. Interestingly, however, he may not be responsible for my happiness, but he sure can interfere with it!

In many of my friend's marriages, separations weren't good; there was infidelity in more cases than I want to remember. Too many adulterous relationships are started when there's a geographical separation. Although in our marriage we were apart for long stretches of time, we both had a very strong sense of loyalty and commitment, and—most important—I just didn't have time or energy to get involved in something like that. Murph has always been the good-looking sort that you notice in a crowd but was always introverted— the strong silent type. To this day he still shies away when women appear to be interested in him, so infidelity was not high on my list of concerns.

No two summers were the same. While my husband was busy with the military and his government obligations, my girls and I would drive, fly, or take the train to Canada, North Carolina, or South Carolina. The summer that Murph spent in Southeast Asia during the Vietnam War was particularly worrisome for us, but we were able to spend a couple of relaxing weeks in a house on Cape Cod. In his absence, my husband would have preferred that we spend our summers at home even though he was not there. He worried about our free and easy style of travel, but we did it anyway. In hindsight, I am glad that we did take off on our different adventures and were not held back because Dad wasn't there. Now married with families of their own, our daughters have a wonderful sense of independence and never hesitate to go off and have adventures with their own children.

My life was not unique. In many ways it followed the lives of our original settlers whose husbands and fathers were routinely absent for extended periods of time. Abigail Adams, wife of one president and mother of another, had a similar life with frequent separations, although our lives are spaced two hundred years apart.

We were both born in Massachusetts, just thirty miles apart. We both married strong-willed local boys and we proved that we were equally as strong. We're both descended from church leaders, which may account for some of our foibles. As good New Englanders, we did what we had to do without complaint. Abigail wrote, "the mind is stretched when contending with difficulties." And difficulties there were, but being eminently practical and possessing a strong work ethic, we persevered. I suspect that like her I have an overdeveloped sense of right and wrong, am intolerant of fools, and am proudly self-sufficient. While our husbands pursued active careers, we were left behind. Our marriages stayed strong as we successfully raised children and tended home and hearth very much on our own. Somehow, while busy raising children and keeping the home fires burning, we each were able to carve out time to pursue our own special interests.

Today's mores and customs in our country are so far removed from where we began that our forefathers would surely not recognize our lifestyle. We are currently in a throwaway mode. If something doesn't work, we don't fix it, we find a new one: a new car, a new toaster, a new marriage. No longer do we spend time mending and repairing. We replace. The consequences to a throwaway marriage can be heartbreaking, for you and for your children.

Many times in my marriage we were tempted to throw in the towel, which would have been the easy way out, but we stuck with it. Now, I'm more than thankful that some inner strength kept me tied to the life I'd chosen. Through our forty-four years together we were challenged with trials and upheavals, but it created a solidarity and appreciation for each other. Through all the years of struggle, we've created a history, and it's a history that belongs only to us. Bickering and disagreements are still part of our lives, but it's temporary. We're now life companions and we're very aware and appreciative of what we have as we face our own mortality.

I, too, am very appreciative of my Chuck and our lengthening history as I'm sitting on the curb of Baltimore/Washington International Airport, waiting for my husband to retrieve me from my California getaway. He pulls up in our mud-splattered silver Ford Escape, and he is wearing his John Lennon sunglasses he's had since I met him in 1985. His salt-and-pepper hair is its usual mess. The familiarity of this scene overwhelms me with a sense of what a good marriage should feel like—*I am home*—and I am surprisingly relieved that my summer streak of independence is over. A half hour later, we park in our driveway and Chuck grabs the faded brown leather suitcase he has carried for me for going on twenty-four years. We are walking toward the house where our strapping sons have lived since they were tiny boys; the russet shingles are now faded pewter in places and the teal blue paint that rims the windows is coming off in curls.

I see the abandoned wooden swing set and sandbox our toddlers used to play on and in for hours every day. We are standing on our front porch about to enter the door, dodging the six bicycles in all sizes. There is even a rusty red tricycle. We keep our swing set and our sand toys and our collection of bikes because our grandchildren will love these relics. I look at Chuck and he looks at me and the unspoken exchange is that we know we will be together as the next generation runs wild in our yard on a river like their fathers did.

IV

Through Sickness and Loathing and Death

"The fantasy is that I could leave and be happier.
The truth is I could leave and still be unhappy."

—ALICE

THE KITCHEN IS the heart of my life, as it has been for centuries of wives, starting with Sarah in the book of Genesis who braised pigeon with pomegranate in her tent for Isaac and Abraham. When we serve up food, we serve up love. "I just love y'all," drawls Paula Deen on the Food Network, pumping butter into artery-clogging pastry dough and surrounded by her adoring sons. When my own boys are in my kitchen, I, too, feel rooted in multigenerational love. Wistful images of my lost parents and the swift passage of time come to me often while I am slapping together school lunches and chopping garlic and sautéing fish. My mother, flushed from the oven and wiping her hands on her red-checked apron, still seems as if she is joining me when I am enveloped in pungent fumes, although she passed away a week before Christmas in 2006.

The kitchen is where I am flooded with the most gratitude for the home we have created, a wash that dissolves any residual distress, little and large, that surfaces each day.

On this Indian summer morning in October, I am standing at

the oak center island making turkey sandwiches for Jack and Zane, one on rye, one on white, one with Swiss, one with American, one with mayo, one with mustard, one with cucumber, one with tomato and a sprinkling of salt. I grunted about it when the job required double this duty: four made-to-order sandwiches before two sons left to be fed by college cafeterias. And I grunt about it now. At the same time, I am attached to this ritual of motherhood, and I am holding on to it as long as I can. I love it and I loathe it, and damn, I will really miss making sandwiches at dawn when it's just me in the kitchen alone, drinking coffee and watching *Morning Joe*.

This yo-yo of emotions is a lot like marriage: You love him and you loathe him and you can't let go.

Chuck is seated at the kitchen table with his young clones; their arm movements and slurps are nearly in synchrony as they shovel in Honey Nut Cheerios. It's a moment I want to freeze, my boys in my kitchen, and I'm remembering something my mother told me. She, too, was the mother who made every meal and often complained she was sick of making meals, although she kept her apron on all day, poised to wipe up any spill or to whip up a snack for any hungry kid. During one of her visits eight years ago, she watched as I mashed black beans and garlic into ground turkey for a meat loaf. I was clucking my tongue and huffing about how icky the globs felt squishing through my fingers.

"Stop complaining," my mother said sharply. Easy for her to say. She was sipping cold Grey Goose and not kneading cold meat at five P.M. like she often did when she was my age. She continued with a sigh: "The happiest I was in my life was when I had you three children seated around my kitchen table, eating food that I made. Now, you kids are all over the place." Clinking the ice in her glass, her brown eyes clouded with tears, she talked about how lonely it was to be one person eating at her kitchen table, staring at pictures of her three children and eight grandchildren perched on the kitchen window sill.

"I haven't made a meat loaf since your father died," she said. "It reminds me too much of him."

My dad died in 1986, at the age of sixty-seven, after thirty-four years of marriage and undetected heart disease. She added softly, as if she was talking to herself: "You don't realize what you have until you lose it."

My mother outlived my father by twenty years, went on one lousy date, and kept her wedding ring on. Their marriage was volatile and fun and unfailingly committed: lots of loathing, lots of loving. One abiding memory is of my mom stomping around the kitchen while my dad was in on his cushioned blue-striped chair, feet up on the matching ottoman, flicking through *The Wall Street Journal*.

What wife hasn't stomped around her kitchen while her man lies in repose? What wives, except for those who take frequent business trips or are medicated, don't loathe their husbands as much as they love them? Who among you hasn't harbored the nasty thought, even just once for six seconds, that you'd be fine, or perhaps better, when death does him part?

Will I make meat loaf with turkey and beans, which Chuck adores, when he is gone? Will I cry myself to sleep, with our wedding album open and slumped on my chest? Or will I date the pool man Wayne? Until death do us part could be another forty years, or it could be tomorrow. Chuck reminds me of the unthinkable and the impossible, that *I* could go first, and these what-ifs are moot. His parents both died young, and so did my father. "Who shall live, and who shall die?" are the words we recite during the Jewish high holidays. The answer is uncertain, yet this is for sure: It's brutal for the survivor, no matter how rough the marriage was. We know that no matter what course former senator John Edwards's life takes, he will forever be a broken man.

The following stories track four wives in various stages of loathing and loss and renaissance: two with young children and unhelpful husbands, one with a sick husband, and one whose husband recently died. The experiences that have forced them to own their wedding vows, for better and for worse, should help any spouse push through the "I'm gonna kill him" phases and yield to the advice of my mom: Savor what you have, while you have it within reach.

"FOR WEEKS AT A TIME I hate my husband, but I'm stuck," says a forty-seven-year-old woman from Phoenix named Alice. Their ten-year-old daughter, Julia, was born three months premature and has been plagued with serious health problems, "too much for one person to handle on her own, and so I can't leave him," she adds.

Over a four-hour meal at a Chinese restaurant, Alice describes a difficult marriage defined by urgent collaborations over medical emergencies and intimacy frayed from stress. Recently Alice has been "working on herself" and blaming Chris less, fueling a discovery that he isn't so bad after all.

Standing a fraction over five feet tall, Alice looks more like a schoolgirl than a six-figure corporate consultant. She is dressed in a short navy pleated skirt, a crisp white shirt, and black ballet-shoe flats. Her black hair falls down her back in one thick braid. Alice wears no jewelry, has a spot of blush on each cheek, and speaks in sentences that are as clear as her persona.

ALICE

I can't remember when we were happy for more than a couple of days at a time. I am trying very hard to balance work and the enormous needs of our sick child, while living with someone I don't recognize anymore as the man I married. I admit that I wasn't madly in love when I got married. I did love him. I felt like we had shared values and I was confident that we would be a good team in life and as parents.

When we decided to marry, we agreed we didn't want our parents' lives, which we considered traditional and ordinary. They lived very safe lives. We wanted more passion. We wanted more adventure. We wanted more spontaneity. Over the course of our twenty-year marriage, we have done a lot of work in therapy, on ourselves individually and as a couple. My takeaway realization during this process was that I had no idea who I really was, and that my inhibitions came from a mother who was sexually frozen and from a father whose favorite line was "Whatever you want, dear." I never heard them talk about sex or intimacy. I grew up as the youngest of five children in a very traditional Presbyterian family and never did develop a separate sense of self. My identity was built on being responsive to others.

With this upbringing, my challenge has been to work on hearing my own voice and to be open to feeling passion. I spent the first several years of marriage without even thinking about having children, because I knew I had to find my own identity first.

We started trying to conceive when I was thirty-five, and within a year I was pregnant. Chris and I were both really excited; this news came at a warm and loving point in our marriage. I had an uneventful pregnancy and I worked full-time until my emergency delivery. Things spiraled downward from that point on, and neither of us has fully recovered, nor do I think we ever will.

Our daughter arrived at twenty-six weeks with a multitude of grave medical issues, including autism and epilepsy. We couldn't bring her home from the neonatal ICU until she was nearly four months old, and she nearly died dozens of times. Ten years later, I am still fighting to have the extraordinary life we said we were going to have. I know, deep down, that we can never reach that dream. But I refuse to just give up.

There is no way we can change what is going on with Julia. She attends a special school and requires speech therapy, physical therapy, you name it. This has created a lot of conflict in our marriage because we both cope with her illness in very different ways. My way has been to dig in and to keep fighting. Chris's way has been to be in a state of denial, that everything is going to turn out okay.

Things are not okay and will never be okay. I know that mothers feel more; we are lions fighting for our cubs. But I sense no fire in the belly at all coming from him. Our startling differences as parents and as people were made clear to me almost from the second our daughter was born, clinging to her life. I was on the waiting room floor crumpled in sobs, and Chris was in a chair, numb and cold, reading a magazine.

I left my job for the first three years of our daughter's life. We also had a nurse and a physical therapist come in every day because there were so many medical challenges. Julia couldn't walk and couldn't hold down food and couldn't tell us what she needed, because her speech was delayed. Her speech is still hard to understand. It killed me inside to go back to work, but I had to, financially.

I have always been the major breadwinner in the marriage, and even with insurance, the extra medical help our daughter needed was impossible to pay for on only one salary. Disparity over money is one of the major reasons couples get divorced; compound that with dealing with chronic illness and that's our happy little family. It became excruciating for me to be away from Julia all day, so I convinced my boss to give me a part-time schedule. I'm still making more in four days than my husband makes in five.

I am so tired of being the architect of everything. A girlfriend sent me an e-mail last week that I printed out and stashed in my wallet: It said, "Help! I hate my whole f—ing life!" That made me laugh and made me cry.

That's often me. I'm sure this happens a lot in special-needs households, that it's the mother who is the creative thinker, the force behind trying organic foods or researching stem cell procedures or acupuncture to make our child better. Carrying this weight alone has left me exhausted and resentful.

I want an equal partner.

In the beginning of our marriage, Chris was very much a teammate. I married a man that I believed would duke it out with me in life and help me figure out hardships. Dealing with our daughter got to be too big of a hardship for him. He became meek and lost his fire.

I am left with this sense of betrayal. I have lost the man I married. He doesn't fight the fight. He doesn't share the dream. He has surrendered to our parents' patterns, to the default mode of being dispassionate, of accepting the status quo. The man I married would never have tolerated going a month without sex. Now he will tolerate going a year without sex. In the old days, if I put on a few pounds, he'd say, "Why don't you go to the gym?" Now he doesn't say anything about my body.

Honestly, it feels like we both got hit by a truck when our child was born and we got back up on our feet in different ways. My coping mechanism is to get so angry that I start beating up on him and yelling, "Why don't you ever do this or do that?" His coping mechanism is to retreat, to do what he's told and not offer any original ideas, so as not to rock the boat even more. Maybe this is what happens to most married couples, even those with healthy children: You are hot for each other. You get married. You have kids and mortgages, and things never get hot again. This seems like a dismal road ahead since we could be married for fifty or more years. Both sets of our parents are still alive and married. No matter how bad things get, they stay together and endure begrudgingly. That's not the life I want.

My parents just celebrated their fifty-fifth anniversary, and I often wonder what kept them together in what seemed like a dull marriage. What it comes down to is that they both have an unshakable faith. They both believe that God definitely wants them to stay together, that Christ willed it to be. That is their common bond, and it's been really strong glue. I consider myself to be a devout Christian, but God is not enough to put me at peace. I am really angry, and though Chris doesn't speak up, I know he's angry, too.

The big question for us is: Can we forgive each other? Can we make a commitment to try anew when I feel like we have nothing left? Will we ever have good sex again? We had a lot of sex when I was trying to get pregnant, and I feel that I got punished for that—see, that's the good Christian in me, still considering sex a sin. Wanting children was a wonderful period of our marriage; we were really working at loving each other and toward the shared goal of parenthood. Then came our little sick girl, whom I love more than I have ever loved anyone in my life. But caring for Julia is a lonely and painful fight. It has been hell.

Last month I just lost it. Chris came home from work at eight thirty on a night I had worked in the office all day, picked up Julia from school, got home, fed her, bathed her, and put her to bed. I became completely unglued and started screaming at him: "I'm making more money. I'm doing most of the child care. I'm taking care of all her special needs, and doing all the heavy lifting myself to find better ways to meet those needs. Things have to change!" He sat there calmly, then said, "I can't listen to this. You are a drama queen, and this is just theatrics." I shouted back at him, "You don't understand how much pain I'm in. You need to change, or I will leave you."

I have not threatened to leave him before. Hearing that, he looked up, really shaken, speechless for a while. Then he said, "You know I do love you. I love our family. This has to work." That softening on his part, I feel, I hope, is the beginning of us finding our way back together. Recently, we were having a rare day alone. Our daughter was with my parents, and we were driving to go out for dinner. I looked over at him and I thought, Oh my God, this is the guy I married. He had his sunglasses on, he was humming to the radio, and he looked handsome and young. Maybe we will start being sexual again. I want that. I miss being touched.

I don't know any details of my parents' sex life, but I know they sleep next to each other in a double bed. As kids we'd go in there in the morning to talk to them and they'd be lying snuggled up on one side of the bed. Touching is so important; it keeps you connected. When you are not touching your husband at all, the loneliness and resentment builds up over time. For me it has led to a lack of emotional connection. I look at my parents and ask myself, "How can they still love each other after fifty-five years?" Hate feels horrible. But it grows, it festers. What if it gets worse? I cannot let that happen. Finding a new husband isn't the answer: Who will love Julia like he does?

I never imagined marriage could be this hard. It's next to impossible to live with another human being, particularly in our family situation and with my demanding work situation. My girlfriends with big jobs whose kids do not have special needs also really struggle to have a successful professional life and a successful personal life. A big piece of this struggle for me is that between giving all of myself to my daughter and having to work full-time, too, doing anything for myself is the first thing to go.

With young children, you just can't expect to spend a lot of time on personal pursuits and hobbies. You can't stop taking care of your children. You can't stop showing up for work. So, like in my case, you skip a few photography classes. You cancel lunch with girlfriends.

And because of these compromises, whom do you resent? Your husband—who somehow continues to make it to the gym and is calm because somehow all the stuff that is stressful is getting done by someone else. This is a big clue on why marriage can suck. So the answer for me has been to be more fierce about doing stuff for myself. Remember that no one wins when you are the martyr. On airplanes, you are instructed to put the oxygen on yourself first if trouble arises, and, you know, lately I've been rigid about making my husband take over the couple times a week I need a break or else I will break.

The fantasy is that I could leave and be happier. The truth is I could leave and still be unhappy.

So I've been pressed to figure out how I can possibly make the other parts of my life happy. I'm forty-eight years old, and I have only just begun to figure out that yelling at my husband isn't going to make me a better person. I have always loved art, and during the past year I've started painting and doing photography again. I wake up on Saturday mornings and I have all this pent-up energy so I go to art classes—most of the students are elementary school kids! But I'm a much happier person if I'm doing something creative. Expressing myself artistically gets negative feelings flowing out of me and my whole life goes better. When you are faced with a lot of hard issues you have to get really aggressive about doing things that feed your soul. I have also started to write furiously in a journal, and I can't tell you how good that feels; it's as if I'm talking to a friend who is just listening and not judging. Writing really lightens my load.

Chris encouraged me recently to try to sell some of my pictures. He said, "These are really good. Let people see them. Let people buy them." That was really endearing. I am seeing more and more that when I expand into my writing and art it eases the frustrations of raising a child who has so many of her own frustrations. I am working on all the places in my life where I can make things better, and not just saying to Chris, "I'm unhappy, you need to change."

As a couple, we are unable to live the progressive life we imagined we would lead when we met; we are bound by our daughter's endless needs. But I can work on myself. I can ask, "How can I become the person I want to be?" We know other parents of kids with disabilities who get divorced because they think being with someone detached from their problems will lessen their own problems. It's just bullshit. Chris and I are together in this pain, and there is no escape. The biggest challenge for me is that by nature I'm a perfectionist and our life will always be imperfect. I am finding out, slowly, that releasing the fear and the anger through creative outlets keeps me from feeling like I am going crazy.

Any writer knows that pouring out thoughts on paper releases negativity and opens up space for hope and humor. I urge my media students at American University to keep journals in which they write their hearts out, especially when they are hurting. I've got a large stack of my own journals, with fraying covers and pages stained with wine and tears and ecstatic love. The pile starts at age thirteen and chronicles adolescent crushes and hot homecomings, the birth of children, angst over aging and youthful yearnings, marital malaise. Our children are healthy and I can hear Alice's pain but cannot feel the depth of her sorrow, though I do know the fragile filament she describes that separates love and hate in a marriage.

Studies that measure long-term marriage satisfaction show

that young children and teenagers, even those who don't demand layers of extra care, are high stress factors that contribute to marital flares. This is amplified by the tension between two career parents who tussle endlessly about who is doing more. We need to be reminded that a majority of couples who soldier onward through the frantic phases of sleepless infants through turbulent teens hit a more peaceful plateau. Brad Wilcox, director of the National Marriage Project, spoke of the first eight years of marriage as the ones in which most couples part ways. Another peak for divorce is around fifteen years, the era of rebellion when a mom and a dad frequently disagree on dating rules or how much back talk merits being grounded. It is also a time when we as parents are entering midlife and women particularly are mourning the loss of their youth. During this period of discontent and the first sighting of wrinkles, there is an urge to start anew, perhaps with a fresh romance. (I don't recommend this unless the marriage is really crippling; you take yourself with you wherever you go and even if you are leaving for someone hot and new, the new becomes old, and so it goes. You are still stuck with you.)

The sight of the swing set in our yard makes me nostalgic for chubby toddlers and the nights when my sons' adolescent friends were raiding our refrigerator. Yet at the same time, the stationary teeter-totter and empty sandbox awaiting grandchildren remind me of the burden that was lifted when the boys became responsible young men who drive, hold jobs, and can do a Subway run without me or my cash.

I am talking to a forty-six-year-old woman from Ohio who has a fifteen-year-old son and an eleven-year-old daughter. One day she finds pot in her son's room, and the next day she is dealing with a distraught daughter who is the brunt of mean-girl bullying on her basketball team. Her husband was raised by a Greek mother who waited on him like a prince and never punished him. "So I inherited a man who doesn't lift a finger with housework and counts on me to be the disciplinarian and the shoulder everyone cries on—including him."

It's 11:20 A.M., December 28, 2010, and Renee lets out an exasperated string of sighs as she cleans up after Christmas and picks up her husband's dirty socks mixed in with the shreds of wrapping paper. Raised by first-generation Armenian parents who collided constantly and stayed together, Renee says, "I'm turning into my mother," a woman who did all the domestic chores and gauged which of her six kids needed to be punished while her husband said, "You handle it." Her cotton-candy pink fingernails fly through the air, and her black eyes blaze as Renee talks about loving and hating and being wholly committed to her marriage.

RENEE

I'm always the heavy with the kids. My husband gets to come home, change out of his suit into his sweats, and flop down on the couch, and the kids practically jump on his lap they're so happy to see him and flee their strict mother. Meanwhile, we both have just worked a full day, and I'm in the kitchen throwing dinner together and he's on the couch watching the news. I always feel like there's some anger burbling below the surface with me. It's hard to describe but it's always there. Like I could spend all Saturday cleaning the house and he comes home after working out, grabs some food, then leaves the refrigerator door open, jars open on the counter, and his smelly undershirt and wet towel on the bathroom floor.

He's just like a child; he grew up with a mother who did 100 percent of everything for him. When we got married he was thirty-seven, and it's going to take me a lot longer than the seventeen years we've been together to undo all the damage and retrain him. This is where I often am at in my marriage right now: I'm exhausted and I'm mad and I'm disgusted. He's like a frat boy slob, clothes everywhere, farting loudly without an "excuse me" and it's like, "hey, show me some respect."

Lately I have started to let his dirty dishes and dirty clothes sit where he left them. I feel like sticking his nose in his mess like you do when you train a dog.

I talk to my mom about this because she had three times as many kids to raise as I do, and she just shrugs and says, "Renee, that's marriage." How do wives slug forward when they are always angry? I have noticed that my one glass of wine at the end of the day is turning into a half a bottle or more. That takes the edge off kitchen duty and children duty. Sex, what's that? We are down to once a month if he's lucky. I am too pissed and too tired for sex most of the time. You know what saves my ass? My husband makes me laugh. And our children worship the very ground he walks on. Why wouldn't they? He says "yes" and I say "no."

But I have hope. My sister just sent her last kid to college, and she tells me that she's starting to like her husband again. So I'm thinking there are easier times ahead for me, too. Another thing to his credit: As much as I complain that my husband always looks like he just woke up, I'd hate to be married to some fussy guy who slicked his hair and preened in front of the mirror more than I do.

My mother said this to me yesterday when I was complaining that my slob of a husband peed all over the toilet: "Renee, you are lucky to have a husband. He has a good job. He gave you good kids. When you were a little girl you would say to me, 'I can't wait to get married and have my own family.'"

It's true. I remember seeing so many of my friends' parents divorce, and I knew I wanted a traditional life. So marriage can be disgusting, but I am constantly renewed by the wondrous parts. Like at Christmas, my husband heaped buckets of presents on all of us, and as we opened them under the tree it did seem like that storybook fantasy I had when I was small: the mom surrounded by her family, all together in their little house while it snowed outside. The emotions from the holidays really put me in a better mood for a good couple of months. I would go to therapy, but he is dead set against it. As my husband says, "Whaddya want to fix? Whaddya want that you don't have?"

I want that burble of constant anger I feel to go away. So maybe it never does. But to answer my husband's question, there really isn't much that I don't have—except a hands-on husband.

The December holidays filled with festivals and rituals revolving around family do fan an immense rush of gratitude like Renee expressed. For all of December, I am generally lovestruck with not only my husband, who heaps presents on us, too, but with everyone—the mailman, the guy who changes my oil at the Ford dealer, the lady at the dry cleaner. Christmas carols make me delirious with good tidings, even though I'm a Hanukkah girl. All the children's birthdays are at the end of the year, and I am always grateful we made it through one more year, healthy and safe.

The holiday season of 2010 was also a season of thankfulness for Karen, whose husband of thirty-four years is in his fourth round of chemotherapy for lung cancer. Arnold's last scan in mid-December showed that his tumors were shrinking. At the age of twenty-two, Karen married Arnold, then thirty, a rugged dentist, jogger, golfer, fisherman, windsurfer, and equestrian. At sixty-four, Arnold is still a charismatic old hippie who wears a navy blue beret to cover his red hair thinning from chemo. But he now tires more easily and now walks the three miles he used to run every day.

With their only child in college, a self-described "rebel," Karen and Arnold were entering a second honeymoon phase, free to travel often to their newly purchased second home in North Carolina. Then came cancer.

Karen is a chic wisp of a woman in all-black Donna Karan,

yet she speaks in a big voice with a broad Michigan accent. Grand hand motions accompany each rapid sentence, jangling her four gold bracelets. Having endured many swerves in a marriage with lots of loathing and now sickness, today Karen and Arnold are in a stage that could be characterized as happily-ever-after, after-all.

KAREN

I was not head-over-heels infatuated with Arnold when we met. It wasn't like that, ever. We just always got along. He made me laugh. We had a lot in common. From our first date, really, we just kind of settled into a comfortable relationship and never turned back. Arnold was really larger than life, and I got caught up in that energy.

When I look back at all of this I think, "What is love, anyway?" For me, it wasn't this incredible romantic yearning. It's that we were good companions. Arnold was always upbeat, very smart but not overanalytical. He had this way of just moving on and not getting bogged down by problems. This trait has served us both well as he deals with his cancer. As a doctor, and as someone who had been around a lot of illness, Arnold has an incredible strength when facing life-and-death situations.

I loved being married to Arnold at the beginning. I never questioned whether we had made the right decision. Arnold was rugged and real. I had never met anybody like him, and he had never met anybody like me, an unpretentious Midwestern girl. He was used to slick East Coasters. We were intrigued—this is a good way to start a marriage, to be curious about each other. We were having such a good time that we decided not to have children for a while.

Arnold and I were together for about fifteen years before we had a child. We were so happy when I got pregnant, words can't describe that happiness. By the time Chas was in second grade, though, and for about the next ten years of raising him, my husband and I fluctuated between best friends and scalding enemies. I will be honest: I was very unhappy and many times considered splitting up.

I know a lot of women look back at their children's births and they are absolutely beaming with joy. I had an emergency C-section because the cord was wrapped around the baby's neck. Then, I was given too much medication during my epidural, and I nearly went into respiratory failure. And I lost so much blood I needed a transfusion. When I woke up, though, and saw Arnold feeding Chas with a tiny little bottle, I just started crying. It was so great; we were a family.

Almost immediately, Chas was everything to Arnold and I was like chopped liver. We both directed all our love toward our son and weren't very loving toward each other. Chas grew from an adorable baby into an edgy and opinionated boy, and Arnold always sided with him. He would say, "Isn't it great how he's not afraid to be his own person and speak his mind?" and the two of them would gang up on me. I used to think, "These are supposed to be the best years of my life; why am I so sad?"

Arnold thought it was cool to have a renegade son because he had been a renegade himself. My husband was a bad boy. He started smoking when he was eleven. He hitchhiked to Atlantic City when he was thirteen, and his father told the police, "Throw him in jail until I can get there." He was bad, bad, bad.

So there was no big mystery as to why we would have a rebellious son. During our hardest times, I would say to Arnold, "Let's go to therapy," and he would always say, "We can figure this out for ourselves." I would tell him that I felt very unloved in this relationship, and he would insist, "You are the love of my life." I'd say, "This feels more like hate than love." And he'd say, "I'm not leaving." The only reason we didn't get divorced during those bad years is because he would never move out and I wouldn't either. Finally, I was really agonizing over whether I should leave, and I actually looked at apartments.

Around this time we discovered that Chas needed heart surgery. He had a murmur since he was a baby, and it turned out that one of his valves was deformed. Arnold and I became united again quickly during this ordeal, and Chas is fine now. It's strange, but medical problems have been the glue that keeps our marriage together. Maybe it's this way with other couples, too: When faced with obstacles in your family, you know you can depend on each other.

Within a few weeks of the surgery, Chas was back at Gold's Gym lifting weights and back into full-throttle terrible teens. Arnold wanted to be his best friend, so he would just let things roll. I was the bad parent who said, "Guess what? It's not okay to come home at three in the morning."

Many parents I know who have one child break down when their kid goes to college. For us, this began one of the most tranquil periods of our marriage. Arnold had retired from his medical practice, and we became a couple again, like we were in the old days. We bought a condo in North Carolina and we would take long golfing weekends there, go to antique stores, relax, and laugh. Chas blossomed at college; he got a lot more subdued and was getting great grades so he wasn't an object of dissent for us anymore.

It was during this peaceful time in our marriage that Arnold was first diagnosed with lung cancer. Our whole lives changed, just like that. One day we're hanging blinds and pictures and laughing in our new condominium; the next day he's in the hospital having an emergency CAT scan. Two weeks later, Arnold was in surgery getting a third of his lung removed. His doctors assured him the cancer was completely encapsulated, that they got the whole thing, and that it didn't jump to anywhere. So we're thinking how lucky he is, they got it all! Soon he's back jogging three miles a day and playing eighteen holes of golf with no problems. He's going for checkups every three or four months and doctors keep giving him a clean bill of health.

Almost two years later, Arnold was having a tight feeling in his chest, and a CAT scan showed something new. I get a phone call on a rainy Thursday morning, and it's my husband. He says, "Karen, sit down. My lung cancer is back, and it's really back. There are tumors in both lungs." He is now in his fourth round of chemotherapy, and so far the tumors seem to be shrinking slightly, which is hopeful.

This is the first time in thirty-one years I have seen him sitting on a couch for longer than an hour at a time. But now he tires easily, his hair started to fall out, and he blows up at little things, not that I blame him. He's the one dealing with cancer, not me. But sometimes I get so down at the changes in him and worried about what lies ahead that I think, "Arnold's cancer is killing me."

So that's where we are at. We're coming up on the three-year mark from his first diagnosis and he's happy to be alive. Arnold will sometimes ask his oncologist, "How long do I have?" And the doctor tells him, "You could have five years. You could have five months. I don't know, Arnold, but we will try everything we can to keep you going."

Immediately we started doing things we've been putting off. We have an old-fashioned marriage in that my husband has always handled the money and the bills. I left my job when Chas was born, and Arnold has literally taken care of me. Over the past months, he has been educating me about all our financial matters and teaching me accounting skills. He'll patiently show me things about the maintenance of the house. He'll tell me, "I'm not going to be able to tell you this from my grave, so listen carefully."

I am not afraid of tomorrow; I'm too exhausted right now to think about the future. I am stronger and more independent now than I've ever been; I've had to be. Our relationship has gone through a lot of ups and downs during his illness, and basically since he started treatment a year ago I haven't left his side. I know more than most wives know what the vow means to stand by your spouse through hardship and sickness until death do you part.

He has days when he says, "I love you, I love you," over and over, and he hugs me and kisses me and won't let go. The he says, "I didn't treat you well enough," and hugs me again. On other days, he's back to the old Arnold—snapping at me and treating me like shit. I am actually glad when I see the old Arnold; it means he's feeling okay.

I've been with this man more than half of my life. He is my partner, and I'm going to be really lost without him. We are both very sad about how the treatment is affecting him. He is nauseated and has bouts of feeling really blue. Who wouldn't? It is hell on him, and he can be hell to live with. I told him yesterday—it was sort of a joke—"I just hope I don't die before you do."

Overall, though, Arnold has remained incredibly positive, and he is living every second of his life as fully as possible. He just got back from a trip with some guy friends to a ranch in Wyoming, and he rode horses and went fly-fishing and they drank a lot of beer. I am trying very hard to be calm when he has those moments of being totally freaked out and he's screaming at me. Right now, he needs me to be his rock of support; he really doesn't even want me out of his sight. He took care of me all these years; now it's my turn.

The week that Arnold was away, I did a lot of reflecting. The house was so calm, and I thought about what it will be like when my house is always quiet and I am alone. I'm sure Arnold will still be larger than life for me even when he's not in this house or in this world. When I remember that I was actually thinking of leaving him, it seems like another Karen because this Karen is sitting here talking about a person who is really her best friend. No matter how bummed out I've been in this marriage, I could always talk to Arnold about anything. I know if we would have been able to grow old together, this could have been our happiest time of all. Arnold is a good husband; he's not always nice, but he is a good person. He hasn't cheated on me. Arnold has never said to me, "You're ugly" or "You're fat" or "You're a terrible mother," like I hear from girlfriends who put up with husbands who insult them. I am really learning a lot now about what it means to love someone. It means you swallow your own anger and put up with their shit when they need you to. We would love to go to Italy; we've been talking about that for years, but I don't think Arnold and I are going to Italy anytime soon. He really just wants to be home, sitting at the end of our dock, drinking a Heineken and staring out at the water like he's done our whole marriage.

When I look down the road I sometimes laugh and think, "Well, at least I know I'm not going to be stuck with him for the next twenty-five years." Of course, the way I'm feeling now, I'd love to be stuck with this man even ten more years. And I was always the one asking, "Why don't we just split up?" And Arnold would say, "If you want to leave, leave. I'm not leaving this house." Those fiery moments reminded me of that scene from the movie *The War of the Roses*, in which Kathleen Turner and Michael Douglas are in this nightmare marriage but neither will leave the house. In the final scene they are both fighting and hanging from the chandelier.

Well, Arnold never did leave the house, did he? He got his way, as usual.

Like Karen, I am fifty-six and could easily live another thirty, maybe even forty, years. The prospect of another chance at love untainted by the bruises of an old marriage is sometimes appealing. Then I look over at my partner of twenty-three years and think, "With this one at least I know what I'm getting." Moved by Karen's story of living urgently in the moment, I am poignantly aware how fortunate we are. I surprise Chuck with a random kiss and whisper, "I love you," my lips seductively grazing his ear, and he coolly remarks, "Wait ten minutes. You will feel differently." I know that he is right. I also know if the day comes that his maroon La-Z-Boy is empty because I am the last one standing, I will miss his silence and his sarcasm and our fights. His imperfections will be muted in my memory by a glow of perfect love, like my mother's airbrushed recollection of my father.

Yet—until death do we part? Damn, that seems long. I ask Chuck if he thinks we will be married forever, and he says, "Yes." I ask, "How do you know that?" He looks at me—he actually turns from the TV—and says solemnly, "Because you are my wife."

Hearing the words "my wife" shakes me. Those words are so

simple compared to the depth and complexity of the actual role. Being a wife can mean that you need to buffet every morsel of crap and wave of sadness that comes your way. And decades later, if you are tough and lucky, you have dropped your weapons and your armor and you join the old marrieds who claim that the longer they are together, the loathing is less and the loving is more. This sweeping feeling of gratitude is enlarged by a call I get during Thanksgiving weekend from my childhood friend Donna Farris Outlaw, who recently buried her husband. She found fifty-eight-year-old Jerry slumped over on the living room couch one evening when she returned from the beauty parlor. He died two days later in the hospital of internal bleeding. Red-haired, freckled, and Irish Donna's partner of twenty-six years was a black Chicago cop, with whom she had two sons, now ages twenty-three and twenty-one.

Donna met Jerry in the mid-1970s while she was working at a suburban McDonald's that was a popular hangout for Cook County police. Her father told her he would not speak to her until she could tell him she was no longer dating outside her race. Donna never spoke to her father again. "He died without knowing his grandsons, and not knowing the man who was the love of my life," she said. A widow at fifty-seven, Donna is a chilling reminder of what we take for granted.

DONNA

I had worked at this McDonald's for thirteen years and had become good friends with many Chicago policemen and policewomen. Jerry was not a classically handsome guy; he was about five feet eight, pudgy and muscular, a star among the Cook County Sheriff's police. Well, one thing led to another and we got engaged, had two kids, and lived together for twenty-three years before we got married in 2007.

It was really hard for me to be cut out of my father's life, but my mother grew to love Jerry dearly. There was never a problem with his family; they were very open and receptive. At his funeral, his mother told me that I was the best thing that ever happened to her son.

Jerry had high blood pressure. He was a smoker until about four years ago; he smoked long brown More cigarettes and a lot of them. He ended up having a heart valve transplant, but he recovered quickly and was back at work within a couple of weeks. His death came out of nowhere. I was getting a pedicure, and I came home a couple minutes after nine at night, and I found him sitting on the couch, very disoriented. Even the dog was acting weird. Jerry's eyes were not right, his breathing was labored, and he was out of it. I called 911 and we got him to the hospital, where they found massive internal bleeding.

They took him into surgery to repair the veins going to the small intestine that had burst. His heart stopped during surgery and he died shortly after—it was just too much for his body to take. I am still numb and disbelieving, and I know I will be like this for a long time to come. It's weird; there are so many things you do as a couple in a long-term relationship that become so routine you don't even notice you are doing it. It's the little things I miss.

Like when I came home from work, he'd be watching TV, I'd be in the kitchen cooking, and we would yell back and forth about what we did that day. I miss his amazing stories that only a Chicago cop knows. I feel empty a lot of the time.

Jerry was a cop for thirty-five years, and although he was involved in many dangerous situations, I never really worried about him because I knew he was a good cop. I knew he wouldn't rush into anything and play hero. Sometimes I'd hear about murders in Chicago on the news and he wasn't home, but he would always call me and say, "I'm not there. I'm okay." I've had moments when I thought marriage was a pain. I've had moments when I thought, "Man, is this hell even worth it?" I would say in the end we do it for the children. Because my boys are mixed race, I didn't want them growing up without a father; there are so many fatherless boys in the black culture. We didn't want our boys to become statistics.

And Jerry was such a strong father figure for them. All he had to do was look at those kids if they were misbehaving—we called it the "Jerry Look"—and they would straighten up right away. That look even worked on the dog. When the dog was acting up, Jerry would stare at him and the dog would creep back into the corner and lie down quietly.

I had a lot of respect for my husband and his ability to leave his work on the streets and not bring it home with him. A cop's job means he answers calls for shootings and car accidents; he sees people with their heads blown off and their heads sliced through windshields. It takes a certain type of person to handle that type of work and not come home in a horrible mood. My husband was the one all our friends called when their kids were in trouble. He was the go-to guy with any issues they had with bad behavior or brushes with the law. He was a hero in our home and in our community, I can tell you that. More than five hundred members of the Cook County Sheriff's Police Department and friends came to his funeral; an honor guard stood by the casket, in uniform and at attention, as he was put into the hearse. It was an elegant finale for a really great husband, father, and policeman.

He's been buried for only a few weeks and my friends are already asking me if I'd get married again. I'm not opposed to another marriage; I think every person you do love you love differently. Even though you have a great marriage, you look for something different at different times at your life. When you are younger, it is more like a lusty, madly-in-love feeling. When I'm in my sixties I might remarry for companion love. Whatever I do, I'm getting buried next to Jerry. That's all set. I want to be next to him for our next life together.

I have no tolerance now when my friends complain about the piddly little things they have to put up with in their marriages. I tell them, "I wish I still had a husband to complain about," and that shuts them right up.

V

Resurrecting Childhood Passions

"There is an inner calm and intensity of spirit that
comes from pushing yourself to your maximum
potential."

—GABRIELLE

I AM LOOKING OUT the kitchen window at four young men
hurling fallen pinecones and walnuts into the woods with
lacrosse sticks, bare-chested and howling with each shot. They
measure from six feet five down to six feet tall, and their torsos and
arms are bands of muscle. This sweaty tribe, made up of my grown
sons, is within earshot and within my reach, a gorgeous and whole
moment in the late summer dusk, a finger snap of time.

Theo is off for a junior semester abroad in Prague, and Isaac
is starting as a freshman in college. In one week, I will Skype and
text message my two eldest children instead of hugging them good
night. Twins Jack and Zane, age seventeen, are rising juniors in
high school, and then in two years it will be just me and Chuck
and two fat white cats, T.J. and Maxx, named after my favorite
store.

Scouring bean-and-cheese burritos off of plates, I am standing at my spot near the sink where I have stood for years, the place
with the best view to watch the boys playing outside. As four taut
teenagers lope and whoop on this hot night, I am seeing instead

four soft toddlers in tiny red sweatshirts and terrycloth bibs, falling over each other like a pack of puppies. It was yesterday, it seems, when I washed baby bottles at this sink and cherished my good fortune of being a new mother who had years to go before college depleted her dinner table.

I see preschoolers with velvety cheeks in Power Rangers shirts sprawled on the sidewalk, writing words they've just learned in pastel chalk. I see third graders in Michael Jordan jerseys taking turns throwing a basketball, underhand, to land in a rickety hoop Chuck installed in 1994. I see a huddle of pimply adolescents playing capture the flag, boxers rising from their pulled-down shorts, and high school graduation parties with clusters of teary parents. I will soon be alone in a big, empty yard to tend to my fig trees and irises and to figure out who I will be when no one is calling for Mommy anymore.

It's both staggering and energizing, the sharp turn from the woman at the center of the lives of needy children to a woman who must rediscover—or re-create—her own center. Mothering young children provides a huge distraction from having to deal with your own growth issues. Women at my stage faced with shifting life cycles and emptying nests need to ask ourselves: Who was I before my kids came along? Who do I want to be now? Splayed by domestic chores and professional pursuits, often we spend much of childrearing not remembering who we were.

I am lying on Isaac's bed as he gleefully packs for his first year of college, which starts tomorrow. He is shoving a pair of yellow gym shorts and an iridescent Frisbee into his duffel bag. My head is buried in his sea green pillowcase I ordered from a Garnet Hill catalog for his first bed when he moved from a crib. "Mom, quit the waah-waah," Isaac says with a mock huff, giving me a little kiss on my forehead. "I'm only two hours away." I smile back, sniffle back my snotty nose, and don't tell him what's on my mind—that he will soon be a lifetime away.

Rarely do I go a week without hearing from a reader or a girlfriend about how emptying nests are tossing them into slumps that are more severe than expected. I ask them, "What was the passion of your soul when you were young? What did you once love to do but had to leave behind because of marriage and your profession and exhaustion?" Lost hobbies are filled with raw childhood energy that can be a transformative fertilizer to grow new parts of ourselves and reboot early joy. What sport of the soul did you abandon with age? Resurrecting passions of our youth can take some of the sting out of hard, but necessary, transitions.

Riding horses is a sport I loved, left behind, and started again, thanks to a random conversation at a school play. I was telling my friend Steuart that I've spent most of the past twenty years on the sidelines watching my kids star in sports and school plays. I've known him since Theo and his daughter Jessie started prekindergarten together. His family owns a four-hundred-acre farm twenty minutes from our house, where he trains horses and gives riding lessons. We were watching our then-seventeen-year-olds leap across the stage.

In the role of the Pharaoh, my Theo was wearing a gold headpiece with a matching long skirt, and he was twirling Jessie, the show's lead dancer. She arched her body over Theo's arm in a Cirque du Soleil–caliber back bend that formed a perfect O with her lithe body. The audience gasped and applauded, and I am seeing my mom and dad in the roaring crowd at my high school football games when I was the cheerleader in the center, doing a round-off and landing in a split.

After the production, Steuart and I waited together for our children to emerge from the dressing room. He is a champion dressage rider, and he told me about a first place he had just won. I admitted that I was jealous that in his late forties he still got to indulge in athletic endeavors he loves.

Over the years, I have shared with him how much horseback riding meant to me as a girl. When I was growing up, my father used to take the family to a ranch in Arizona where we rode most of every day, led by tobacco-spitting cowboys on perilous mountain trails and tearing through the open desert. In the past three decades, I've been on a horse fewer than a dozen times. Yet the silver-plated sculpture of a stallion I won in the 1970 Camp Aga-wak horse show is in my constant field of vision just behind my computer screen, goading me to get back in the saddle. Steuart offered: "Well, come out and ride again."

That Saturday, I went to his farm and mounted his mom's old gentle quarter horse. I placed my head on River's coarse mane and stroked her tawny neck and just lay there for a while, while my whole girlhood shot through me. I now ride whenever I can. Lop-ing on a horse, I feel my whole self open, like it did when I was ten and riding my pony, Chico, through the parched Tucson terrain, dodging cacti, dust flying. Resurrecting this old passion of mine has given me a piece of my primal self that's been missing.

As much as we accomplish in our professions, there is nothing like dipping back into something artistic or athletic that we once excelled at yet discarded with age. When I'm on a horse, fluid with the animal's muscled body, I am newly assured that I am too young to be old. I feel the same way when I'm writing, lost in the flow of words and thoughts so that my fingers and my mind are a unified machine—it's a pure state of being. In Mihaly Csikszentmihalyi's bestseller *Flow: The Psychology of Optimal Experience,* the author concludes after twenty-five years of research that the happiest peo-ple are those absorbed by creative and challenging tasks, people wholly involved and flowing, mind and body, with their work. We achieve optimal joy, according to Csikszentmihalyi, when "the action carries us forward as if by magic."

Tracey Karsten Farrell's childhood sails with her father across the lakes of Michigan formed magical memories that remained at her core, though a hectic job and three children kept her off the water for years. Recently, at the age of fifty-seven, she is often on boats in her new position as a yacht broker in the Bay Area, a flow back into an old life that has left her "totally energized." Tracey was a nineteen-year-old sophomore at Mount Holyoke College when "this big tall guy with beautiful hands" entered her life, shaking up her early 1970s feminist views that women should postpone marriage and motherhood to first rise in their careers. Standing six feet tall, Tracey was drawn to the six-feet-six Glenn Farrell, captain of the Amherst College basketball team, for his relaxed manner, honed in his native Southern California. She was a Connecticut girl reared in a traditional family, a continent away from his free-spirited surfing roots. Yet on June 3, 1975, two days after her college graduation, Tracey Karsten became Tracey Farrell in the Mount Holyoke chapel.

Throughout her climb from young feminist to marketing ace to mother of three daughters to mother of the bride, Tracey, like many midlife women, lost track of her original self. Here is her story of recovering that person.

TRACEY

My first memory of sailing was when I was four and my dad took me out on Lake Erie in a very small sloop and a howling wind. I've never been more scared or more exhilarated in my life. That began my lifelong passion for sailing and for boats in general. A few months ago, after years of consulting in corporate marketing and only intermittent boat time, I decided to become a licensed yacht salesperson, and I feel that pure excitement once again. My kids are grown. One daughter is married. Glenn and I can now do what we want, when we want to. This freedom means I can pay closer attention to my own growth and to the continued growth of our marriage.

Glenn and I were college sweethearts, and that raises the bar in many ways. Of course, you cannot go back to the early hot years when time absolutely stopped with a look into those blue eyes. Yet, we are a couple that still holds hands wherever we go. I love that about us; we've done this since we met.

When Glenn and I first hugged, it was electric. We pulled back and looked at each other with surprise, and with some kind of weird understanding of what was about to unfold. There were so many things that drew me to him. His long hair and patched jeans and cowboy shirts. He occasionally smoked cigarettes and could blow smoke rings like Gandalf. Our first date was in October 1973. We danced all night and sang and laughed, and it was like we had never been apart. We completed each other in a really crazy way, and we did it so quickly.

This was the seventies, and things were really opening up for women at that point in time. My group of girlfriends were educated to be the best and the brightest, and the last thing any one of us planned to do was get married right after we got our degrees. Yet by March of my junior year, I was engaged—six months after that fateful first date. After my graduation, Glenn was recruited to play basketball in France, and so, after three months of marriage, we ended up in a walled village of about seven hundred people in the agricultural community of Bruch. A whole new world opened up to us, filled with fruit trees, vineyards, tobacco farms, and rustic food. We lived in a tiny cottage with an outhouse and a chicken coop, and were the only Americans within miles. There was no heat in the winter months, so we would move our bed over beside the wall we shared with the village bakery. Daily, at about three A.M., we would begin to feel the warmth of the ovens and smell the incredible fragrance of fresh-baked breads and croissants.

It may sound bucolic, but at first we were miserably homesick; it was a big adjustment for both of us to be living in such a fishbowl, and our French was still pretty limited. I trembled at the thought of going to the local stores and having to ask for goods. One day I was so down, and so frustrated, I packed a backpack and said, "I'm going to hitchhike to Albi." This was the *ville* that was the hometown of Toulouse Lautrec. Glenn looked at me and said, "You can't go by yourself." I said, "Sure I can—watch me."

This was our first argument. I told him, "Look, you are down and I am down and we need a change of scenery to regroup." So he grudgingly packed and we took off together for the most wonderful little adventure. Along the way, we found ourselves relaxing into the moment again, laughing and remembering why we had agreed to head to Europe in the first place—to experience life in a different way. It was the best thing we could have done for ourselves, and it forged an attitude that was to define our relationship.

In our darkest times, over the years, we have had to both be willing to make changes to find the light. Now, thirty-five years of marriage later, France remains a metaphor for us when things aren't going well. One of us will say, "Hey, let's go do something different. Take my hand. Follow me."

Once we got over the initial culture shock we grew to absolutely love our life there. Glenn became the star of the Division III basketball team. He was bigger than Michael Jordan to them, and they would have festivals in his honor. We made friends that truly became like family to us, nurturing us in our early years of marriage. The day we left France I felt like I was splitting in two and leaving my true self there.

Glenn graduated from UCLA with his MBA, and we relocated to San Francisco. I moved into corporate marketing for Levi Strauss, and Glenn joined Peat Marwick Mitchell. In my head and my heart, I thought, like so many women of my generation, "I can do it all. I can have a great career, I can have kids, I can have a successful marriage." Looking back, I think I felt overly invincible. Then my own personal challenges began to get in my way. First, there was the sudden loss of my father to a heart attack at age fifty-nine. Then, every couple of years, I suffered huge medical setbacks: I ruptured a disc in my lower back right after our second daughter was conceived, and had to spend close to five months of that pregnancy in bed while Glenn very capably cared for our firstborn. After months of physical therapy and alternative treatments, I had back surgery a year later. We had another baby—and two years later, there was an emergency appendectomy. Then, not too long after that, a second back surgery. All throughout this period, I was trying to be a good mother and wife/partner, but it became a very difficult time for me both physically and emotionally.

Then Glenn made partner at the firm, which was great for him but very tough on our family life. I was deeply proud of him. But, up to this point, things had been pretty much fifty-fifty on the home front, splitting childrearing and household chores. Becoming partner meant a whole new level of responsibility for him, and I would often be home alone day and night with small children. I was also still juggling a career and dealing with health issues.

By the time our third daughter was born, my corporate clients had grown to include major Fortune 500 businesses, and I was frantic to make deadlines, let alone dinner or participate in my kids' school activities. It was apparent that Glenn and I were evolving away from the tight unit we once were.

There were a lot of stupid arguments during this time, and in many instances the stress was forcing me into throwing tantrums like a two-year-old, seeking attention of any kind. Where I had always loved the Tracey that Glenn seemed to evoke when we were together, I started to really dislike myself. I had so much, but I seemed to have no happiness. I was no longer Glenn's primary focus, and many deep insecurities set in.

During this period, and up until recently, the girls and I would spend every summer sailing on the Chesapeake Bay, near where my mother and my brother and his family now live. With Glenn often obligated to summer work deadlines, we would pack up and head east to spend some quality time with my East Coast family. My father had owned a forty-three-foot sailboat, and after he died my siblings and I all came together and decided we would restore the boat and share it with our families. It has been a real point of connection between us as a portal of memories and as a vessel for new experiences.

My three daughters and I have gone on long chick trips up and down the Chesapeake Bay. We've caught and cooked fish and crabs, and we've weathered many a terrible storm. Each summer on the water, we have all learned about risk-taking and teamwork, and about responsibility and our own inner reserves. My father was a true sailor, and he gave that gift to me. I have passed that gift on to the granddaughters he never knew and shown them as well the true spirit of their mother.

Over the years, I've shared with my daughters personal experiences that might guide them in their own life journeys. I tell them to pay attention to what makes them the happiest and to be open to new adventures. I tell them that the most interesting people are those who have zigged and zagged, and that they should never be afraid to try something new as long as they keep moving forward. As parents we encourage our children to follow their passions, and too often we leave our own passions behind.

As the children moved out or married one by one, I found myself relapsing into depending again too much on Glenn to make me happy. Honestly, that was the blessing and the curse of our next chapter together. On the one hand, it's such a wonderful feeling to still be living with my college boyfriend. On the other hand, you just cannot expect someone else to be responsible for your well-being. I looked at other marriages around me, saw the breakups and divorces, and wondered about my own periods of sadness.

Was I expecting too much, again, of myself or of my husband? Here I am, a woman in a good marriage, but I rarely see the guy because he's so busy. The girls are living on their own. There are no sailing trips, no adventures. Everyone has moved on.

All of a sudden, I was seeing myself as a wife and a mother, standing in the middle of an empty house, wondering, "Okay, so what do I do now? Nobody needs me." Glenn was meaningfully occupied with a long, fulfilling career. Where was my parallel existence? I found myself staring, kind of like Luke Skywalker when he confronts his demons and they turn out to be himself, at a lot of emptiness. I did not want to just wait around for Glenn to retire.

I needed to reengage with something that fulfilled me. And I needed to stop dwelling on the physical changes and challenges. You go through this period in your fifties when you are looking at every gray hair and every wrinkle, and you can turn yourself into a cottage industry with Botox and plastic surgery, or you can forgo all that and go get a new life.

It was during this time that I met an engaging woman in her sixties who was heavily into sailing. She told me that she had turned her love of sailing into a career as a yacht broker. She started talking about her daily activity on the docks, and it was as if this tiny lightbulb went off and sent a little flicker through my soul. I almost started crying, as she said that she was retiring in the fall and the firm might need someone. That little flicker started to burn a lot brighter. I sat on the idea for a while, discussing it with Glenn and really weighing if this was right for me. I thought, "Am I moving backward and doing this because of the prospect of recapturing the old Tracey? Or am I moving forward, like I tell my daughters to make sure they are doing, and also taking away the pressure I tend to put on my husband and marriage to completely sustain me?"

I realized that the old version of the Tracey-mom-wife doesn't exist anymore. I do not have to juggle everyone else's schedules. I can become a new and improved Tracey that builds on all of the richness of life before and reaches new heights with the prospect of doing something I had never done. I needed to go forward, and what better way to do that than with sailing and with the wind literally at my back?

I did get the yacht salesperson's job—and it's as if the best of my past is coming together with dreams for the future. In yacht sales, I am able to use my expertise in corporate marketing and at the same time build on my lifelong experience with boats. Since yacht sales are all commission-based, it feels good to be able to again contribute financially to our family.

Every morning when I arrive to work and look out over the water and the masts, I exhale deeply, thankfully. I watch the burgees change when the next weather front moves in; I see the tugs and sailboats and Coast Guard ships come and go; and share the friendly camaraderie of all the folks on the docks. There is a family of stingrays that hover in the lagoon surrounding the brokerage boats, many herons, and the occasional errant sea lion. This new world is something that I have created for myself, a second life that now belongs only to me. My love of water and my love of boats have circled back to me in a powerful way.

I took my daughter Devon down for a test sail of a yacht last week. As we were getting the boat rigged, my boss was walking toward us, and she said, "Tracey, you bring a great new energy out on the docks." My daughter looked at me after my boss left and said, "Mom, this is the happiest I've seen you in years." Out of the mouths of babes come many truths.

Sailing always gave me some of my highest highs, and I found that no matter what was going on in our lives, if I could get back on the water, things seemed more hopeful. Now Glenn sees me so fulfilled with this new activity that I believe he sees hope for himself as well, for what lies ahead after his retirement. Aging is not easy for the guys, either. So with this reinvention of myself, I feel a little like I've taken a first step again, toward a new future together—and I am saying to him, with all my love, "Hey, let's go do something different. Take my hand. Follow me."

Tracey describes a dramatic repositioning of a family that is now a party of two at home, and not five. Who will we be as a couple without the boys that have formed a glorious wedge between us for so long? What if we don't like each other, apart from the gaggle? The looming vision of our large dining room table with me on one end, Chuck on the other, and nothing in between already leaves a lonely sting. There will be plenty of rough days ahead, I presume, as he wonders, like I will wonder, "What do I need to do to want to stay married?" As long as we keep asking that question, we should be okay. The answer for me will be to keep doing work and play outside of my marriage that I love.

Lots of aging adventurers are too young to be old ladies gazing wistfully through photo albums filled with pictures of us as girlhood riding or sailing champions, with cheeks flushed from adrenaline and wind. We need to keep reinventing ourselves with every phase or else we will wither inside. I have a forty-eight-year-old acquaintance who is blasting through every fertility procedure available to have a third child. Her oldest is a boy entering his senior year in high school, and she hasn't practiced law since he was born. "I know exactly who I am when I am surrounded by children," she says.

I understand why some women are driven to keep having babies. It's a way of staying distracted from working on our own unfinished selves. Those selves catch up to us, though, and we can't escape this cold fact: Snuggly babies turn into surly and independent teenagers, even if you have a dozen of them. Ultimately, at some point, we are left behind, moms staring at themselves in the mirror, asking, "Now what?"

Who are you beyond Mommy? It's crucial to start birthing a new self while you still have kids in tow so that when the empty nest does hit, you aren't flailing in despair. You know the old saying: Look for a new job while you still have your old job, so you're standing on firm ground while you're scouting. Gabrielle Redford knows this from her profession and from her home life as the mother of twin eight-year-olds.

At forty-four, Gabrielle Redford is the editorial projects manager of the Washington-based *AARP The Magazine*, a publication formed in 1949 as an arm of the American Association of Retired Persons. Guided by the prevailing mantra that fifty is the new thirty, *AARP The Magazine*, which reigns as the world's highest-circulation magazine (35 million readers), has become an edgy bible for aging readers who work hard and play hard through their seventies and eighties and feel great.

In her twelve years at *AARP The Magazine*, Gabrielle, whose position includes serving as fitness editor, has introduced lifestyle trends that have helped fan the boomer health and longevity movement. A head turner with golden hair, a model's lithe physique, and pale blue eyes, Gabrielle has the zeal of a woman in her twenties. That's because the nationally ranked teen swimming champ has resumed the sport that made her soar as a child. Two racing suits are draped over the towel rack in the downstairs bathroom of her home, sexy numbers in bold colors and cut with low backs.

Tonight, Gabrielle will stretch into one of them and head to the nearby Naval Academy to practice with the masters swim team. Her twins are in an elementary school nearby as this Texas native talks about resurrecting her true self, under water.

GABRIELLE

Competitive swimming has been my identity for as long as I can remember, and I know I will be a swimmer long after the children are in college. When I was young, swimming was all I did aside from going to school. I swam three hours a day, as a butterflyer, and I was very good at it. That's where I got my confidence. The sport of swimming is very wrapped up in looking good and feeling healthy, so that has always been a big part of my identity, too.

At fifteen, I won the Texas state championships in butterfly, and I went on to the YMCA Nationals and was ranked as one of the top swimmers of my age in the country. I looked like an Amazon woman. I was very lean but I had huge shoulders and a big neck. You've seen Olympic swimmers; they're just built. That was me. Thick and muscled. Going through adolescence I looked like this super athlete, but I wanted to look more feminine. At the time, I didn't equate being strong athletically as being feminine. Now I do. Now I see them as two pieces of the same pie.

That summer in high school I developed an eating disorder and I lost a tremendous amount of weight. I went from 120 to probably 95 pounds—not good. If you're an elite swimmer, and even if you dropped substantial weight like me, you can still swim at an impressive level. But I never got to the elite champion level that I was before.

At fifteen, if I had kept those skills, I believe I could have gone on to the Junior Olympics. My eating disorder cut short the potential I had to become that great athlete, and I've always had that void. One big reason competitive swimming is so thrilling for me now is that I get to chase after a dream that wasn't fulfilled in my childhood. I look back and think, *"I could have been a contender nationally,"* but I got too skinny. I didn't have the energy to propel myself through the water. I did end up swimming in college for a Division III school and I did well, but I still had a distorted body image. I was very concerned about appearing thin, and the last thing I wanted to look like was a big-shouldered Amazon.

I am so different now; today the happiness I feel with swimming is a deeper contentment. It grounds me in a lot of ways. I'm a better mom. I'm a better editor. I'm a better friend, when I have that part of me fulfilled which is the swimmer persona. When I'm swimming hard sets through the water, I am free from everything else: I don't think about my deadlines. I don't think about the kids. I am proud of my muscles now, not ashamed: I'm forty-four, and in the best shape of my life. I will always be conscious of body image, but I never weigh myself anymore. I know how my jeans fit.

I taught my kids how to swim when they were very young because it was such an important part of my growing-up years. When they tried out for the Navy Junior Team last year the head coach called to tell me they made the team. I said, "Oh, that's wonderful; I used to swim myself," and I went on and on, excited to talk to someone who lived the sport like I did. Then he said to me, "Well, your kids are on a team. Why don't you swim for the Navy masters team?" Anybody twenty-one or older is considered a masters swimmer.

So I started swimming with this group about a year ago, and I adore my teammates. There's something about being in the water, half naked—you get to know people really well, very quickly. It's an instant intimacy, and it's very sexy. I'm one of a couple of women in my group with about eight guys. The men are in their forties up until their early fifties. We're all married, but, well, there is harmless flirting going on and at times we'll go out for drinks after practice, then go home to our families.

Intense workouts, I realize now, are something I really missed. There is an inner calm and intensity of spirit that comes from pushing yourself to your maximum potential. I feel like I did when I was a kid swimming at an elite level and doing back-to-back hundred-meter sets that leave you entirely breathless. I did this at nine and at fifteen, and I'm doing it at forty-four.

By the end of it, you're practically dead. You've worked so hard, and the euphoria is huge because the whole team feels it; it's a shared experience. I always felt alive when I was swimming. You've heard of a runner's high—I get a swimmer's high every time I pull through the water.

I have reconnected with a force that is pumping my self-esteem, maybe even more than when I was young. My anorexia is long gone. I feel strong. I feel sexy. I feel powerful. And this translates to a lot of different areas of my life. Before I took up swimming again, my life was mostly about work and family. I kind of fit in a run or a bike ride every once in a while before the kids woke up. There was little time in between to devote to relating to friends or having a real relationship with myself.

Although my husband appreciates that swimming makes me a happier mother and a happier wife, I do worry sometimes that I'm leaving him behind. Team sports are not his thing; he's very much a solitary outdoorsman who goes off in the woods by himself to fish or hunt. My husband and I have different interests but very much the same values. My mother used to say, "You cannot rely on one person for all your needs." And I am definitely a person who requires a village of people. I can't tell you what a charge I have gotten out of becoming part of a community of swim buddies in midlife, competitive athletes with like-minded interests. It has just opened me up in so many new ways.

I go to swim practice three nights a week, and my husband watches the kids on those days. I'm not in the office. I'm not in the house. I'm somewhere else doing something just for me. Swimming is this wonderful combination of feeling both vulnerable and like Superwoman.

Your libido shoots way up in your forties. Compounded with the adrenaline rush of swimming, your sex drive feels like it is off the charts. This is definitely something good to bring home after practice. As you get older, I think you forget what makes you tick, the magic of sexuality, the real stuff inside that is the real person you are. I hear from so many of our AARP readers who feel they are doing everything for their families and doing nothing for themselves. Unhappiness often drives you to a therapist's couch. You come out thinking that counseling was a bit helpful; it was very expensive, but you are still the same person. I really believe that physical activity can transform your whole life. Swimming for me is a lot cheaper and gives me a lot more lasting power. I feel very feminine and strong at the same time, something I was unable to achieve when I was younger.

Women often get depressed at the prospect of turning fifty; I would never trade who I am now with who I was in my thirties. The early years of our marriage and early motherhood were a heartbreaking struggle for us.

When the twins were four months old, our daughter Allie was hospitalized because she was going into heart failure. She has a rare congenital condition in which her arteries are transposed; the artery going to her lungs and the one going to her body are switched. Her heart compensated by flipping its functions so that her small ventricle now pumps to her body and the large ventricle pumps to her lungs.

This put a terrible stress on our marriage. Looking back, I honestly believe I was borderline psychotic. We were so sleep-deprived from having to get up every couple of hours to administer any one of her twenty-one medications and to monitor her feeding tube—she had to be fed throughout the night. Every time you picked up this poor little baby, she had a backpack of fluids trailing her. On top of this, I had a healthy baby to take care of. My mother, thank God, moved in for about five months.

At first, my husband was scared of the whole situation, and he was hands-off. Dave is a marine biologist, and his escape was being able to spend all day at the office through these early months of trauma; I took a year off from my job. I did not exercise during this time. No swimming. No running. Nothing. And talk about skinny? I was scarily bone thin. That was the low period for our relationship, and it unfortunately came at the early part of our marriage, not at midlife when many people experience problems. The hurt came for me because Dave maintained his steady-rock demeanor, and in some ways, that was really good. He was the calm in the storm. But I also needed a partner who was just as urgent as I was. I was the one who was always trying to figure out what was wrong with the baby and what can we do today that's a little different to fix the baby? The journalist in me took over. I was really aware how the worrying and problem solving for children is mainly up to the women, because we do that instinctively.

Basically, in order to get my daughter off the feeding tube I had to teach her how to eat—not easy for someone who is not a doctor. I had an occupational therapist come once a week to give me tips, but mostly this enormous responsibility was on our shoulders.

When Allie finally got off the feeding tube at two-and-a-half years old, Dave and I went into post-traumatic stress. We had held it together for so long that we finally heaved into a meltdown. We had used up all our reserves dealing with the heart disease and had neglected to address the primary communication issues a couple needs to deal with to make a marriage work. It was awful. We were in such urgent mode with our daughter we had lost sight of each other.

It took a while—months really—to climb out of that abyss. We had to come together because twin babies need the attention of two healthy parents who are on the same team. Allie and Will are eight now, and I'm finally at the point where they are in school all day and I have climbed back fully into my career and into my own mental health. My daughter had a stress test yesterday at Johns Hopkins, and her heart is strong for now, though she may eventually need a heart transplant.

I am so happy when I watch her on the swim team; she's not one of the fastest kids—as a matter of fact, she is one of the slowest kids. But she's out there and she's making her heart stronger by exercising.

Good marriages have this yin-yang quality to them. When one partner is strong, the other gets to be not-so-strong, and vice versa. You'll always have one parent that's better in some area than the other. Say, when the kids get sick, they usually want Mommy. My husband is much better at just playing with the kids.

Wanna play chess? Ask Dad. So one parent gets time off while the other is on.

The kids are front and center always when they're young, but both parents don't always have to be front and center with them. I think problems arise when one parent feels overwhelmed and the other parent doesn't recognize it enough to step in. That's when you just have to say, "Listen, I've had the kids after school every day this week and I'm going to go to the pool or the gym tonight to get away from it all."

Exercise is more healing than anything, I know that firsthand, and it is a fundamental lesson I am passing on to the children. When Allie was born the doctors told me she would never be able to exercise, and I never accepted that. I thought, "You just watch her!" I want her to grow into a confident woman, and exercise has shaped my identity and given me courage. Allie will never be an Olympic athlete, but she can swim and she can ride her bike and she can figure skate like everyone else.

As the magazine's fitness editor, I am constantly getting letters from women who tell me things like, "I'm sixty-five and I ran my first marathon" or "On my seventy-fifth birthday I took up salsa dancing." At midlife and older, people are achieving athletic goals they haven't had the time, or the focus, to achieve when they were young. Scientists are discovering that our bodies can do much more than we previously thought we could, and that exercise has an anti-aging effect at the molecular level of cells. I'm discovering that personally; at forty-four, I am swimming at nearly the speed I did in my teens, and I am more determined than ever to break my records. And I feel more youthful and energetic than I've ever felt.

I swim as much for my head as I do for my body. My children recognize this about me. When I'm grumpy they will say, "Mom, why don't you go swim for a while." When the time comes for the children to leave home, I see myself competing in swim meets internationally. There was just a competition in Puerto Rico that I qualified for but didn't attend because of the children. My mentors are the seniors out there still swimming hard into their eighties.

I'm a swimmer. That's who I am. That's my identity. In my youth I was ashamed to have an Amazon body. Now I have serious leg muscles and serious arm muscles and I'm proud of them. Muscles represent not just strength of body but strength of character. Moving swiftly through water—that's freedom.

AARP studies and a slew of other research over the past three decades underscore the impact of a healthy diet and physical fitness on longevity. Exercise strengthens the immune system, lowers blood pressure, and staves off heart disease and stroke. Wives often joke about their couch potato husbands who lounge while they wait on them. I've been known to join in those conversations; it makes for entertaining girls' night out chatter. But immobility for our mates and for us is actually a death sentence, and not a subject to take lightly. Kenneth Cooper, a founder of the modern fitness movement, coined the word *aerobics*, taken from the word *aerobic*, which means to live with oxygen. He integrated the term into the name of the world-renowned Cooper Aerobics Center he built in Dallas in 1970. Cooper's pioneering work in the fields of fitness and sports medicine helped turned "aerobics" into a household word and a multi-billion-dollar business.

The media's obsessive messaging on the benefits of regular exercise has revolutionized the way Americans view aging. The first baby boomers turned sixty-five in 2011, and damn if they are going to let themselves get fat or old! Breaking health news dispatches endlessly stream as tickers on cable TV, trumpeting just-released studies on the correlation between exercise and beating everything from diabetes to dementia. Data from the Aerobics

Center Longitudinal Study that examined twenty-seven years of participants tells us this: Thirty minutes of moderate-intensity exercise, such as brisk walking, five or more days each week yields a 50 percent reduction in mortality risk.

Witnessing Tina Turner at seventy-one stomping around on stage in stilettos or Mick Jagger at sixty-eight making love to his mic has ignited all our boomer fantasies of growing wilder and sexier with each passing year. Some anti-aging doctors are telling today's Peter Pans that these dreams are within reach. In short, you *can* teach old dogs new tricks.

I did a *Washington Post* article on the growing numbers of Americans turning one hundred and had the opportunity to speak to John Rowe, coauthor of the book *Successful Aging*, based on a ten-year MacArthur Foundation study of seniors. His news is good: "Our most surprising finding is that we are responsible for our own old age. Only about 30 percent of aging is inherited."

I heard from other researchers that brain regions in humans do not have significant cell death as we age. Rather, as the brain is stimulated it sprouts new projections called dendrites that proliferate like limbs on trees. As we keep feeding our minds, these cells continue to grow throughout the entire life cycle. So keep doing those crossword puzzles!

While an aging brain can sprout new branches from "intellectual sweating," a term used by the late Gene Cohen, founding director of George Washington University's Center on Aging, Health and Humanities, so can a sweating body sprout muscles in later years. One classic Boston study done in the early 1990s tracked nursing home residents as old as ninety-eight who worked out on weight machines three times a week for eight weeks. Results showed muscle strength to increase an average of 174 percent, and the subjects' walking speed increased 50 percent.

Long-range studies of seniors also point to the validity of the burgeoning field of mind-body science, with statistical proof that staying engaged in hobbies that open up creative channels also adds years to the lifespan. These activities grease neural connections and also pump dopamine, a chemical messenger similar to adrenaline that affects our emotional responses and ability to experience pleasure, through the body. This mutes stress levels that trigger illness and contributes overall to a sunnier outlook, which makes for a more tranquil marriage.

Movement as a tonic for sanity and sustenance was my mother's survival secret. When I went through spells of sadness and inertia as a girl, she'd say, "Move your *tuchas* [Yiddish for 'ass']. Things could be worse." Born Jewish in Warsaw during the Nazi massacre, she survived the Holocaust through intense and frantic movement; her mother, sister, brother, and five nieces and nephews were killed. That was the barometer of "worse" she measured everything else against.

My mom didn't wallow in tortured backward glances. When her last child left her nest, my parents sold our house in Oak Park, Illinois, where my siblings and I had lived our whole lives, and they moved into a new condo and into a new life on Lake Michigan. She stepped effortlessly from her role as a stay-at-home mom into becoming the leading saleswoman in the men's department at Lord & Taylor, her first paycheck in a thirty-four-year marriage and a position she held into her eighties. She walked the nine blocks to work every morning, even in the winter, against the frigid lakefront blasts. Going back to retail was a return to one of her own youthful passions. When she immigrated to the United States in 1953, she was hired as a salesgirl in cosmetics at Saks Fifth Avenue, a block from Lord & Taylor. Immersed in glamorous customers with mink stoles, cinched waists, and stable families helped transport her from the horrors of her past.

My mother's legacy of moving onward is one that will get me through my own empty nest and other passages. She showed me that staying active and engrossed in work you love can be a cure for anything. We should all listen to Bob Dylan who in his song "Forever Young" instructs us: "May your hands always be busy. May your feet always be swift."

And with movement comes a fortified self to stay forever youthful.

I am sitting with a buff grandmother with silver hair in a Beatles cut that is still wet from an hour-long swim. A retired high school administrator, Lois Levine has never been busier, having revived her childhood love of arts and crafts. She is the poster child of senior mind-body health; swimming has given her new muscles past age seventy and her artistry hones her mental clarity. Married to Saul for fifty-five years, Lois now spends much of her time in her Florida studio making pots, vessels, animals, and masks for private commissions and to exhibit at local arts fairs.

When seventy-seven-year-old Lois effuses about the works she sculpts by hand without the aid of a wheel, her blue eyes shine as if she were a kindergartner telling her mom how it felt to dig her fingers into cold clay for the first time. I am not equipped to study Lois as a neurologist would, but I can sense the dendrites sprouting in her brain as she talks about finding her way back to art.

LOIS

As the years pass, you tend to lose touch with your creativity if you are not using it. But as a young child growing up in the country of Spring Valley, New York, I would draw and paint, and I loved assembling things. It came very naturally to me; I was just a very creative child, putting together all kinds of costumes for dress up and making collages. We always had crayons and glue and yarn and scissors around my house.

On Thursdays during summers, which were my father's days off, we used to go to the lake in Bear Mountain State Park. When everyone else was swimming, I was constructing sand castles. Our winters were long and snowy. When the other kids were sledding or having snowball fights, I would be making snowpeople. I definitely had an early affinity for sculpture.

I had a long career in education, starting with teaching kindergarten and ending as the dean of students at a high school. That was twenty years of my life, a time where I wasn't doing art at all; I was teaching and raising children. After I retired from the school system, I started taking intensive pottery lessons, and I took to clay like a fish takes to water. I joined professional pottery-making groups. Getting back into art really has reconnected me to some of the happiest parts of my childhood. A few years ago I started teaching pottery to children at a Montessori school, and I give private lessons on weekends in my home.

My studio is in my garage, and we may as well put a bed in there, because I work day and night. I just lose myself in that clay. I forget about everything. I forget about food. I forget about anything I'm worried about.

When I first got married, my husband traveled a lot, and I was not very sure of who I was or what I wanted. When I hit forty and the women's movement was unfolding, I went through a major metamorphosis. I would say to myself, "I'm not Mrs. Saul Levine. I'm Lois." I did all sorts of things: I went to Israel by myself, and even volunteered in the Israeli army three times. I got very involved in local politics and sat on the board of Planned Parenthood. I began to find my own interests and my own voice, and to establish my own place.

I realized pretty early on that marriage alone couldn't make me happy. I never wanted to break up our marriage; it was never a thought. But I knew I needed something else. When the other women teachers left school to go to Loehmann's, I would head to the swimming pool and do an hour of laps, which I still do three times a week. Along with my art, swimming gives me youthful energy. At the age of seventy-six, I am thinner and in better shape than I've ever been.

I can't say I don't have aches and pains. But I've got a lot of stamina. I can work in my studio from morning until night. I do believe if more women recognized that they need lives and passions of their own, we wouldn't see so much divorce. My husband has his own interests. He reads. He bikes. He plays tennis. He joined a theater group recently and now acts in plays. He is proud of my accomplishments and never ceases to brag to people about my art, though there is probably a part of him that would love me to spend more time with him. But I need this.

When I go into my studio and pick up my clay, I discover many new parts of myself. As an artist who wants to keep developing, I would love to travel to Peru and Bhutan and Southeast Asia for inspiration. Maybe I'll be like Grandma Moses, who started her artistic career late in life and worked vigorously almost until she died at the age of 101. I feel like I am just beginning, really. Right now I feel better about myself than I've ever felt. I love what I do, I'm good at it, and I'm respected as an artist. My two children are grown with their own successful careers. My grandchildren are grown up.

It's Lois time.

This is a grandma with vigor and optimism, a woman who springs out of bed each morning because of a creative pursuit that awaits her. My advice is don't wait until you are in your seventies to resurrect a sport or hobby that once filled you with purpose and direction. At every age and every stage, do what Lois does: Keep thinking. Keep exploring. Most important, keep moving.

My husband's grandmother Mattie Anthony outlived Grandma Moses because she remained engaged in her passions and in growing her mind. This woman we called Granny died last year a month before her 105th birthday, outliving her husband by twenty-four years. Her body was strong until she hit 102, and her mind didn't start softening until 103. When people asked Granny for her secrets she would answer plainly: "Muscles have memory, and I drove my body hard all of my life."

As a young girl, she used to help her father as he plowed the family's farm on the Eastern Shore of Maryland. For recreation, she spent afternoons playing hours of baseball with her first cousin who lived across the road. That cousin was Jimmie Foxx, who was drafted by the Philadelphia Athletics and became one of the greatest sluggers in all baseball history, a winner of the Triple Crown and a Baseball Hall of Famer.

As a young woman, Granny rode horseback through dense woods to the one-room schoolhouse where she taught grades one through seven. When she retired from teaching at the age of sixty-five, she never stopped "pulling and bending" in the sprawling vegetable garden she tended, hauling hoses and doing deep knee bends into the earth, for seventy-five years. As a senior citizen, she toured Asia, Africa, and Antarctica.

"Had I just gone home and sat down after I retired, I wouldn't be here today," Granny would say, surrounded by photographs of twelve great-grandchildren and two great-great-grandchildren. "All of my life I have never stopped moving. My friends who stopped aren't around any more."

VI
Why Love Lasts

"Tom and I have never had a lot of money, but we
had the important things: faith and family and each
other."

—MARIAN

I AM A NATIVE of Oak Park, Illinois, a village just west of
Chicago that is also the hometown of Betty White, Ernest
Hemingway, and Frank Lloyd Wright. Dozens of venerable
Victorian structures and Prairie-style Wright houses line the wide
streets of Oak Park along with centuries-old maples, gingkoes,
and oaks.

When I return to Forest Avenue, the street I lived on for my
first eighteen years, the word that resounds in my mind is "solid."
The buildings are solid and the citizens are solidly committed to
the historic preservation of their community. And many high
school sweethearts I noticed kissing by their lockers in the late
1960s are still standing together, committed to the historic preservation of their marriages.

The midlife couples in this section (including two that began
in Oak Park) are like the grand trees of my girlhood. They have
been battered by storms and age, yet they remain firmly implanted,
with deep roots and thick trunks and new growth each year. While
each story is unique, there are four central qualities that these still-
besotted spouses all share: They communicate well, they fight

well, they believe marriage means forever, and they profess to be more in love today than they were when they met thirty or forty years ago.

They made it through periodic itches and prolonged agony (one couple lost a twenty-four-year-old child in a canoe accident) because the omnipotent force called love soothed the pain at even the most excruciating of turns. What is love anyway? We know it blends sexual chemistry, friendship, loyalty, and respect. But it's really the mystery of love, the incomprehensible, that draws us in and keeps us in a relationship. The late Presbyterian minister Bruce Larson, a founder of the 1970s Relational Christianity movement, used to say that a love that endures has a mixture of "guts, gonads and God." That is glib and brief for such a grand sentiment, yet those alliterative words say everything: Staying married takes fortitude and guts to keep your commitment in the face of upheavals. Hopping in bed with your mate can get you through the nastiest of fights. And there is a spiritual force that attracts you to each other and holds you in its embrace—and keeps you from being too naughty.

Indeed, I felt a sense of spiritual rightness when I first met Chuck in 1985 at the Washington bar Déjà Vu, French for "already seen," as if our old souls were converging again. His eyes were kind and the clearest of blue. He stood six feet three, and with my height of five feet eight, my immediate thought was "we will have tall children." This before we had had our first kiss. On our honeymoon, we shared our intention of having four children by the time we were forty, and damn if we didn't do just that.

I was thirty-three and he was thirty-one when we took our wedding walk to the John Lennon song "Imagine" down an aisle lined with red and white roses, me in white silk shantung with a red garter high on my right thigh. His hair was too long, just like I like it, and I felt a rush of relief to be surrendering to an ancient tradition with a man whose parents managed to stay married, as mine did. I had already pinned my dreams on a couple wrong princes and learned through heartache what the right prince needed to possess. On top of that list is reliability, the sexiest quality of all, and that's the core of Chuck. While this book is designed to give wives permission to rewrite the rules of their own marriages, this is one rule I suggest every wife insist on with her spouse: "Do what you say you're going to do." Predictability is the greatest gift you can give each other in a marriage, as you know from your girlfriends who never know where the hell their husbands are.

Most of the people in this chapter were at least a decade younger than I was when they made the mature choice to get married, trusting that their first love could be their last. Although they were barely out of their teens when they innocently took this high-risk gamble, so far they are winning. It comes down to what psychologist Florence Wiedemann of Dallas spoke about: mastering the ability to fight fairly, let go, and move on. Each wife in a successful marriage I interviewed is still hanging in there because she and her spouse have been able to resolve most conflicts and accept those that are irresolvable.

This mirrors the theories of psychologist John Gottman, the author of *The Seven Principles for Making Marriage Work*, who introduced a type of therapy that focuses on increasing positive interactions among couples, which enhances the ability to resolve differences. He is renowned for his Love Lab at the West Coast Gottman Institute, in which he has studied hundreds of couples figuring out how to get along since 1986. Of Gottman's seven principles for marital success, these three have factored most prominently in the happiest wives I've met:

- "Interact frequently, tell each other about your day, your thoughts, your experiences." I would add to remember to kiss your spouse hello and good-bye, and hug them hard—oxytocin will start surging and you will not only feel better but research shows those embraces pump bursts of chemicals that help you live longer, too.

- "Solve your solvable problems." Gottman asserts that in both happy and unhappy marriages, more than 80 percent of the time the wife brings up marital conflicts while the husband tries to avoid discussing them. Being one of those nagging wives, my addendum to this principle is that when you want your clam of a husband to open up, don't start a conversation with "You should," and instead use the words "Why don't we . . ."

- "Overcome gridlock." This, of course, is essential; if you don't let go of antique blame and vintage rage you will forever be stuck in anger, which is the closed door to friendship and sex, and leads to divorce.

Gottman stresses that not all negative behaviors contribute to marital dissolution, but four behaviors in particular do, which he labels the "Four Horsemen of the Apocalypse." First comes "criticism," which brings on contempt, which in turn elicits "defensiveness" and finally ends up at "stonewalling," or total withdrawal. All of the following wives have displayed one or more of these destructive behaviors during their long marriages but have managed to avoid gridlock through focusing on the positives of their partnerships. Here are more of their secrets for keeping Gottman's "Four Horsemen" at bay.

Paula was the goddess of Oak Park and River Forest High School's class of 1970, who graduated two years ahead of me. She was a cheerleader with long blonde hair and an exquisite face—part Sharon Stone and part Doris Day. Stereotyped as what she calls a "two-dimensional rah-rah girl," she shocked her acolytes when she broke up with the star quarterback to date the quirky and enigmatic Rian, one of the class valedictorians who hung out with the alternative crowd of political activists, not the jocks. "We are two people who no one could ever have imagined would have gotten together in the first place," says Paula. That was forty years ago. Today the couple perceived as clearly mismatched still sleep wrapped in each other's arms. Here is Paula's account of what it's like to be fifty-eight and still dating her high school boyfriend.

PAULA

There is definitely something about growing up in a deep-rooted community that affects how you value marriage as a long-haul vision. I am keenly aware that my father's parents, grandparents, and great-grandparents all raised their families in Oak Park, and those marriages all lasted, which is a legacy of sorts. My mother's parents, who also stayed married, raised their family in Oak Park as well. It may be easier to dissolve a marriage if you grow up in a newer community where nearly every family is from somewhere else, and without relatives nearby and the souls of ancestors in the air.

It feels really comfortable to still be with my high school boyfriend. I am not worried that my husband will leave me for someone younger. Because we met so young, in many ways that sense of youthful love will always be with us.

I will always be able to picture Rian as that teenager I fell in love with my senior year of high school, and that vision keeps rejuvenating our old marriage. Rian was my first true love, and though that early passion is wonderful, I think intimacy gets better as you get to know each other over the years. Frequency may diminish a little, but the quality improves.

He has always done thoughtful things in sort of a secretive way. He'll put my favorite candy, a Heath bar, under my pillow, or he'll leave me a poem written in his microscopic handwriting on a little piece of paper on the bottom of my clean tea mug. We live in a lovely setting on the edge of a small town on nineteen acres of land in southwest Michigan. I'm looking out at our backyard toward the Kalamazoo River. My husband mows the lawn in the backyard except for a twenty-five-yard patch of grasses that he leaves in the shape of a big heart. We've had a heart in our backyard for years, a constant valentine.

I didn't really know Rian until senior year, although I had heard his name. People would kind of whisper about him because he was so bright and he pushed boundaries. His friends were the early hippies of the mid-1960s who were always testing authority, and they were the alternative group that made him their candidate and elected him to student council our senior year. That's how I met him. He certainly did not fit the mold of anyone else on council.

At the time I was dating the quarterback, a smart and funny guy, and I was wearing a small football charm he had given me on a necklace. Rian and I were both assigned to sit in the student council room at the same time. I would bring a pile of books and start studying, and any time I would look up Rian would be sitting there, at the other end of the long table, just staring at me, with a very serious expression. I assumed it was a stare of contempt for this rah-rah cheerleader. He has since told me many times that he was staring at me due to attraction.

Gradually we began to talk, and he was unlike anyone I had ever met. He played football and he wrestled, but he also worked at a bookstore and had helped start a coffeehouse in a church basement. He liked all different kinds of music, not just rock. Rian introduced me to the jazz legend Miles Davis and to the albums of folk guitarist John Fahey. No one whom I knew in high school was already into jazz or listening to a musician as esoteric as Fahey. Finally, at Christmas break, senior year, the quarterback and I broke up and Rian and I started to date, which really surprised my crowd of friends.

Rian's friends also couldn't understand how he could possibly date a cheerleader. It was a breach of countercultural beliefs. I was only seventeen, yet I felt powerfully drawn to him, almost with a sense of destiny. He was an athlete yet also a brooding scholar, and I just found that combination so appealing. I still do. Rian remains a brooding scholar and he weighs almost the same as he did in high school. He is a biker and a cross-country skier, and he keeps himself in great shape.

I was going through some old photos recently of that first sweet time we were falling in love. Pictures of Rian as a teenager still make my heart pound. That's the magic of sustaining an old romance: The memories from long ago are good ones. I have friends who look at pictures of their husbands with their high school and college girlfriends, and that causes a lot of jealousy. When Rian and I look back at old pictures, we are together.

Then I went off to the University of Wisconsin in Madison, and Rian went off to Oberlin College in Ohio. He hitchhiked to see me several times during that freshman year, and one day that spring I get this call, "I'm transferring to Madison." Honestly, I had mixed feelings about it. I thought, "What if our relationship doesn't work out?" Well, it did work out, even though we got married quite young—between junior and senior years in June of 1973. I was only twenty, and he was twenty-one. He had applied to Jefferson Medical College in Philadelphia to see if he could be admitted a year early, and he was accepted early—two weeks after our wedding. I only had one semester left of college, so we figured, why not? When we left Philadelphia four years later, Rian had graduated from medical school and I had a master's in art therapy. During those years he was in medical school, I juggled several jobs but I was also able to do my thing—taking painting and printmaking classes to finish my undergrad degree and then pursuing art therapy. I certainly wasn't a wife waiting at home. I always had my own interests. That has been really important in making our marriage last.

I would say that, most recently, money issues have been the biggest stressor in our marriage. Finances are tough with a solo medical practice, which Rian has had for the last eight years, so I have put my art on hold to work as Rian's office manager and receptionist. Truly, though, the strongest stressor over the course of our marriage has been Rian's lack of free time on evenings and weekends. I know it's a common problem for spouses of physicians.

Since I started to work with Rian I've only been able to do my art around the edges of my life, designing some cards, a creative project here or there. I haven't really been able to dig in, and I feel a strong desire to do so now. When Rian went out on his own eight years ago, I offered to be his office manager. He is this devoted mad professor type who cares about his clinical work but who doesn't want to think about the business end of things. I jumped in with both feet and said, "I'll tackle this. I'll get this rolling."

Now it's been long enough. I really want to focus more on creating. I was just in Spain and Italy—a generous gift from my mother for herself and all six of her daughters. Seeing Florence, Rome, and the Amalfi Coast, I am now filled with inspiration and ready to focus on art. But financially I can't abandon my job at our clinic yet. Rian supports me in my desire to do my art, and I support him in his need right now for me to continue to manage his office. Sacrifice and flexibility are so important in a marriage. Rian's first position after residency was with a family practice in rural Wisconsin, twelve miles from the nearest town. The nearest neighbor was around a bend almost a mile away. I remember being holed up in our farmhouse with two toddlers while he was stuck at the hospital covering the ER and delivering babies. I would get so frustrated, thinking, "What am I doing here? I am so far from my family and friends. I am just going crazy with cabin fever."

Believe me, it hasn't been all roses. We argue. Sometimes we are petty. Sometimes we are stubborn. There have been serious arguments, like the day I was digging in our vegetable garden on the Wisconsin farm while also trying to entertain our squabbling children. Rian was heading off to work and I was frustrated that he wasn't helping with all the chores and needs around our little farm. I started to accuse him of being selfish and our dialogue escalated. Suddenly, rather than continuing to argue, he said pointedly, "Well, if you are so unhappy, why don't you divorce me?" I was flabbergasted. I didn't want a divorce then and I certainly don't now. I love Rian and I'm committed to being with him forever.

Moment to moment in a long relationship you flip back and forth: Who is in control? Who is willing to acquiesce? We are by no means a couple with a perfect marriage. We have a very good marriage. It comes back to our children. When we think of our children, both grown and both good people, it makes us both more grateful for our marriage. The kids add the glue to the marriage framework that makes it stronger.

How many couples do you know that share the same e-mail? I can read his e-mails and he can read mine. There is total trust, yet we don't have tight reins on each other. I have friends whose husbands have tight controls on their free time and who seem jealous of time they spend with their girlfriends. Others have husbands who expect that dinner is served at a certain time, and if not, they are in trouble. I cannot imagine living like that—being afraid of my husband's anger if we have dinner an hour later or being worried because I went to a movie with girlfriends.

After thirty-seven years of marriage, I know all of my partner's idiosyncrasies, his weaknesses, his strengths, and his vulnerabilities. I know what it means to truly love someone. We kiss every day and nestle together at night in bed, falling asleep with various limbs intertwined. Some friends tell me they don't like sleeping up against their spouses, and this always surprises me. Rian and I sometimes dance all alone. There's a favorite Van Morrison song, "Someone Like You," on a CD that's in our player at work. When that song comes on while each of us is working at our respective desks outside of clinic hours, we crank up the volume and dance slowly to it right there in our waiting room.

I remember when I was twenty, people told me I was crazy to marry so young. My instincts told me it was right, and so we jumped in. My feeling at the time toward those people who didn't believe in us was, "I'll show you, baby." It turns out that I made a good choice.

This is the indescribable mystery of love, the instinctive tug that compels old lovers like Paula and Rian to get up and start dancing. It's a spontaneous act that comes from soul-deep arousal. This is the magic that drives divorced husbands and wives to find their lost loves; this is the magic that makes trouble at high school reunions when ex-sweethearts arrive with new spouses and the one that got away seems more appealing than the one you've got. I interviewed one woman whose twenty-five-year marriage imploded after she spent the night with her seventh grade boyfriend at their thirty-fifth high school reunion, an event they both prophetically chose to attend solo. I met her right when it happened, and she updated me with this e-mail six months later: "I am still MADLY in LOVE! I am getting divorced and my children are still having a tough time. But I am more sure each day that I have made a good decision to be in a truly loving and fulfilling relationship, physically and emotionally! It is a dream come true! He is heaven on earth and it has been fifteen months!"

Hmm, I wonder what "MADLY in LOVE" will feel like after fifteen years, when the infatuation phase has long fizzled out.

While love has mystical components, there is no mystery as to why growing numbers of disgruntled spouses or divorced singles are reuniting with their childhood sweethearts. First off, many people have Facebook profiles and are findable with the click of a computer key. And as Paula describes, high school honeys can make you feel perpetually young and sexy. They don't see you approaching sixty; they remember the first kiss. What boomer with acid reflux and arthritis doesn't want that? Even if your original lover is now thirty pounds overweight and has not a hair on his head, you always see that teenager who first sent flutters throughout your body and became the ruler of your imagination. The what-ifs about the one who got away never stop tantalizing.

And if you end up back together, or if you never left each other, you are fortified by having all your life cycles linked—past, present, and future.

Marian Brandstrader Garrigan needed that spine of old love more than any other wife I know. She described the boy she met at fifteen and married at twenty as "the rock of my life" that she leaned on when the couple was dealt the cruelest blow a parent can endure. Their youngest of four daughters, Kathy, drowned at age twenty-four along with two others in a boating accident on Harding Lake near Fairbanks, Alaska, while working for AmeriCorps.

Kathy was a three-sport high school athlete and a varsity volleyball player at St. Joseph's College, a vital and cheery young woman whom Marian called "the icing on my three-layer cake." Three years after the tragedy, Marian is just starting to heal, warmed by the womb of the Oak Park neighborhood she was raised in and never left, and by the new life in her family, two grandchildren she takes care of while her daughters are at work.

Marian sent me a recent photograph of her and Tom, a carpentry contractor; they are dancing and her mouth is wide open in hysterical laughter. Still slim and very brunette, Marian is wearing a tight brown dress with a shocking pink ruffle at the neck, and I see the same winsome girl I met when we were high school freshmen. There must be something in the Oak Park water that makes lovers want to keep dancing no matter how stiff and old they get! Here is Marian's view on how the right marriage can "get you through anything."

MARIAN

The thing that attracted me to Tom in the first place is what helped get me through the loss of Kathy. He is solid as a rock. He knows instinctively the right thing to do. I have always felt safe with Tom. He got on a plane a couple of days after this happened with Kathy and he just assumed a very important role. There were different teams working on search and recovery, and often butting up against each other. Tom, even in his grief, was the guy who helped keep the peace. Tom was the cement that held everyone together. You can count on Tom, and that is really important in a long marriage.

I met him my first week of high school. We were part of the same crowd, but all through high school, we didn't date. Although when I'd come back home from a break in college I would always gravitate toward him. He was the rock then, too, the leader of our old crowd, the steady guy you could turn to. He was a good listener and a good dancer—and I love to dance. We were dating other people, but somehow I would end up dancing with Tom at parties. My dad died when I was seventeen, and that loss was also a big part of my attraction to Tom. He felt like home. He felt safe. When you have that void in your life of losing a parent, you turn to someone solid you can lean on. That's Tom.

We got married when I was twenty-one. We were just kids, and we started having our own kids right away, four by the time I was twenty-nine. I'm one of ten kids in a Catholic family, and I knew I wanted to have a lot of children. Kathy was our youngest daughter, a real dynamo. After she graduated from St. Joseph's College, she went to work for AmeriCorps in Fairbanks, Alaska. We got word that there was a canoe accident over Memorial Day weekend, and Kathy was in the boat. There were no witnesses. The search went on for five weeks in and around the lake. Kathy had been swimming since she was a baby. Nobody could believe that Kathy Garrigan could drown in a lake. She had unbelievable physical endurance, and she was an excellent swimmer.

I didn't go with Tom to help find Kathy because one of our other daughters was about to give birth. There was this massive search effort in Alaska. Help came all the way from the top: Even the late senator Ted Stevens and then-governor Sarah Palin got involved by extending the search efforts. When Kathy was found, the sonar expert we hired determined that she was able to swim about four hundred yards toward shore, and that's exactly the amount of time hypothermia occurs in very cold water. Kathy was a fighter, she was so strong, and somehow even knowing how hard she tried to swim away makes us feel better.

As devastated as we were, I was grateful that my daughter was found. I totally relate to mothers of kids across the world who have missing children who are never found. For those mothers of the world, you make me strong. For those mothers, I just couldn't let myself fall apart. I am connected to the pain of other mothers; my grandmother lost three of her twelve children, but she had to get up every morning and raise her other children. The mothers who have no idea where their children are fighting in Afghanistan are getting up and going to work in the morning. That connection with other mothers bolstered me immediately: If they can hang in there, I can hang in there, too.

Throughout everything, Tom and I were able to hold each other up. We did it for each other, and we did it for our other three daughters, Kathy's sisters. Of course, we are forever changed. Tom and I think twice when we walk out the door and say good-bye. To lose a child like this, it's just a central thing in our marriage. Not that we dwell on it, but whenever one of us wants to talk about it we are there for each other to listen. Then we have long periods of time in which we just don't want to talk at all.

Tom and I have always been good at being quiet together; we've gone on long car rides together and we've been totally silent, and it's not because anyone is mad. It's going on three years now since the tragedy, and the pain is less raw. I lead a quiet and happy life, just being Grandma and being near family. I have two grandsons, ages five and three. I have been lucky enough to be able to be their part-time caregiver. All three of my daughters live within a mile of me, and I have ninety first cousins, many of whom live close by. Going through what we went through and coming out the other end, we survived because our family was right there with us. Ultimately, it was Tom that got me through: I understand deeply now why I married this person and why I stayed married to him. I can count on Tom.

And there's something sexy about knowing there is a part of him that looks at me and still sees that sixteen-year-old girl and I still see that sixteen-year-old boy. We get to be young forever in each other's eyes. Tom sees the high school Marian, not the wrinkled Marian.

We beat the odds, I know: Many couples who have babies when they themselves are babies don't make it. You just have to stick it out through all the ups and downs. And don't compare yourself to other people or envy other couples who you feel are achieving more or have more. Tom and I have never had a lot of money, but we had the important things: faith and family and each other. Losing a child is the most profound loss you can experience as a human being. I can understand why couples in our situation would go their separate ways or turn to drugs or become violent. You feel like you have lost your mind. We handled it because we have each other. If anything, Kathy's death recemented our relationship. When love can withstand this, love is the real thing.

It also helps that our chemistry is still there. We just celebrated our thirty-fifth anniversary at a little cottage in Indiana. I'm not going to go into details, but we felt as young as we did when we used to hit a motel when we were twenty.

Rocklike reliability and sustained crackle are what Marian has and what I gratefully have in a husband. I am envious a bit that Paula and Marian found their princes so early, without having to muck through a swamp of Mr. Wrongs like the majority of us did. When they married in the 1970s the average American bride was in her early twenties; today the average age for a woman to get married has been bumped up to twenty-seven, and twenty-nine for the groom. Most of the midlife women I know, though, were professionals like me in our early thirties when we said, "I do."

We came of age jaded about the sanctity of marriage, riding the cultural shifts induced by the sexual revolution and the advent of no-fault divorce laws in the 1970s that allowed couples in conflict to split with ease, for no good reason other than they were tired of each other. We were the Me Generation, who grew up thinking that we were entitled to this elusive thing called happiness, that we could have it all: great jobs, great kids, and a great marriage filled with great sex and nonstop excitement. Anger mounts because having all this at once is impossible, thus our generation's large therapy bills and a constant questioning, "Am I really happy?"

Our Depression-era mothers and grandmothers didn't drill themselves on whether or not they were happy. They were married, period, for better and for worse. "Dig in and hold on" was their motto, like the American soldiers that stormed Normandy, digging in and holding on, through the messiest and bloodiest of battles. They weathered the Great Depression, which took courage and tenacity, and they didn't back down from hardships in life or in relationships. Marriage is messy, and they knew you had to get in there and fight for the relationship's survival.

While I know the self-affirming value of separate vacations and separate passions, I inherited this old-fashioned belief that marriage should be forever, unless you are being destroyed by an abusive spouse. Marriage through the centuries represents hope and stability, and not necessarily that you get to be happy. The expectation of happily-ever-after is a ticket to divorce: Modern marriage is usually the coming together of two defiant and accomplished individuals who retain two last names and two bank accounts. It is hell to navigate a marriage day-to-day. But the goal of marriage remains unchanged: to love and be loved in a permanent state. If you can't accept that prolonged love takes unrelenting work, don't get married. Shelley is a forty-two-year-old woman who survived the unthinkable in her marriage because, as she puts it, "bottom line— I never stopped loving my husband." I was sitting next to her at a Starbucks, making some notes on one of my chapters for this book, when she excused herself for reading over my shoulder, then said, "You are studying marriage? Have I got a story for you."

Shelley's high school boyfriend–turned–husband of

twenty-one years had a yearlong affair with Shelley's best girlfriend—really yucky, awful stuff. Shelley is remarkably poised, in a purple turtleneck and low-slung blue jeans, as she recounts the experience that remains a "scab that hasn't completely healed."

SHELLEY

It was absolutely horrific. I felt like I wanted to die. I stayed indoors for a good year and became seriously depressed. I was blindsided: Throughout this whole affair my best friend still pretended to be my best friend. I am telling you, she was my best of best friends. We told each other everything—big mistake!

I met my husband when I was fifteen years old, and I remember thinking when we first started to go out, "I am the luckiest girl alive! I met the person I'm supposed to be with for the rest of my life." We had a great marriage before he made this awful mistake, and we have a better marriage now. He was so remorseful that I was able to forgive him. People couldn't believe that I could stay with this man after what he put me through. How could I not stay? I am in love with my husband. We have young children together. We are a family.

My husband is a very handsome man and a little narcissistic. I got married when I was twenty-one, and on my wedding day my great-aunt said to me, "Shelley, he is so good-looking. Watch out. He'll never be able to be faithful to you. The girls will be after him." Over the years I have watched as women flirt with my husband, but I have never felt threatened. Our sex life was always good, and he always told me he thought I was beautiful. About two years ago I noticed subtle changes in his behavior. He became more distant and closed off. We made love less often. I passed it off as him just being busy at work. We both come from nothing, and my husband has gone on to build a very big business that consumes him. I would share my frustration that my husband was withdrawing from me with my supposed best friend, and she would give me sympathetic advice when all along she was screwing him.

Right now I can say that my marriage is a remarkable story of healing. When I found out about the affair we immediately went into therapy and deep self-reflection. It was horrendous because I felt like I was reliving my parents' life. I'm from a broken home. My parents stayed together until my brother and I were teenagers, then they split up. This is the worst-case scenario, growing up watching this empty kind of love and hearing from your mom, "We are staying together for you children, then I'm walking." My children were six and nine when this happened, and at first I promised myself, "I will never stay with anyone for the sake of my children." I think what my parents did was a mistake, living a miserable life together because they thought it was best for their children.

I really pressed myself to analyze my marriage, telling myself, "If you are truly unhappy and there is no connection in this relationship, leave this marriage. Do it now while you're still young and you can start over." But there was a profound connection, and up until this terrible point, I was content. We met so young and our love was deep and strong. Neither of us had ever given the other person any reason to doubt that we would grow old together. We didn't fight. We were that great couple everyone wanted to be like.

Although I didn't have an outward clue this was going on, I must have intuitively sensed something was wrong, because one night I had a realistic dream that my friend was sleeping with my husband. I called her that morning and said, "Oh my God, I had this dream about you. Please tell me it's not true!" There was silence for too long, and that told me it was true. As the story came out from both of them, I learned terrible details, like when we took vacations together the two of them would have sex somewhere then both couples would meet up for dinner.

I was horrified and mortified and in shock. She was my best of best of friends. We talked three times a day. We talked about everything, including detailed discussions about sex with our husbands. She used everything I said to her advantage. One thing I learned from this is your best friend should be your husband, and that you should never tell a girlfriend everything. From the start, I was very angry at my husband, but I don't blame him for this. She came after him; she pressed all the hot buttons with him because I gave them to her. I told her about some gaping holes in him and she knew exactly how to fill them. She is a very attractive woman, so this was not an easy thing on the ego and, frankly, still isn't. I still have my days. One of the qualities I most admire in myself is that I was able to walk away from this situation without destroying her.

Quite honestly, what she did to me is much more egregious than what he did. There is something sacred with the bond of women; true girlfriends have heart-to-heart talks and understand you like a man never can. Then when a woman takes advantage of that and slashes you, it is shocking. To this day, I hear from friends that she professes that she loved me through this whole affair and how much she misses me as a friend. What a joke.

To get through this, my husband and I made a deal. We promised each other that we would really move on, and that we wouldn't bring this up every time we have a bad fight. Today we rarely talk about it, but sometimes I have to bite my tongue. But if you really forgive someone you have to forgive totally, you can't turn around and slap him in the face. You have to let go of the poison of the soul. My husband pledged certain things about his behavior that I wanted him to change, and he has changed. He is far less narcissistic, and if I want his attention, now I get it immediately.

The cliché is true: What doesn't kill you makes you stronger. I have changed, too. You have to look at yourself and ask, "What part did I play in driving my husband away?" I was very insecure, stemming way back from my childhood. I was always scared I wasn't measuring up. As a result, I put my husband on a pedestal, really almost for as long as I've known him. I thought of him as the perfect man: handsome and self-made. When everything came crashing down, the blessing was that I got to see he was imperfect like the rest of us.

Today I am really proud of who I am: I lived through one of the worst things you can possibly live through and I'm still standing. And my marriage is better than you could ever imagine a marriage to be, because I don't have the same fears anymore about what people think of me. I don't care about measuring up to other people, and I no longer view my husband as a superior being. My family is all that matters to me. I am born again.

A few months ago I saw this woman at a party. I called her over and said, "Honestly, you did me a favor. I have the greatest marriage on this earth because of you." I do feel like I have the upper hand: I have the man I love.

I've got three lessons for other vulnerable wives on how to protect your marriage. First of all, it is dangerous to tell all. If you are so close to another woman that you are revealing everything about your life there is something lacking in your marriage. Your husband should be the only person you can let down your guard for, 100 percent. And two, don't talk about the sexual parts of your marriage with anyone but your husband, not even the girlfriends you totally trust. If you start talking about details like penis size, that is just really stupid. And third, you can recover from an affair if you're in the right marriage.

When I got to the point where I finally felt it was okay for my husband to touch me, it felt like a honeymoon. This whole tragedy really was a sexual jump start to our marriage. I am haunted sometimes, imagining her with him. But honestly, what's the choice when you're the mom of young kids and you're in love? You have to go on. My husband will feel terrible about this until his dying day. The humility and regret he has shown is my reminder that he does really love me. We grew up together, and we're still growing up together.

Over the many years I have reported about intimate relationships, sex is definitely a recurring hot (or cold) topic. Nearly every wife I interviewed was curious about how much sex other people were having in a long marriage. I can tell you that swinger Mimi in the next chapter is the only person I've met who told me she is still having sex four times a week with her husband of thirty years. Many longtime couples do not have sex even once a week, or even once a month. When it's down to once a year, that's trouble.

When there is not a medical condition involved, such as erectile dysfunction, which strikes some one third of males over the age of fifty, slackened sexual activity generally stems from fraying emotional intimacy, which comes from bad communication and/or too much time apart. In this book I tout the virtues of finding your own passion and hobbies to pursue. But there's a difference between self-exploration and self-absorption. Make sure you put "talk to my spouse" on your to-do list and you will likely find yourself in bed together more. When you're not communicating, you're usually not touching, and that's when it becomes more appealing to seek touching elsewhere.

A forty-nine-year-old money manager in New Jersey, the mother of three adult children, expressed to me what I found to be a fairly typical synopsis of sex, and lack thereof, in a marriage of two people with big jobs and little interface time. "I am still very attracted to my husband, even after twenty-five years, but we only have sex once or twice a month," she admitted. "It's not from lack of desire. I am horny for him, a lot. But we don't have time for sex. We don't have time to talk. I leave earlier than he does in the morning, and I'm usually asleep when he gets home at night.

"I read in magazines that busy couples should schedule sex on their weekly calendars, and that idea seems so calculating to me. People aren't machines; there should be some magic to the timing of sex. A few days ago I was so frustrated, I yelled at my husband when he walked in the door, even before he took off his coat, 'I'm not fat. I'm not ugly. Why don't you make love to me anymore?' He smiled at me and in a soft voice said, 'Why don't you make love to *me* anymore? You are never around when I am around.' So we had sex, really good sex, right then and there.

"After my temper tantrum, we both got to be reassured about something really important: He still wants me and I still want him, even with my droops and his shiny head," she concluded with a wry laugh. "We're up to having sex twice a month now and for us that's a big accomplishment. Ask for what you want, and who knows? You just might get it."

"Ask and you shall receive" is indeed a mantra to remember in marriage. Sit and stew and you get nowhere. My rule with Chuck is that if one of us wants to be intimate we need to tell the other person, and instead of sulking get on with things. Luckily, neither of us will ever forget the heat of the moment when we first realized our connection, and that memory is a place we can always turn to rev things up.

It was an icy night in early January 1986, and we were having dinner at the Lebanese Taverna in Arlington, Virginia. The restaurant was cold, and I was shivering. Chuck took off his crew-neck sweater with chevron stripes of barn red and olive green. It was soft and worn, and it smelled musky. I was enticed by his muscled twenty-nine-year-old chest, which was now adorned by only a white T-shirt, and impressed by the sweetness of the gesture of wanting to warm me up. Remembering our earliest combustion is a sexy point of reference we can always go back to and never fails to bring on a thaw. Remember that first blush of knowing that you wanted to sleep with your mate and you, too, may be more conscientious about remembering to have sex. Sex makes a husband and wife equal in their vulnerability, which brings on more empathy and more curiosity about each other, no matter how long you've been together. Sex with one partner over the course of a long life opens up your whole being. But it's really an ability to keep growing together that opens up your soul.

Along with sex, money was another popular, often exasperating, topic of conversation among the wives I interviewed. Indeed, therapists and divorce lawyers always put finances among the top reasons couples end up in their offices, particularly now. As the recession is flattening many professions, their practices are flourishing. Remembering your marital commitment to hang in there through the pits has never been more challenging as more husbands who for years went to work in Duke of Windsor–style suits are schlepping around in bathrobes scouring want ads, and women have to pick up the slack.

Jade, age fifty-two, was recently laid off from her $200,000-a-year executive position at an international media corporation, a Washington-based job that meant being on the road ten days each month. Instead of feeling frantic, Jade was relieved. Throughout her twenty-year marriage, she has earned two to three times more than her younger husband. "Not a problem at first," she says. "I figured his earning capabilities would eventually catch up or exceed mine, at which time he would take over as the family's major breadwinner." Step up he did, landing a senior position in finance that paid nearly as much as Jade's old salary. "Finally, I could relax," she says. "I could spend more time with our only son and more time with my aging parents."

Her relief was short-lived. Within four months of her husband's new employment, he, too, was laid off as the recession struck his company. A woman who has worked full-time since college graduation and is yearning for a break, Jade is instead a midlife woman who is scouring the job market for employment. Jade is not pleased. Hers is a story that is hardly rare as women ascend in corporations and the economy has headed south. She is a stressed six-figure wife who is ready to downshift and have her five-figure husband accelerate his pace.

JADE

When money is a problem in marriage everything else is impacted. Money worries can negatively color pretty much everything else in your life. Money is the thing that enables many of the wonderful dimensions of your life to exist, and the lack of money kills so many other dimensions. If you are worried about day-to-day sustenance, guess what? Are you going to be in the mood for sex? Are you going to be pleasant and happy? Probably not.

Money problems put pressure on every area of your marriage and family, because not only are your discretionary desires threatened but your basic needs are threatened.

We see it all around us with our friends: middle management and top management people looking for new work after twenty and thirty years with the same company. People are forced to come out of retirement as their 401(k)s have crashed and burned. I understand why there are rising numbers of midlife divorce.

I love my husband, and our marriage is strong. We will stay together, but it's a challenge, I will admit it. I just wasn't expecting this now. I have carried the load for both of us for our whole marriage, and it was our understanding that even if I wasn't laid off, I would start winding down. Then this happens, and I say to him, "You can do this! Find another good job!" I've been out of work for all of a few months after twenty years of making most of our family income, and he says to me, "When are you going to get a new job?" In my mind, it's his turn, or at the very least let's dial down our lifestyle to better fit our new financial circumstances.

When my husband's employer filed Chapter 11, to his credit he didn't take up guitar lessons or start working on his golf game, like some of my friends' spouses have. He's been looking for a new job every single day. And finally it looks like he is about to get an offer. The issue right now is that this potential job pays about half of what his old job paid out. I've picked up some freelance consulting work, but the way I feel is, "It's your turn to outearn me, buddy."

With age comes an appreciation for the limited amount of time you have for people you love. At this stage in life I want to be able to spend time with our sixteen-year-old son before he goes off to college in two short years. My parents are well into their eighties, and I want to spend time with them. So I say to my husband, "You need to step up. I shouldn't have to be the one that gets back into the rat race when I've been the one doing it for so long."

And I'm getting some pushback from him. He does expect me to get back out there because he's always been able to rely on me to be out there. I understand that financial contributions of each partner in a marriage can ebb and flow, but I've been the flow and I'm more than ready to ebb. When I lost my position after fifteen years with that company I also got a very big severance package, and that's what saved the day for our family. I could still cover 75 percent of our bills, as I've done since I married this man. I could still pay the mortgage. I could still pay our insurance. I could still buy the majority of our groceries. But that money is running out and the way things stand, it looks like I can't really downshift now; I can only tread water, then I will probably need to go back out into the workforce full-time.

I am not happy about this, I can tell you that. I can see where money problems can cause a flight response in some couples. As I said, I'm not checking out on what has been for the most part a really good relationship. But our tension level is definitely ratcheted up.

You know, he should be saying to me, "Look, you've shouldered the financial weight for the first twenty years of our marriage; it's my time to take over this responsibility, which will allow you to be available for your parents and our family." Instead he says little things that make me feel guilty that I'm not bringing in the six figures that I've always brought home. The question "How can I help?" never gets asked. We are at a standoff that needs to be addressed, but as of now, he is not willing to have the real conversation we need to have about money and lifestyle.

When I say to him, "This new position does not financially value your education and experience. You can get a better job than this," he says things like, "Just give me a year to get my finances back in order." Your finances? How about our finances? I paid my dues for a long time, and I'm looking for a little relief and I'm not getting it. So when he says to me, "When are you going to go back to work full-time?" I feel like saying, "Maybe never," but unfortunately that doesn't seem possible with our situation right now.

Oh yes, I am upset about this. Even when I was working seventy hours a week and I was back and forth on airplanes, I still did the lion's share of work around the house. I would leave home for a business trip, and when I got back three days later the same dishes would still be in the dishwasher and the sink would be filled with dirty dishes. It would make me insane.

A good marriage includes communication and intimacy, and financial stability is a big piece of it, too. When you have those things going, a relationship rides along pretty well. When finances get rocky your whole life feels rocky. Communication and intimacy take a real hit. It's this conflict I have as a woman with great earning potential; on the one hand I love making the big bucks and my financial independence. On the other hand, I am more than ready for a break.

Marriage? I'm in it for the long haul, but so far this has been our biggest obstacle, and if we pull through this one, we're going to be okay. What I need to do is really be honest, without being angry, about what I need right now and why I believe, after twenty years, I deserve it. And I'm open to hearing what's in his heart, too.

Marriage? Here is my nondictionary definition: frustration ratcheted into rage; empathy melting into compassion; letting go of anger and moving on. So goes the cycle if you want to "be okay," as Jade puts it, until death do you part. She understands that ultimately the key to dismantling conflicts is to make sure each partner sees beyond herself and himself and hears the other out. Psychoanalyst Erich Fromm, author of *The Art of Loving*, spoke of true love as being a concern for the life and growth of one's beloved. Concern for the other's growth means doing what Shelley did; although she was the victim of a despicable act she didn't let what she called "poison of the soul" demolish the couple's foundation, or their family. From her loving gesture of forgiveness, her husband is growing and Shelley is growing and they are closer than ever, sexually and emotionally.

Love can be perfect, if you know that it will never be perfect. Most of the longtime wives I interviewed openly admitted that children were the most perfect part of their marriages, an elemental bond holding them together, "the glue," as I often heard. Maryland filmmaker Cid Collins Walker, childless and fifty-eight, has relied on the pure essence of love itself and a spiritual "divination" as her long-running octane in her thirty-year marriage to Richard. She also presents one of the best definitions of happiness I've ever heard. Here's more from Cid, a calming and luminous earth mother who knows what's really important.

CID

It's almost a supernatural force that people who are meant to be together stay together. I am currently doing a film about artist Anna Campbell Bliss, and she believes the universe is ordered, and so do I. If you don't believe in the structure to the universe, then your life and your marriage are likely chaotic.

The wedding promise I made is very important to me, but it's deeper than that. Richard and I are spiritually well-matched. Opposites attract for a reason: A lot of people may think that just because a potential mate is different than you that he isn't good for you. They seek people who are just like them, and it's an error they make. They are the ones who are constantly moving through relationships, because they're seeking something that doesn't exist: the perfect relationship.

I call it the "Christina Aguilera syndrome"; so many popular actors and artists like her have a marriage and make beautiful children, then they see someone on the set in the same profession they like better, so they dump the marriage. Then they say things like, "Well, neither of us was happy," and they are thinking only me-me-me and not about the destruction they caused. These pop culture stars are heroes to the younger generation, and they are establishing terrible role models when it comes to relationships. Taking a wedding vow means accepting a responsibility. But they want happiness, or so they say, and that wins out over anything else.

I'll tell you what happiness is: Simplicity is happiness. Simplicity in your diet. Simplicity in all the crap you acquire, whether it be bling or clothes or houses. Happiness is about simplicity in your relationships; you honor your commitment and do the right thing. There are tremendous ups and downs in a great marriage, phases where there is great difficulty, phases of illness, phases of loss, be it financial or the death of your parents. Frankly, for me the biggest challenge is that I had a big love before my marriage, and although it was a star-crossed love, I was deeply in love.

I was so damaged coming into my new marriage, but because of that disappointment it really enabled me to go on and have a great marriage. I saw what I didn't want, and that paved the way for me having what I really need. Because of what I went through, I knew that hot romantic passion is not what is going to sustain your relationship; that is fleeting. What sustains your relationship is love, and there is a big difference between love and lust. Sexuality of course is a part of love, but love is a much bigger thing than passion. Hollywood players get their heads turned because they are turned on sexually to someone else, and this whole notion of marital commitment doesn't enter their minds. I have news for them: You aren't going to get anywhere in marriage, or in life, if you cannot make and keep your commitments. And in marriage, when there are the inevitable lows and blows, you've got to recommit every day.

I work with a lot of younger people, and they don't know the meaning of hanging in there. They are in the computer world, where you can dump someone just by pressing the delete key. They look outside themselves to find quick hits of happiness when we wives of a certain age know you first have to figure out who you are. Most people don't spend enough time alone to figure out why you are on this earth. It's not just to sleep with a lot of people. It's not just to go to the hairdresser. That's why I am a filmmaker, to probe deeply into the authentic lives of people and subjects.

I became a Buddhist in my early twenties, and even if I leave the practice from time to time, I always come back to it, and it centers me. People blame their unhappiness on other people, and Buddhism doesn't subscribe to blame. You need to go inside yourself ardently, whether it's through walking or yoga or meditation. This makes you a better spouse, more disciplined and more open to just letting the other person be who they are. I picked a spouse who is 100 percent supportive in watching me galloping ahead in my career. He is fine with me being the dominant force, and I am fine to let him gallop ahead at times, too.

In retrospect I would have had at least one child, but I came of age living in Manhattan during a time when women put their careers first and denied their maternal instinct, which I believe all women have. Instead I am able to act on this instinct in my work and in all of my relationships.

So I don't have kids going "Mom, mom, mom"; our marriage is a very tight unit, and it is sacred to us. Buddhism really teaches you to recognize death and to intensely savor and live each moment. I understand the fragility of life, and I also know there is great strength to life. None of us knows how long our life will be, so you have to dig in, dig into your passions, and dig into your life partners. In the beginning and in the middle and in the end, it's all about love.

VII
Naughty Girls

"Seeing this man makes me get along better with
my husband. I am a nicer, more tolerant person
because of this affair."

—CYNTHIA

Okay, I admit to being distracted sometimes. I'm on a
plane and a man is sitting next to me and he smells good
and he has straight white teeth. We start talking, and his
eyes twinkle at my jokes and he says something about his childhood in Brooklyn, and I am pulled toward his story and toward
him as if we were raised in the same leafy borough.

He buys me cheap airline cabernet and we drink across the
country, and I want time to stop right there, suspended in an aura
of possibility. My hand brushes his accidentally and we catch each
other's eyes. The jarring voice ordering us to put our trays and seats
back up snaps me back into this moment when we are about to
land. The flight attendant rustles through the aisles with her bulg-
ing garbage bag, and I look at him and he looks at me. And, well,
anything could happen from there. We are landing in ten minutes
in a foreign city with no dinner plans.

But I leave him. Fantasy is way better than reality in these
situations.

Some women like Shauna, who tells her story in this chapter,
are able to compartmentalize, separating boyfriend love from

husband love without getting befuddled. Don't be swayed when a person you are not married to makes you think naughty thoughts. A compartmentalizer can glide through an affair; a traditional romantic cries in her coffee and her wine, always wishing she were somewhere else. Romantic temptation awakens our sexuality and makes us feel youthful and fully alive. I say ride that hormonal surge straight into your own bedroom and initiate great sex with your spouse.

A colleague who became infatuated with a seatmate on a flight from Las Vegas to Baltimore reminds us that the tingles you feel from rubbing elbows at 34,000 feet should perhaps be left on board. Lucy says she knew within the first hour airborne with Greg that she "could be in love," and that he was everything that Michael, her husband of twenty-four years, was not. Greg is a wiry high school science teacher with a forceful personality. Michael is a mild-tempered podiatrist.

Flash forward seven years and Lucy and Greg are married and Michael is remarried to a woman twenty years younger. The two couples are in the same room together several times a year for holidays and birthdays, so Michael and Lucy's grown daughter can celebrate with both of her parents. Over the years, Greg has gained weight and Michael has lost weight. Greg has lost hair and Michael has a gray mop. Greg, who is twelve years older than Lucy, isn't moving so fast anymore. Michael ran his first half-marathon at age fifty-eight.

"I miss Michael," Lucy says. "We just spent Thanksgiving together, with our spouses, and our daughter. I kept looking over at him. He really has aged well. Michael and I have a history I will never share with anyone else. I am not unhappy in my new marriage, but it's not quite the ecstasy I expected. If I knew then what I know now I would have not gotten divorced. But things were dull when I met Greg. I was ready for an affair. Greg really energized me as a woman.

"I should have taken that sexual boost and used it like a magic pill to go back home and revive my husband, and revive us as a couple," she continues. "If you avoid getting caught, a little affair can perk up a marriage. I've seen it happen with close friends. What I tell them is 'let the affair run its course, enjoy the ride, then go back to your husbands.' For me, the thrill of the chase was more exciting than landing my prey."

That Thanksgiving night that Lucy found Michael so appealing she walked him to his car and they had a teenage make-out session, like they used to when they first met. She says it felt "delicious and old, yet deliciously new," and that if she had kept her affair a secret, she could still be married to him today. Adultery has been a well-kept secret and an ill-kept lie since people first tasted the bittersweet suffering that goes along with philandering. As early as 18 B.C., the very horny and very advanced Ovid addressed the promiscuous times of Rome in his seduction manual *The Art of Love*, with insights that could have been issued today: "People don't resist the temptation of new delights. . . . The crop is better in our neighbour's field; his cows more rich in milk."

The players I am about to introduce you to believe that keeping secrets is far better than having to concoct elaborate lies. These stories—hot, sad, delirious, and naughty—show us again that there is no normal path in modern marriage, and that, despite blessed vows, many people veer from their promises, with bumbling turns and dangerous detours. All humans need to eat and sleep and poop; lots of humans also feel a need to break rules and feast in their neighbors' fields.

Taboos are seductive, starting in childhood when we frolic on property that is posted NO TRESPASSING. Knowing you could get caught at any moment is both frightening and invigorating. Adultery is the ultimate naughty behavior, and while the act is wrong, the ancient human impulse to sample the forbidden will never die.

Why would it? We're not living in Pakistan, where some husbands have their wives' eyes gouged out when they *suspect* (even without proof) they are screwing around. Thankfully we are not wives in the Middle Ages, an era when the Church decreed that the sexual act should take place only for the purpose of procreation and not for pleasure. Instead, we are living in times when sexual pleasure is deemed one of our basic rights, and if people aren't getting it at home, an affair can be prompted with the ease of a two-word text message.

There are no hard repercussions in our lax sexual culture for adultery, except for temporary disgrace and perhaps a divorce. In marriages with deep roots and commitment, an affair is often tolerated, and can even force open channels of communication. For other couples, infidelity is the final brick that cracks a marriage that was already faltering.

"It is a general assumption that the main reason people get divorced is that someone is having an affair," says divorce lawyer Robert Liotta, who has handled many of Washington's illustrious breakups, among them Nora Ephron and Carl Bernstein's. "Nearly all of the cases I see in which adultery is an issue, the affair is not the cause of the destruction of the marriage. Marriages fall apart because the relationship has been a disaster for years and the affair is just a symptom. You wouldn't believe how many people haven't slept together for years, and someone will finally say, 'I can't go on like this.'"

Despite more than a thirty-year passage of time since women's liberation, the macho and prevailing myth is that it's the husbands who are more susceptible to temptations. With women making up more than half of the workforce and beginning to outearn men in professions that demand lots of travel, adultery is an equal-opportunity diversion. There are no accurate statistics on adultery because most people don't tell the truth about sex. A composite estimate from all the top therapists and relationship researchers I have spoken to put the number of marriages in the United States that are tarred by infidelity between 40 and 60 percent.

Chemistry is chemistry. Some women walk away from it, and others can't help but follow the sexual crackle, wherever it may lead. In the arms of new men, weary wives can escape old husbands and piles of bills, locked in surreal scenes of strip-teasing off their silk undies and push-up bras, their cotton husband-wear stashed in drawers at home. They pledge their love to men who seem like soul mates because they are not married to them and not sharing a bathroom with them every morning and every night.

When fantasy becomes reality, things may not seem so hot anymore. I talked to one female insurance broker who had a year of breathless lunches with a male coworker crush. One afternoon, they decided to take it to the next step and checked into the nearby Days Inn ("not the most romantic of places," she recalls, "but the closest, and we were ready!"). As he did his striptease, she said he had so much hair on his back that "I nearly gagged. He obviously didn't know that men can get waxed, too." Sex did not happen, and the flirtation died.

I spoke to fourteen wives who are engaged in extramarital liaisons. They range from loose hippies to starchy conservatives, and go up to the age of seventy-eight. Yet these women share this common and significant trait: Wanderlust occurs when the relationship at home turns lonely, stale, or cold. I would say this to you: Don't judge a book by its cover; apple-cheeked women in Amish-style dresses could be wearing black garter belts and have lovers on the side.

However blasé we have become as a culture accustomed to broken marriage vows and sex on the sly, there is a timeless fact about women in love and in lust that remains unchanged: Females, even the toughest of us, are hardwired as a species to be tender of heart. Therefore, fleeting passion usually takes more of a toll on us than on our husbands, brothers, and sons. We are not the weaker sex, but we seem to bruise more easily. It is biological and ancient and nonretractable.

During a United Press International interview with Germaine Greer I found that the formidable feminist had even at one point cowered to a man. Tall and taunting and bisexual, Greer is known as a harsh critic of traditional relationships, this after trying her hand at marriage once at the age of thirty—an experiment that lasted less than a month. The Amazon of the women's liberation movement, who used to ride around in her car and sip from a Jack

Daniel's bottle, remembered that brief, unhappy period: "I was only married for three weeks, but I think I was forced to burst into tears and say 'I'm sorry' three times in those three weeks," said Greer, now seventy-two and a professor emeritus at the University of Warwick in England. "There was a power struggle going on, and my job was to lose it. There's something about testosterone that is scary. It is hard-nosed and aggressive and cruel. I think you have to be out of your brain to want a husband."

What Greer was speaking about is the "little woman syndrome," the archaic yet still popular mind-set held by many men that their wives should concede power to them. Yet for a woman torn between two lovers, often the mental cruelty she suffers most is that which she piles on herself. We are the caregivers, the softies, the gender programmed to take care of the needs of everyone else before we care for ourselves.

Adultery severs a woman from her primal instinct to be responsible. The torment between guilt and lust of an unfaithful wife may be something we'd never want to emulate, yet we can't get enough of her fractured sagas. Two of the most enduring literary classics feature heroines in adulterous distress: Leo Tolstoy's *Anna Karenina* and Gustave Flaubert's *Madame Bovary*. Besotted with her lover and married to a man who refused a divorce, Anna throws herself in front of a train. In *Madame Bovary*, Emma's affairs drive her to swallow arsenic.

Modern philanderers are more likely to drink heavily and see a therapist who tells them to leave their lovers. When given that solution, this woman chose to leave her therapist instead.

Shauna is a refined fifty-five-year-old wife, married for thirty-two years to a wealthy Texas developer and in love with someone else. She greets me in a high-collared lace blouse and a billowy black skirt that grazes her ankle. Shauna is unlike any woman I have ever met. Demure and very feminine to the eye, she is a portfolio manager who makes $250,000 a year and thinks like a man, in compartments, cool about her double life, with no crying jags. She has managed to hold together a long marriage and a long affair with a landscaper she met in 1990, while he was planting succulents in her sprawling yard.

On her husband, Paul: "I can't see ever leaving him."

On the landscaper: "I can't see ever leaving him."

Shauna praises Paul as a good father, a good grandfather, and a "good man." The landscaper loves sex; her husband needs to be begged to have sex twice a year. So this wife gets to have it both ways: a committed marriage and a committed boyfriend. Very naughty—and, she would claim, very necessary.

Yes, the cliché is true: Women are suckers for guys who can fix things. Chuck worked as a carpenter before he became an architect, and he built much of our house with his own hands. Having a handy man is convenient *and* sexy; I love the sight of a man in a worn-out leather tool belt. One really naughty grandma recalled a time in the late 1950s when her one-year-old was asleep in the next room, and she shtupped the man installing her refrigerator—in her kitchen.

Is Shauna a wretched wife? Is she merely trying to survive? Is a secret life okay to pursue as long as you are not hurting a spouse? Our interview lasted an entire weekend, most of it seated on a butterscotch-brown leather couch in her Houston living room. I sat bug-eyed and open-mouthed as she wove together her riveting and contorted story, a mink throw covering her legs.

SHAUNA

My husband is only capable of doing so much, and it's not enough. He didn't like sex when we got married and he doesn't like it now, thirty years later. We have gone to therapists all over Texas, and in New York and Los Angeles. But you can't turn a Popsicle into a flaming torch. I am a very sexual person and I am not willing to live without intimacy. Period.

I got married when I was twenty. My husband came from the same kind of background I did, affluent white Anglo-Saxon Protestant. He was a graduate of an Ivy League business school, and my mother loved him. He is three years older than me, and he had never had sex with anyone before me. After our third date we had sex, and it wasn't very good. But I really liked this person. He was a nice man, and I figured our physical relationship would get better.

We got married after a year of dating, and immediately I realized there was something very wrong about our sex life. He was not a participant; he was a receiver. I was giving all my love to him physically, and I was getting very little back. I was too embarrassed to talk to my mother about this, or to share details of my nonexistent sex life with my girlfriends. So I didn't do anything about it. Now, three decades later, I am certain he is mentally blocked to physical intimacy; that part of him is shut off.

Looking back, I see that I was convinced I should marry him by other people, and not by my own sense of conviction. We were still dating when I left for my freshman year at Berkeley. He kept calling and calling, telling me how much he missed me. His college roommate later told me that his whole senior year he used to just sit at his desk in the dorm. He lost twenty pounds, he wouldn't eat because he was so forlorn about not being with me. Meanwhile, I'm living in a suite with really nice girls and we are going out with great guys. My mother would call and say, "How can you be dating when this wonderful boyfriend of yours is sitting home alone watching football games?" My family was very disapproving that I was ruining my chances with what they considered to be an excellent catch.

It was really important for me to please my mother; I couldn't stand to have her disapproval. So I got engaged to Paul in the middle of my sophomore year. I can't believe that I stunted my whole life when I was at the peak of self-discovery. None of my friends were getting married. But I bought my mother's warning that he would get away if I didn't grab him. Right before I moved back to Texas I had started dating the most unbelievably handsome guy at Berkeley. He drove a convertible Porsche, and he was an upperclassman. He was very seductive, he had this dry sense of humor, and we started sleeping together. Even after I got engaged we continued having this affair. Sex was great, and I figured I'd be leaving soon anyway, so what the hell?

Right after I got married, I used to imagine it was this boy from Berkeley I was with in bed, and not Paul. Even though my husband and I rarely had sex, it was just my luck that I got pregnant, seven months after the wedding. One day, right before I delivered our daughter, I was so lonely I called my old boyfriend from Berkeley. It was really sad. He said, "I loved you, what happened? You're too young to be off the market." Once we had a child, I knew I was really stuck. Paul was very touchy with our son, but there was zero sensuality toward me. One day I asked him, "If you can't stand to touch me, why did you marry me?" His answer was, "Because I didn't want anyone else to get you."

Okay, so you look at a person's childhood and ask, "What went wrong?" His mother was very cold and his father worked all the time and was never around. So he really received very little nurturing or demonstration of love.

For example, he liked me to perform oral sex, but he would never do it to me. Picture a man rigid as a corpse, you are rubbing him and kissing him all over, he has an orgasm, then goes to sleep. We'd have sex about once every three months; after I would lie there, quietly crying. Finally, I did tell my mother what was going on. She said, "In order to have a happy marriage you need to have sex once a week. When Paul gets home tonight, make love to your husband." We did have sex that night, and bingo, I got pregnant again. My diaphragm must not have been inserted right.

Even though I had a two-year-old daughter and a baby on the way, I started thinking about maybe getting a divorce. My brothers, who were both married, talked me out of it. They told me that no one wants to marry a divorcée with two young children. So I stayed with Paul, although I knew I could never have a marriage like my parents had. They couldn't keep their hands off each other, even in older age. They had rich sexual chemistry, and you just can't invent it if it's not there.

Shortly after our second child was born, I told Paul I wouldn't have sex with him anymore. He said, "Fine, I'll go get a prostitute." I told him I felt like his prostitute, that I give him pleasure in bed and he gives me nothing. After that conversation, we stopped cold having sex. I was married ten years when I had my first affair. It was bound to happen, right? I was sexually frustrated and my husband was not treating me kindly. I also grew up with unreal expectations about marriage, since my parents were so happy. My mother taught me that marriage meant a man would swoop you up on a white horse, ride off, and take care of you for the rest of your life. Instead, I felt isolated, alienated, and really mad at my mother. I was tricked into marriage.

I was thirty and living outside of Houston with my two kids when this carpenter came over to fix our door. He was about forty-five, a real man. It wasn't even that I found him so attractive. The draw was that he listened to me, and he had really expressive eyes. I found a lot of other projects for him to do around the house. It got sexual pretty quickly, though we never played around when the children were home. They were in school by then. He was divorced, so it wasn't like he had anything to feel guilty about, and things went on like this for three years. This is the person who taught me fantastic things about my body that I had never experienced. After a taste of good sex, I wasn't able to live without it again.

The affair ended because one afternoon my husband barged into the house unexpected. He forgot his wallet, and he found us on the couch, fondling not fornicating, thank God. My shirt was up and my pants were unzipped and my lover was in his T-shirt and boxers. Okay, you figure this one out: My husband looked at us almost calmly and went upstairs to get his wallet. We dressed quickly, and my lover ran out the door. Paul then said to me in a voice like he was scolding a child, "He can't do any work in this house anymore." I swear to you, that that was it. My husband and I have never spoken of that incident again, to this day. It is totally unbelievable that a person's emotions can be so frozen that he wouldn't confront me. So he knows I've been with other men, but it's just not something we ever discuss. I would be shocked if he has been with anyone else; sex is scary to this man.

That was the first of my two love affairs, and I don't feel guilty about either of them, because I don't think I am doing anything wrong. All I'm doing is getting something I need that my husband won't give me. The carpenter was a beginner's course in sensuality and sexuality. The next affair has taken me to a new level, and it's so fantastic that I haven't been able to walk away from it.

He's a landscaper and he was doing some planting in our yard. One really hot Texas afternoon, he was placing aloes into the ground and I sat down next to him. I felt an instant attraction, and we were very comfortable in conversation, as if we'd known each other forever. Eventually we started to talk about our relationships. I told him that I'm in a marriage with no sex. I guess that sounds like an invitation to men, and it turns me on when someone is turned on by me.

He's six feet three and fifty-four, and looks like a cross between a really good version of Keith Richards and Clint Eastwood. One day I was bending over at the kitchen counter writing him a check and he stood right in back of me—I could feel his crotch gently touching my ass. Neither of us moved for a minute, then I stood up, turned around, got on my tiptoes, and we kissed. Our clothes were off in about fifteen seconds.

After that, I wanted to spend every waking moment with him. I was obsessed. Little things would get me off. Like if I touched his arm, his muscles were hard as a rock and it got me so excited we'd make love right then and there. Another time, I was sitting on his lap in a chair in the backyard; the kids and my husband were at a baseball game. It was night and there were so many stars out, and we did it outdoors. I was like a teenager with him: I wanted him in me and with me constantly.

Meanwhile I would always bring up with my husband that maybe we should go to couples counseling together. We went to three sessions together, then he said, "Nothing is wrong with me. You go alone." And so I did. I found this really good therapist and she took one look at me while I was talking about Paul and said, "If you are having an affair you have to tell your husband. You seem too happy to not be having sex." I told her that my husband caught me one day with another man and he was just blank about it, no blowup, nothing. She said, "Talk to him. Tell him."

I went home that night and we had a nice dinner together. By this time, both our children were out of college and living on their own. After our meal, Paul got up to turn on the TV and I said, "I have something important to tell you. Let's talk instead of watching television." I then started to talk openly about my affairs, and it's just incredible how a husband of twenty-four years reacted.

He cut me off and said, "So that's all you had to say?" He actually looked relieved.

I asked him, "What did you think I wanted to talk about?"

He said, "I thought you were going to tell me that you are a lesbian."

Can you believe this? My husband doesn't have a clue about who I am. Over the years, I have actually thought maybe it's him who is gay. But I've come to think he's asexual; he just has zero passion.

Even with the bizarre double life I lead, I still consider myself to be a good girl and a good wife—isn't that odd? I work hard at my job, and I am always there when anyone needs me in the family. I have a lot of respect for my husband's success in his profession and I am at his side for his important business dinners. This requires a lot of juggling, believe me.

Every six months or so, my lover and I try to break it off. He has never been married, and he has no children to complicate our situation. So it's always me who says, "Look, I can't do this anymore." So we break up for a week or so, he sends me dirty text messages, then I can't stand it so I text back "Come over now." I don't work at an office; I work at home. So it's been very convenient for us to conduct an affair. It's getting harder now because my lover has started talking about me leaving my marriage. He says he wants to have a "normal relationship" with me. He wants to hold hands with me in public. He doesn't see himself as the other man; he sees my husband as the other man.

On top of the sex, we really are best friends. I often wonder: "If I'm this happy now, imagine how happy I'd be if I went to bed curled up to this beautiful man every night?"

I'm not stupid, though. I realize these perfect separate bubbles are going to burst at some point. But the direction I will take is not clear yet. My husband and I are very involved in our children's lives. Our grandchildren sleep over and love to have their grandparents together. It would destroy them if I split up their secure little worlds. Our grown children are old enough to deal with a divorce, and I know it would be far less stressful for me to lead a life that is open and truthful. But I don't have the courage to leave my husband. And I don't have the courage to leave my lover. At this point, he's like another husband, that's how attached I feel. I'm stuck.

Paul is a familiar type to me; we both come from wealthy families and our politics are conservative. The real bond of course, is that we are the matriarch and patriarch for a son and a daughter and five grandchildren whom we both cherish dearly. I don't know any woman who could do what I'm doing without having a mental breakdown. I am able to compartmentalize each of my lives as totally separate and necessary. From my husband I get security; he is a partner in a family we created together. From my lover I feel so loved and peaceful. But we can't talk about politics at all. He's a rabid liberal Obama fan and we don't agree on anything. One morning I had Rush Limbaugh on. I just love him, and I thought my lover was going to throw the radio across the living room. It's the first time I saw his temper escalate. I didn't like him at all at that moment. It was creepy.

Shortly after that episode I decided maybe I should focus all of my energy on making my marriage better. One night my husband came home and I made a candle-light lobster dinner. We drank champagne and after dinner, I told him I had a surprise. I then turned on an adult porno movie and sat right next to him, rubbing his thigh. I was getting very hot, and at the end of the movie I looked at him and there was no expression on his face. I said, "Doesn't this make you want to have sex?" He said, "No." I realized that this man is fifty-eight years old, and how can he learn this now? It would be like going to get a Ph.D. without having gone to high school.

I was back in my flaming liberal's arms the next morning. I figured that I'm entitled to be happy sexually. I'm entitled to be with a man who tells me I'm gorgeous every time he sees me. I'm entitled to feel like a woman. There are many moments in which I do feel like I'm the woman who has it all from her two lives. But what I don't have in either life is a life that is honest and free.

My newest therapist was trying to get me to analyze the fact that I don't feel guilty. I stopped going to her when I realized I don't want to start feeling guilty about not feeling guilty. Not having guilt is liberating in my situation. Having this secret is way different than manufacturing a big lie. A secret is like giving yourself a pass: It's something that's between you and you. I know that everybody has secrets. My girlfriends tell me things about their own adventures with other men, and I don't judge them. As long as you don't get caught and as long as you are being nice to your spouse, I say, do what you have to do. Given my circumstances, I'm doing the best that I can.

I love my husband like you love an old childhood friend. When my lover comes over, I am transported into another world. He touches me everywhere and sometimes we don't even talk, yet our communication is complete.

I celebrated my fifty-fourth birthday last week, and I was thinking about all the years of this splintered existence I still have ahead of me. I said to my boyfriend, "What would you think if we moved in together and I left my husband?"

He got quiet and didn't say anything right away. Then he said that he was thinking about going to Barcelona to live for a while. "Shouldn't I follow my dreams? That's been my dream for thirty years," is how he put it.

I said, "I thought I was your dream." And I started crying at the table because to me that was like an arrow through my heart. My husband and I had intercourse right after that because I figured I should resign myself to this marriage. Sex wasn't great. It was okay. Afterwards, I did feel closer to him. But there will never be fireworks and I need fireworks.

My weakness is that I expect perfection to come from one love relationship, and I'm looking for something that doesn't exist. It takes two for me, and it's still not perfect. Maybe all we can expect from life is 65 percent happiness. I think about what happiness is a lot, because it comes and goes in waves for me. Maybe I've been chasing my tail for my whole marriage; maybe I'm ready for a new chapter. Maybe I don't want to be this person anymore who is thirty minutes here, thirty minutes there, then racing back for thirty minutes here again. Maybe if I stayed in one place I would have sustained happiness. Maybe I will never know any of these answers because I keep doing what I'm doing, just to survive.

I don't talk to anyone about my unusual double life. I don't want their opinions, and I don't want to be judged. Most women I know complain about their husbands, and many of them admit to being unhappy. My situation is so different. Most people who are unhappy with their husbands were at one point happy. I was never happy with my husband. I feel like I was in an arranged marriage. I never fell in love with him. I have remained open to falling in love with my husband all these years, and while I do love him, I know this will never be a romantic love.

Recently my niece told me she thinks she wants to marry her boyfriend. They are both twenty-seven, and she's been dating him on and off since they were sixteen. I said, "Jennifer, are you mostly happy when you are together?" She said, "I would say that 50 percent of the time I can't stand him."

I said, "Honey, if you can't stand him 50 percent of the time, marry him and you won't be able to stand him 100 percent of the time." That got her attention, and there's no wedding date set. I'm not going to push marriage on anyone after what happened to me.

If people knew my survival secret, they'd tell me to come clean and choose one man over the other. They'd call me dirty names. I don't ask for their advice because no one else knows what's best for me. They don't live in my house. Every woman has the right to be with someone who desires her.

During the three-hour flight from Houston to Baltimore, Shauna's love triangle plays over and over in my mind like a film noir I can't tear away from, yet at the same time can't stand watching anymore. She has everything and she has nothing, a realist caught in a standoff with the idealist pursuing an impossible dream. Her line, "Every woman has the right to be with someone who desires her," makes me think about the role sex serves in our lives. If you are having good sex it freezes you in a youthful mind-set and deflects depression about advancing birthdays. Your heart seems fuller and your body appears firmer in the mirror. Even your neck looks better—or if it doesn't, you don't give a damn.

Shauna is getting a lot of action, and she looks great and feels young. Her aloof husband makes her feel angry and old. She is also driven by the thrill of the chase, craving the roaring intensity of the unattainable and unwilling to settle for the low-throttle contentment most long-marrieds are resolved to accept. Whatever you make of Shauna and her juggling act—call her a sex addict or one brave dame—she is indisputably the boss of her own life, though her brand of sovereignty means she must sacrifice truth and inner peace. Her frank sexuality reminds me of Erica Jong's erotic 1994 bestseller *Fear of Fifty*, in which she has an Italian lover she calls "my forest god," a man who says "hello to my nipples, my neck, my lips, my tongue. . . ." Then ". . . he walked me into the bedroom, where he uncovered my body slowly, exclaiming at the beauty of each part, and entered me on the bed, holding firm inside me for what seemed like forever, while I filled with juice like the pears on the pear tree and began to throb as if a storm were shaking them onto the ground." Phew, okay, so now what do you feel like doing *right now?*

Unmarried at the time, Jong's lover had to sneak to her bedside since he had a live-in girlfriend. As Jong writes later in the chapter called "Sex" of their torrid but erratic arrangement: "When he entered me I felt complete. Yet when he left I could not trust him to return. . . . In every woman's heart there is a god of the woods. And this god is not available for marriage, or for home improvement, or for parenthood."

And that's it: Lovers are men who are great at loving you in the moment, and shaky as anchors to hinge your dreams onto.

I am a huge fan of Erica Jong, the irrepressible author of many husbands and many lives who, since the zipless frenzy she caused with the 1974 release of *Fear of Flying*, pushes all women past our comfort zones but protects us on our journeys. *What Do Women Want?* is the title of one of her later books. What I get from Jong and from other unabashed wives is that, more than self-governance, women want to feel worthy. And that gives us dignity.

Shauna feels worthy as a high-earning professional and as the matriarch of an extended family. But she feels peripheral, undesirable—even devalued—as a wife. Not one person or one thousand people can ultimately give you a sense of sustained self-worth; that must spring from within. Yet being told and shown you are needed and sexually desirable is a big boost to your self-esteem, and definitely lops years off the aging process.

When you're having sex the world feels all right.

I am with a woman from St. Louis who has been married forty-five years. Cynthia has white hair, a large body, scraggly nails, and a pale complexion. Her husband is a physics professor and is rarely home. They are parents of one grown daughter and three grandchildren who live in Georgia. Cynthia says her choice to keep up a college romance rekindled at a class reunion was made out of "desperation and desire." Unlike Shauna, they have never consummated their fifty years of kissing and longing.

CYNTHIA

I am absolutely in a committed marriage and at this stage, I can't imagine ever leaving this marriage. One of the major reasons I am able to stay in it is my old boy-friend is still in my life. My husband lectures all over the world and has basically been on the road for forty-five years. When he is at home, he is buried in papers and phone calls. I knew that his career would be demanding going into this relationship, but I didn't imagine in the excitement of courtship that my marriage would turn out to be so lonely.

In the summer of 1980, I slept with five men, four of whom were not my husband. I am not proud of this, but those are the facts. Here I was, alone in rural Indiana, a housewife with a toddler. I think I would have ended up in an institution without these lifelines. As the years went on and my daughter started school, I continued to have male visitors. I have the good fortune of living in a town where a lot of my old classmates still live, including two of my high school boyfriends. One is married, the other is not, and they both were happy to keep me company.

This was around the time that Cyndi Lauper came out with the song "Girls Just Want to Have Fun," and I knew every word and used to sing them very loudly in my kitchen and in my car. That song gave me power. "Girls Just Want to Have Fun" was not only about women needing playtime; to me it meant stepping out from under patriarchal men. That song was sung for us wives of the post-feminist era who were disappointed by the restrictions of traditional marriage. I knew what I was doing was wrong but somehow that song made me feel all right. I had a little secret life that was fun and inspiring.

I felt justified. The intimacy and praise I was getting from other men balanced out the anger I used to feel when my husband came home after a long trip away and expected me to be smiling and waiting, with a great meal on the table. What can I say? Girls need to have some fun, and he was definitely not fun, nor was he physically or emotionally available.

I remain a girl having fun at the age of sixty-eight. My husband just turned seventy-four and still travels more than ever, so I am free to have lunch, or have whatever, any time I want. My friendship with my college boyfriend I honestly can say has saved my marriage. Let's call him Thomas—we met on my eighteenth birthday on a night out at the Boston bars. Back then, you did not screw in high school; you engaged in heavy, heavy petting. I was a virgin when I got married. Thomas was the first guy I really kissed in a meaningful way, the first guy I let touch my breasts, and his was the first penis I ever touched. A girl never forgets those passionate firsts in the backseats of cars.

Thomas was the first boy I loved, and after that first night, we saw each other every day and every weekend for freshman and sophomore years. Even after college we'd sometimes get together over Christmas vacations. By that point, we were simply old friends and the spark was gone.

I didn't see Thomas again until 2003, at the wake of one of the most popular football players in our class. Of our college graduating class, everyone I was really good friends with showed up. When I walked in, Thomas was standing with a group of men and I noticed him right away. The men around him were mostly bald with big stomachs and Thomas had nearly the same body he had when he was twenty, and he had longish gray hair. Here I was, a grandmother of three, but when I saw him it was like I was eighteen again; I felt that same sexy flutter. I walked over to him and he took me by the arm, and we stood together at the casket for a few minutes. Then for the rest of the night we sat in a corner and talked and talked: about his wife, and about my husband, about his three children and my one child, and about our grandchildren.

At one moment, he reached in back of my sweater and tucked in the label, which was sticking out. His fingers briefly touched my back and it was like an electric charge, and I thought the gesture was really sweet. It was as if I were still his girlfriend and he was taking care of me.

When we left the funeral Thomas said, "Let's have lunch sometime," and I gave him my cell phone number. About ten minutes later the phone rang; it was him and we agreed to meet the following week. Here we are, eight years later, and I'm still seeing him, not often, maybe once every other month.

Like when we were kids, we still have petting sessions in the backseat of his car. I never slept with Thomas, after all that dating, so that's something that remains a mystery between us. Probably if we'd done the deed already the infatuation wouldn't have lasted this long. We live within a three-hour drive from each other, and when we meet, we pick somewhere halfway, in some isolated little town where no one knows us.

Starting on our first date as senior citizens, we would hold hands under the table, just like we used to do in college. Then we'd have our arms around each other walking to the parking lot. Then I'd get into his car, we'd drive somewhere and neck madly. I still call it necking, that's how old I am. I'm glad we don't live around the corner from each other or else we'd be tempted to meet more often. As it is, he is always on my mind.

Each time I'm with Thomas it puts a spring in my step, and that lift carries me over until the next time we are together. Thankfully, we have decided not to have intercourse. That would be really confusing, since my feelings are already so strong. Kissing and petting is very romantic, and it's enough for me. I love kissing.

My husband and I haven't really kissed for decades, long, lingering, tongue kisses. We just sort of peck hello and good-bye. I remember hearing Dr. Ruth Westheimer say long ago, "You better make sure you are kissing your husband or else your marriage is in trouble." Maybe if I had listened to her, I wouldn't be running around with an old boyfriend. There have been times when I swear that I will stay away from Thomas, knowing that this relationship may be helping me but is not helping my marriage. He will call and I will not answer the phone. His messages say, "Pick up the phone. You are killing me!" I eventually cave and I call, and when I hear his voice my stomach lurches. He says, "Let's have lunch," and I cannot resist.

He carries Jean Naté lotion in his gym bag—the same lotion he remembers I wore in college—and he rubs it all over my legs and tells me what beautiful feet I have. What husband does this? He says that he and his wife have had separate bedrooms for the past fifteen years, and that there is no intimacy at all. What we have is special and something we both feel lucky to be getting at our age.

I know my behavior is really bad, but I have always been a person who likes to break rules. And this thing with Thomas is really a turn-on, my God, to know that somebody has cared about you for all these years. I am not going to leave my husband, and Thomas is not going to leave his wife. There is no reason to. We've got everything we could ever want as things stand.

With Thomas, it's like a balloon liftoff. Even with no penetration, he is a very hot man; his skin gets very hot. I heard something on the radio the other day about how it's your first real romance that turns out to be the one that really makes the biggest impression on your life. It's your first passionate experience, and that is hard to forget.

Seeing Thomas makes me get along better with my husband. I am a nicer, more tolerant person because of this affair. I spent a lot of years of my marriage feeling very alienated. When I started this thing with Thomas, it brought a sense of warm familiarity. I am a happier wife. Once, I tried to broach the subject of seeing old boyfriends with one of my dearest friends and she cut me short with, "If I wanted to be with other men, I wouldn't have gotten married in the first place." It's not as simple as that, is it? You can be in a long marriage and be in a long affair at the same time and those two worlds don't have to ever collide.

I appreciate my marriage for what it is. We are partners in a long life, and we have grandchildren together. We have our health, and we have sex now and then, and when we do, it is very warm and very nice. But we don't have romance. We don't walk down the beach, holding hands.

I look at my wedding pictures and see a bride with a dreamy expression who believed that marriage would be the best thing that ever happened to her. I expected to be in love for the rest of my life. The disappointments that build up form blockages over time that stop the flow of love. So that's my story. I am a woman in a committed marriage who has never let go of her first real love. How can you walk away from the attraction you have for the first boy you let inside your bra? It takes a great deal of pressure off me psychologically to know that I am still sexually attractive to other men. Thomas will always see me as that young girl who stole his heart and never let it go.

"Mystery is critical to romantic love," writes anthropologist Helen Fisher in *Anatomy of Love*, the immaculately researched 1992 book that broadened the conversation on how brain chemistry affects love. "Barriers also seem to provoke the madness. The chase. If a person is difficult 'to get,' it piques one's interest. In fact, this element of conquest is often central to infatuation. . . ."

Although her relationship is more than a half-century old, Cynthia is still in the infatuation stage. It's difficult "to get" someone who is married, and that unavailability of a love that is unconsummated enlarges the mystery that Fisher says is essential for romance.

"This violent emotional disturbance that we call infatuation (or attraction) may begin with a small molecule called phenyl ethylamine, or PEA," a substance in the brain that arouses feelings of "elation, exhilaration and euphoria," Fisher explains in her book. You've heard enough stories from me and your friends to know that these three emotions hardly characterize a lengthy marriage. The infatuation phase is not biologically sustainable. According to Fisher, the normal duration of infatuation is two to three years. As time passes, other chemicals kick in and lust turns into attachment. If couples learn how to accept the grind of the ordinary and the departure of euphoria, attachment can glide into a comfortable and long monogamous marriage. I am one of those wives who cherish predictability. I'll take the slow burn of a long love instead of the bonfire of euphoria that rises quickly in spectacular flames but ends in choking smoke. Staying married allows me to relax in a crazy world. I believe in a forever partnership.

Yet, this is not a natural state, even for highly evolved animals like us. "The sexual response is primal and animalistic," says Marilyn Charwat, the Florida sex and relationship therapist in practice since the animalistic 1970s. "It is an unnatural situation to have sex with only one person, and many of my clients find this expectation restrictive and impossible. People are living much longer, and they have bigger ideas about self-fulfillment. There is no way any one person can fulfill all of your needs—unless you happen to be one of those very rare women married to a super-communicator, a super-listener, and a super-sex partner.

"In Europe, the concept of extramarital affairs may not be openly discussed, but society has been comfortable with the concept for a very long time," Charwat continues. "American society adapts standards of sexual morality that many find inhumane and impossible; that you marry one person and stay sexually and emotionally true and connected to that person forever. For some women, having more than one love relationship can make the difference between contentment and depression.

"And if the secret comes out? Most marriages can endure adultery. If the partners communicate about it honestly, an affair can even bring positive breakthroughs in the marriage. You'd be stunned how many people have a secret love life, and handle it emotionally and have made peace with it. Of course, an affair does not last indefinitely. When you marry a lover it's no longer an affair, it becomes a marriage with all the day-to-day frustrations of your old marriage."

I have been stunned by the secrets and shenanigans in this journalistic journey through American marriages. Our cultural ideal is that one partner should grow along with you through all the stages of life. The reality is that, for many wives, attaining longevity requires getting growth spurts elsewhere and experimenting with alternative routes. Unearthing real stories about real wives in long marriages underscores the fact that couples are often not what they seem. That gives all of us a break from feeling compelled to live up to a mythical model of what marriage should be. On some level, everyone I interviewed had a secret life, large or small. I'll start with this relatively small one.

For the past four years, Reed, age forty-eight, has harbored a crush on the divorced father of one of her daughter's closest friends, a man she regularly sees in the school parking lot, and a man who is her husband's golfing buddy. She is a stick-skinny gym teacher in an elementary school, securely married, and what she calls "insanely crazy" about this man. Talking fast and with frenetic hand motions, Reed tells me, "Because I am so attracted to this guy I've got to stay away from him. As it is, I can't get him out of my mind, and we haven't even done anything really bad yet."

The lengthy and unspoken attraction led to a spicy encounter that was sort of bad.

She was hosting a small dinner party that included her crush, and she excused herself from the table of eight diners to get another bottle of wine from the basement. When she walked by the powder room, the door was opening, and it was him. He followed her to the basement and closed the door. She gasps and swoons while recounting the incident.

REED

We kissed for one minute, a hard and wonderful kiss. His smell was a mixture of soap and leather, a real manly smell. He picked me up off the floor and hugged me so hard my back cracked. He then brushed the wrinkles out of his shirt, straightened his tie, winked at me, and left me at the wine rack.

When I got back to the table, I was so flustered I forgot to serve the salad course. When the last guest left, and my husband went to bed, I stood at the sink, staring at the plates of untouched beets and feta, still covered in Saran Wrap, and dreamily loaded the dishwasher. Thinking about that one kiss can nearly bring me to orgasm.

I see him all the time and we don't talk about what happened but we know what happened. I sometimes picture him on top of me during lovemaking with my husband. I have really good sex with my husband. Ha! But sex only happens about twice a month, and that's if I'm lucky. I will probably never sleep with my fantasy man, unless my husband keels over. But this one magical kiss has carried me a long way. I am careful to avoid him now at school events. Seeing him may lead to a discussion that would lead to a meeting and throw my marriage in the air.

It's nice that I have an astounding memory, and I can conjure up his animal smell whenever I want. Remembering our very short encounter gives me something extra. Having this man in my life, even from afar, is like having a valuable gold coin secretly hidden deep in my pocket.

Reed's fantasy is hers alone, an infatuation that is causing euphoric feelings because they remain latent, at least for now. Hers is more of a secret lusting than an all-out secret life. Reed's caliber of an encounter was told to me many times by wives—a crush, a kiss, maybe the guy steals a feel and the gal steals one back, then nothing comes of it except orgasmic fantasies. This following story was unique and over-the-top, my most stunning find. And not because I didn't know this stuff goes on, but because the fifty-seven-year-old wife looks like Debbie Reynolds, prim and polished and naïve. In fact, Mimi, with honey-blonde helmet hair and a turned-up collar on her pink polo shirt, owner of an upscale catering business, and her entrepreneur husband, Gerard, are full-tilt swingers. Their gold coins are not secretly hidden away; this Oregon couple have openly integrated their joint fantasies to sleep with other people into what she considers "an honest, traditional marriage." Their three grown kids have no clue, nor do their closest friends, that these pillars of the local church have been sleeping with other couples for the past decade of their thirty-two-year marriage.

Five feet nine with flickering hazel eyes, Mimi toys with her two-karat diamond wedding ring as she reveals what it's like to be part of what swingers call "the lifestyle." Those of us who choose to sleep only with one person are called "vanillas," bland and colorless. Here's more from Mimi on her release once she "crossed over."

MIMI

What a relief to be able to open up about this. It's not like I can sit down with my parents and brothers and say, "Guess what, guys?" Well here it is: Gerard and I are partners for life, only we've added a little twist to the relationship. You would be very surprised who else is in the lifestyle; it's not low-life porn stars. We are normal, successful people. We are attorneys, doctors, CEOs, educators. We are your neighbors. Gerard and I have a monogamous mentality, but we play the marriage game differently.

I've been with five Roberts, and four Daniels. Some of the people I've been with I can't remember their names. I could never turn back now, knowing the satisfaction the lifestyle brings. I think the key to a long marriage is sex. And the secret to great sex is to get a Brazilian wax. My husband and I have always had incredible sex in our relationship. We are a couple who have sex at least four times a week, and it always brings us closer together. When you are having a fight, or when you are not communicating, we know we can fall into bed and everything just melts away. We are relaxed. The lines of communication are suddenly open again. You look each other in the eyes, and you start to talk. This sense of relaxation and communication is intensified tenfold when you are having sex with another couple.

My children would be flabbergasted if they knew about their parents' secret life. I'm in the Garden Club and a leader in our church. Several years ago we crossed the line and discovered this whole underground world of swingers. Most people picture our world as scum with tattoos. The people we choose to be with are highly educated leaders of their communities, people of our socioeconomic group. They are people who know what we know: By expanding our worlds, we get to have our cake and eat it, too.

I can tell you that if more wives and husbands were as honest as Gerard and I, there would be much happier marriages. What you have instead are affairs going on behind people's backs. Or, the husband wants to sleep with someone and the wife wants to sleep with someone and they are afraid to talk about it. Being open about wanting to have multiple sex partners just makes the marriage stronger. We aren't hiding anything from one another; it's out there, and we're able to do it together.

We got into it a few years ago when we started going to resorts where clothing is optional. We discovered that it was nice to sunbathe naked; it was so liberating. And the people we met were so open and warm; when you have your clothes off, everyone is equal. There you are, naked on the beach or naked in the pool, and Gerard can openly have his hands on my breasts with all these people around and it is just very erotic. Some of the behavior is definitely not erotic; I'm not into watching blow jobs, but you may see a woman holding on to the rocks of a waterfall, and the man is entering her from behind. It is an amazing turn-on.

Our first experience was with a couple from Kansas. We hung out with them on the beach and got along very well. He and I were in the shade, and Gerard was with his wife in the sun. I told this man my fantasies, and all of a sudden I was fooling around with him and I saw Gerard fooling around with her. Seeing him giving someone else pleasure was a huge turn-on, and it was the same for him. That evening we were all in one bed together.

Each couple establishes their own rules, and our rule is that the girls rule. That means that when we are first meeting a couple, I get to make the decision of whether we're going to proceed, because girls are much pickier. Guys can find something sexually redeeming about any female. Another of our rules is that when we are with another couple, we are all together in the same bed. And Gerard and I always make sure parts of our bodies are touching each other while we're with other people; it may only be a finger or a toe, but this keeps us connected.

Gerard is totally straight; he won't even touch the other guy. I am bi-lite, which means from the waist up a woman can do anything she wants to me as long as it feels good. It's so nice to kiss women; their lips are so soft. If my vanilla girlfriends knew what we do they'd be shocked beyond belief, though people always comment that Gerard and I are such a hot couple. Now you know why. After he's been with someone else and I've been with someone else, then I go back to him and she goes back to her husband. Every time, Gerard tells me how much better in bed I am than anyone else. I am never jealous. I know Gerard loves me and how great we feel together.

We are really careful about who we choose. We always use condoms, and right now we are semi-monogamous with that couple from Kansas. I am very attracted to this husband, and Gerard and his wife have good chemistry, and when it's over we all lay there and talk about sex and our fantasies. I've never felt closer to two people in my life. Being part of the lifestyle has definitely held my marriage together. It has kept sex new and exciting and unconventional.

It's very erotic for me to be next to Gerard as he's giving another woman pleasure. He loves watching another man get me hot. It's funny, though, of all the partners I've been with, he is still the best. He remains the only man who can bring me to orgasm. So why mess around? It heightens everything when it's just us. We talk about our fantasies, we talk about what turned us on with other people, and when it's time to make love it's incredibly powerful.

I am fifty-seven, and I feel like I am at the peak of my sexuality. Our kids are college graduates and we are free. I'd say we see our Kansas playmates two or three times a year; we will meet them for a long weekend some-where and rarely leave the bedroom. Leading up to these weekends is unbelievably sexy; Gerard and I will talk about what we're going to do with them for weeks before we see them. The buildup is one of the best things about the swinger life; you get to really be explicit about your fantasies. Then when we do get together, it's unbelievable.

I talk to my friends in the lifestyle and none of us feel like our marriages are threatened. I would be jealous if Gerard did something behind my back, but, as I said, everything goes through me. I am the decider of who makes it into our beds. When we first started out I saw on Gerard's e-mails that he was communicating with one of the women we met at Hedonism. I went ballistic. So another of our important rules became that you can't have your own emotional relationships with these people.

It's easy for me; I don't have feelings for these other men. I like to have sex with them, and that's it. I've got the greatest thing going. I am happily married and I get to be with other men. It's such a turn-on to be with other people; your whole body is aroused, mentally and physically. It's like it felt when you first made love with your husband.

I am sure this is a life that the vanillas think of as filthy *Penthouse* stuff, but it has really revived our marriage. I remember when we first got into this there was a tremendous amount of stress in our marriage. Our son had all sorts of developmental issues and I was always tense, and that drove Gerard away. We got in a horrible cycle where I was mad at him and he was mad at me and we were at a standoff. The only time we got together was for sex.

Opening up our love lives has been very healing for our marriage. I don't care what a psychologist might say about our mental health. It works for us, and it works well. We have a solid marriage with each other, and the icing on our cake from others is always delicious. Just talking about our upcoming weekends with our Kansas friends makes our juices flow, and we end up in the bedroom. People are not meant to be monogamous. If people were more honest about this fact, there would be less lying and a lot more long marriages.

Well, Gerard and I do lie about our ages; we tell people we are ten years younger than we actually are. We are both fit, I've had just the right amount of work done on my face, and the couples we are most attracted to are in their forties. Could I ever go back to just one man? I don't think so. This is too much of a charge. And there's full disclosure, total honesty, and that is the root of a good marriage.

I have the most incredible orgasms with my husband. Still, it's like this: I can have a good meal at home but it's really nice to go out and be served at a different restaurant. Everyone has a different style of doing something. You learn different tricks and techniques and you add that to your marriage repertoire.

With images of new tricks with new bedfellows dancing in my head, I am relieved that opening up our marriage has never been suggested. I am liberated and open-minded, but the lifestyle sounds exhausting, though I must admit Mimi is one peppy wife. But damn, if your husband is giving you intense orgasms, why even bother with five Roberts and four Daniels? Although Marilyn Charwat says many of her clients have found peace with their secret love lives, I have not spoken to anyone other than Mimi who is really peaceful about adultery. Yet we lap up their stories of erotic gallivanting with insatiable hunger and curiosity. In her 1994 book, *A Natural History of Love*, Diane Ackerman describes the reason for our rapt attention. In a passage that follows the escapades of African pilot and adventurer Beryl Markham, a woman the author calls "fluorescent with life" and given to "flagrant promiscuity," Ackerman writes: "We may be spiritual beings, but what greater rapture is there than living a life hot on the senses, one augustly physical. With vicarious longing, we search their lives for the outlines of what we have lost: risk, passion, curiosity, exuberance."

Mimi embodies all these qualities, yet it's impossible for most women to adhere to her "no emotional ties" rule: The intimate act of lovemaking is inexorably tied with our spirits and our psyches and all other parts besides gonads.

A shrewd young woman friend who was a virgin when she married told me how aghast she was at the number of sexual partners her girlfriends had by the age of thirty. One twenty-four-year-old had hit the number twenty-four on her birthday. "Every time you sleep with someone you don't love it's like tearing off a little piece of your heart," my friend said. It's a message I share with my sons as they are perched on the cusp of adulthood: Sex is a sacred commodity, and not a cheap giveaway.

VIII

The Man Next Door

"Each time I leave one of these men friends I feel
validated and energized in a way that no one else
does for me."

—LANA

LISTENING TO STORIES from wives who stray, it's clear that their primary motivation isn't about a hankering for more sex (except for Mimi). These women seek solace in another set of arms because they are feeling emotionally starved. While I did find some merry spouses married to men who are consistently fawning and garrulous and straight, most women I interviewed are like me—they wish their spouses listened better and spoke up more.

Taking on a lover may be a temporary fix, yet I've heard enough fractured tales to make me certain that sex on the side is no lasting cure for conjugal lethargy. Here's a healthier idea: When the home front becomes blah and blue, hang out with your close male friends. These bonds that are passionate of mind and chaste of body can fill you up without wrecking your marriage. In fact, boyfriends with boundaries can be a huge relief for harangued husbands: With other doting males filling in the gaps, their wives expect less from them. Men and women, together in spirit and separate in body: When this just-friends connection works, it's magic.

"If your togetherness is not out of lust, your love is going to deepen every day," said 1970s spiritual sage Osho.

A college friend, Annabel, admits to using her men friends to restore the vitality of her ego: "Whenever my old relationship settles into a rut of sweatpants and Netflix, I book drinks with my six-feet-four Dutch friend Ronald," says Annabel. "We talk about sex and marriage and politics, and the air is charged with energy and intelligence. The attraction between us is smoldering and benign. After these sessions I go back home to my man of seventeen years, high on the reaffirmation that I've got sex appeal and a fascinating mind!"

Indeed, the right male pals give you blind adoration and unconditional support, and augment your highest image of yourself. Unlike a husband, with whom you share a toothpaste-splattered sink, men you don't live with find you fresh and extraordinary. They appreciate your views, without judgment or dissent, since what you say has no direct effect on their wallets or their daily lives. Your mortgage is yours, and his in-laws are his. In marriage, a clash of opinions can threaten each other's territory. Extramarital males view you through gauzy spectacles. However well they think they know you, it's still knowledge from afar; you remain a woman of mystery. They don't see your foibles and shadows that emerge in everyday living, faults that make your partner at home aloof and cranky.

Yes, the ancient art of flirtation, when it doesn't ruffle a mate, is easy to do, sexy without the sex, and very fun. Women who love the company of men should be able to have more than one man love them back. Our many men's unswerving affections expand our ability to love and to think, and to be happy. We all know that gay men make awesome boyfriends; this is different. These men pique pheromones—made all the more potent since there is no sexual release. I am not a fan of the very in-vogue term "emotional affair" as a blanket classification for cozy mixed-gender relations.

All deep friendships—between men, between women, between men and women—are emotional affairs, are cerebral affairs, are spiritual affairs, go soul to soul. We seek out people who titillate our whole beings, and even if there is sexual chemistry, it doesn't mean the sexual act will follow.

You've entered the danger zone in a tight friendship when the participants are calling and texting each other every twenty minutes. You've entered the danger zone when you are compelled to share the worst and best news of the day with your platonic suitor before your husband, thereby leeching emotional intimacy from your marriage. Beware of boyfriends who are strangling your marriage, and not strengthening it. On the flip side, don't shy away from a truly galvanizing male friendship because a doomsayer article along the theme of "husbands always come first" makes you feel guilty about something you haven't done and have no intention of doing.

It's a big girl who knows how to choose for herself which deep friendships, with women or men, are healthy and which are poisonous.

When selected wisely, trusty male pals are so precious only a foolish woman would ruin things by taking them to bed. An indelible warning to steer you away from this temptation comes from the 1983 film *The Big Chill*, which depicts a group of University of Michigan friends who gather a decade after graduation, following the suicide of their enigmatic leader, Alex. Glenn Close's character, Sarah, is despondent as she grieves for Alex, a man she enjoyed a lovely, sexy rapport with all through college, then finally slept with multiple times years later, while she was married to Alex's close friend Harold, played by Kevin Kline. Sarah laments tearfully: "We consummated an ancient, lurking passion and all it did was put up a wall on our friendship."

The film *Once*, which premiered in Ireland in 2006, is a more recent cinematic exploration of a man and a woman who love each other chastely (they are not given names in the film). Both are musicians and they meet on the streets of Dublin. They connect over their shared profession and the heartbreak over their romantic estrangements, hers from a husband and his from a long-term girlfriend. They come close to consummating their passionate friendship but eventually return to their other relationships, stronger and more hopeful from their brief time together.

The film gained fame with its 2007 release in the United States and after the theme song from the soundtrack, "Falling Slowly," won an Oscar. The pivotal scene comes nearly at the end of the movie, when the couple takes a motorbike trip into the country. She is talking about her husband left behind in the Czech Republic, and he asks her if she still loves him. She answers with a Czech phrase that means "No, I love you." Still, she urges him to return to his girlfriend in London, which he does.

He sends her a piano as a parting gift, and in the last scene of the movie, the audience sees her playing that piano, newly stimulated as an artist and a wife, with her husband and baby in the background.

My own need for greater stimulation is definitely not about wanting more sex. That's available at home. What I need and want most, and what I'm missing, is more talking. I need conversations, long ones, laden with details and juice. I need to feel connected on the level of soul. I want what Julia Child had when she first starting taking cooking lessons at Le Cordon Bleu in Paris: "I am satisfied in my hands, in my stomach, in my heart, and in my soul," she effused.

My husband has many admirable qualities; he is artistic and loyal and predictable. Being schmoozy is not one of them. Chuck and I do not lie side by side, propped up on pillows at one thirty A.M., talking about our childhoods and eating cold shrimp lo mein like couples do in the movies. Comedies featuring older lovers chatting and chowing down in their beds, like Diane Keaton and Jack Nicholson did in the 2003 film *Something's Gotta Give*, leave me teary. I go to bed at nine P.M.; Chuck stays up watching hockey, then Conan, then he reads biographies of Civil War heroes I've never heard of.

When we plot out trips we will take as empty nesters, his first pick is to explore the ancient castles of Scotland. Mine is to lie on a beach in Corfu. I hate guided architectural tours. He hates lounging in the sun. I love camping in a tent. He hates bugs.

He sits for hours. I can't sit still.

We are twined but separate, the "other" to each other,

strangers who met at a Washington bar, married, and produced a cohesive tribe. Surrendering to motherhood—as I titled my first book—was easy. I am bound to my sons by blood and genes. Surrendering to marriage is another story: Husbands are not our relatives. We can walk. We should walk away for a while when we are feeling bristly or ignored.

"Let there be spaces in your togetherness," is what Almustafa advises in Kahlil Gibran's *The Prophet*, precursor to the boomer mantra "Give each other space."

I love this husband but I am a whole self without him, as he is without me. We are soul mates sometimes and enemies sometimes and lovers sometimes and probably married always. That intuitive knowing we would ride on parallel tracks frightened me as a bride of thirty-three; that same knowing as a fifty-six-year-old wife is oddly soothing. We are free.

We have given each other permission to fuel the numerous tracks of our lives with different people and solo experiences. In early marriage, women are often consumed by living up to in-laws' ideals of a "good wife" who is deserving of their brothers or sons. So we behave like we think we are expected to behave. We suppress urges to reach out to other men, when these outlets make us more interesting and less bitchy.

These friendships need not be decades old. I have a new best boyfriend a mere driveway away. I'm on my way over there now, at Chuck's insistence.

It's six forty-five P.M., and I'm just home from Washington, D.C., where I am a journalism professor at American University. Chuck is sitting, like a petrified rock, transfixed on a clump of hockey players beating each other on TV. Breathless as a first grader who has just seen her first rattlesnake, I start telling him, spit flying, hands flying, the news that I may take my college class to Vietnam.

He remains immobile and asks me gently, "Can this wait?"

I respond not so gently: "NO, THIS CANNOT WAIT. I AM NOT GOING TO A VIETNAMESE RESTAURANT IN

ARLINGTON, VIRGINIA. I MAY BE GOING TO HO CHI MINH CITY. LOOK AT ME!"

In his low, slow voice, he says back to me, "If the Caps [Washington Capitals] lose this game, the season is over. Why don't you go see Derrin?"

Derrin is our next door neighbor, and since he moved in sixteen months ago, my marriage has never been better. This Derrin is nothing like Samantha's goofy and gangly husband on the 1960s TV series *Bewitched*. This Derrin is divorced, sixty, curious, and extroverted, and has a sweet, well-trained Portuguese water dog named Max. When given the silent treatment by my husband and sons, I look out my kitchen window, check out the kitchen next door, and pray that I see Derrin. Once sighted, I call him, tell him to look out the window, wave, and invite myself over.

Needy for conversation, I practically sprint through his door and he pours me a glass of wine as he stirs his homemade mushroom soup, a house specialty, laden with sherry and leeks. Derrin is a master chef who follows intricate recipes from grease-splattered cookbooks. He is also a rare opponent who can beat me at Scrabble, and he has a huge smile, with dimples.

Perched on stools in his kitchen overlooking the Severn River, Derrin and I eat, drink, and talk about Vietnam. I am lucky to have this man next door who piques my intellect and my palate and is always eager to listen to my stories and to share his own private thoughts. He's an adorable man with an adorable dog. Chuck likes him a whole lot, too. They do guy stuff together, like go to the shooting range and discuss power tools. But what Chuck likes most of all about Derrin is that he makes *me* less grouchy. I hear "Go see Derrin" a lot from my husband.

Chuck's birthday was approaching, and I asked him what he'd most like to do. He said, "Let's go to Derrin's and have him cook dinner," an offer Derrin immediately accepted. When we got to his cozy kitchen on an eleven-degree night, our neighbor was rolling slabs of dough on his black marble counter and placing vegetables in small, neat mounds for homemade pizza.

Decked in a white apron, Derrin chopped mushrooms, onions, olives, and artichoke hearts. He then shredded four kinds of cheese. Fat Gulf shrimp bubbled on the stovetop in a bath of butter and red pepper flakes next to a pot of garlicky tomato sauce. When the shrimp were tender, Derrin sliced them into succulent, symmetrical strips.

"Do you like anchovies?" he asked. Simultaneously, I said, "I love them," and Chuck said, "I hate them." It turns out Derrin loves anchovies as much as I do, and he tenderly laid some out on one of the pizzas. I was relieved that Chuck didn't hold his nose and pretend he was going to puke like he does when I open a can of the smelly little fish.

Sipping red wine from large goblets, my husband and I witnessed an impeccable performance befitting the Food Network. Derrin tossed dollops of each topping onto our individual pizzas, sprinkled cheese, drizzled on olive oil, then slipped the pies onto large wooden trays, grabbed the long handles, and placed them into the oven. I felt like we were at a pizzeria from my Chicago hometown, where red-faced chefs wearing white aprons freely roam among their patrons. We ate like pigs and made a couple drunken promises: to never call Domino's again and to never move from our adjacent homes so we could grow old together.

The wine served was a 2007 red called Rosso from Francis Ford Coppola, a blend of zinfandel, syrah, and cabernet. I picked up the bottle and was transfixed by the label that pictured a vineyard against a backdrop of mountains shimmering at sunset in shades of purple and rose. Chuck and Derrin were yakking about plans for a fly-fishing trip, shrieking like boys the age of Huck Finn. I noticed that Chuck was far more animated than he generally is with me.

In that moment, like Coppola's Rosso that swirls together three fine grapes, Iris, Derrin, and Chuck were a delicious blend, each enhancing the unique character of the other better than Chuck and I often do alone.

Walking down our driveway back home, I said to Chuck, "I love Derrin." And Chuck said, "So do I." Since this little birthday party, Derrin now has a girlfriend, Regina. She is open and real and they are delirious to be in later-life love. Best of all, Regina is welcoming to the wife next door.

My wish for readers is that you, too, get to cultivate and retain male friendships throughout your marriage. My wish for you also is that you use these friendships for renewal, and never become overly dependent on someone you are not married to. Liza's close friendship with a man friend nearly severed her relationship with her husband.

During their early years of marriage, while her husband was building his law practice in Northern Virginia, they had stability of income but intermittent face time. Her own career path toward a psychotherapy degree got sidetracked once their first son was born, and that was quickly followed by the birth of another boy. At the peak of her maddest housewife phase, often left alone to care for two toddlers, Liza started having "little nice talks" with a man in the neighborhood as he walked his dog and she walked hers at the same time.

Innocent chatter about canine behavior and the weather turned into a decade-long friendship Liza calls "the most intimate and important adult relationship I have ever had," even though their only body contact was to hug hello and good-bye. A call list on Liza's cell phone discovered by her suspicious husband destroyed the friendship and nearly decimated her marriage. Two years later, Liza is still mourning the loss of a fellow dog lover who became her "best friend."

LIZA

Once we had our kids and my husband was working all the time, our marriage turned into this nightly contest of who's the most tired. It wasn't passionate and it wasn't fun. I would go out walking our poodle and noticed this man who would always be out there with his black Labrador. He wasn't attractive to me, but there was something extremely magnetic about the way that he spoke. He was so gentle, with a very sweet smile.

We became instant friends, and after a few months he'd call me before he took his dog out and we would meet up, and walk together. It was just so easy being with him. I was never one for close girlfriends, but I felt that natural kinship with him that women have with other women. My dog-walking friend and I would discuss my stalled career a lot, and he would counsel me since he is also in the mental health field. We would talk about our families, too. His marriage was falling apart and I would just listen to him.

He didn't hit on me, and I didn't hit on him. We enjoyed being together. I could advise him about his marriage without being personally invested at all, though I could tell it wasn't a marriage worth saving. I would only speak positively about my husband, but I did share that I was lonely at home with just little kids. We clicked on every level, except there was never a desire for physical intimacy, at least on my part. If he felt attracted to me, it wasn't ever discussed.

After a couple of years, we would say "I love you" to each other when we were going our separate way. I did feel love for this person. It was a pure love that was effortless love. As my kids started school the walks got longer. It was better than any girlfriend I ever had because with a man and a woman, there is an element of flirting even when the relationship isn't sexual.

I began to feel as if our friendship was an addiction for me. He is fifteen years older and wiser about almost everything, about money and politics, and really about how to manage my family life. My father died when I was fourteen, and it became really obvious to me that the void he was filling for me was that of a father.

My dad was my best friend in the whole world. I was the apple of his eye and he was my hero. Just going to the hardware store with my father was like the grandest adventure, I'd be so glad to just be around him. I always felt secure when I was with him. When I was with my man friend, I felt protected like my father protected me. I did not feel this way with my husband. My husband doted on his work, and I doted on the kids. It was a pleasure to have someone worry about me.

One day my friend walked me home, the kids were in school, and we sat on my couch, talking and drinking tea. His boot touched my sneaker and he left it there. That feeling of his foot next to mine was so comforting, I can't even explain just how good that felt.

I would mention my dog-walking friend casually from time to time to my husband. One day I was recounting that his Labrador had to go to the veterinarian for some ailment and my husband started yelling at me, "I don't want you alone with him anymore. I don't give a damn about his dog. I'm sure he wants to sleep with you. That's how men think."

I told my husband so many times that there was nothing physical between us, and that I didn't even find him attractive. Still, he did not believe me. So I started to lie. I told my husband the friendship was over, this when our dog walks had turned into lunches, even a movie once in a while. Cutting off the relationship was not something I could possibly do. It would have been like having my father die again.

This man talked to me in a different way than my husband did and I needed that fatherly voice in my life. For many years I had everything: a husband and a family and another man who loved me. It is definitely possible to love two people at once, if you love each of them differently. I never felt like I was falling over the edge in love with this man, but I see now I was definitely perched on the very edge.

It wasn't until this relationship almost ruined my marriage that I realized the friendship was more of an addiction and had left me dangerously vulnerable. Basically I got caught with him one afternoon, and the way it happened quadrupled my husband's suspicions about us.

We were at a restaurant, and I had told my husband I was at a book club meeting. When I got home my husband stopped me at the door and screamed, "Where were you?" I said something stupid, like that I was at the grocery store picking up milk, when I didn't even have any bags in my arms. He said that I left my cell phone on the dining room table and there was a phone call made that morning to a number that I had called every day that week. My husband then just exploded.

On paper, it looked like I was having an affair, no question about it. My husband left the house for a few weeks, and we went through this terrible, painful, horrible period. When he finally came back, he said, "I know you have been sleeping with him. How could you not be?" It took the past two years to try and convince my husband I was not having sex with this man, and I am not sure even now that he is convinced.

My husband actually called my friend on the phone, and yelled, "I know you are screwing my wife." He then called him a string of vulgar and ugly names. That ended my long friendship with this man in about fifteen seconds, and I haven't talked to him since. Not one word.

No one will ever again fill that void for me, and I miss him like it's a death in my family. I miss just talking to him. He was the first phone call I made every day. I miss that he is not hearing about how my kids are growing up, which is exactly what I grieve about with my father.

It's only now that I would say my marriage is almost 85 percent back on track. We have talked a lot about the void this man was filling for me. I told my husband that my main attraction to this man was that he really listened to me, even if the story I told took an hour. With my husband, I would start talking about my day, and he'd interrupt me after one minute and say, "So what happened at the end?"

We are working on better communication, but patience is not something my husband has much of, and I know it's because he always has a lot of work on his mind. Meanwhile, I've realized some essential things about myself.

Most importantly, I've realized I'm not a little girl anymore, and I've got to learn to cope like a big girl who doesn't have a father figure to take care of her. I have to take care of myself, and take care of my children. I do think it's possible to have a good man friend in your life and be married, but I went about it the wrong way. If I could put this whole experience on rewind, I would have introduced my friend to my husband and made him a friend to both of us. If I had conducted this friendship appropriately and openly, he would still be in my life.

I wasn't careful about my emotional boundaries. I became too dependent. It was a hell of a lot easier to be friends with him than to be friends with women. There is a lot of bullshit with women, a lot of pretenses. Women are always second-guessing each other. I don't have the time for relationships that have little substance, and my relationship with this other man was all substance. My women tennis partners are court friends, but we don't see each other beyond the sport. There is part of me now that is closed to forming close friendships, since losing this man hurts so badly.

Use my story as a warning to other wives who may find themselves in a needy state. My husband was never home, and I was hungry for a connection. Tell them to focus on their inner reservoirs and not depend on someone else for strength. Recently I went back to school to train as a social worker, and what I was looking for in this man friend of mine, more and more I am finding in myself. He was an escape from the monotonous, exhausting tasks of being a housewife. Now the kids are older and I can reengage with the world. When I'm with my husband at night, we both have something of value from our days to bring to the table.

I miss my friend every day, still. It is sad. He is the one who made me always feel like I was a person of value, even though most of what I was doing was jogging and playing tennis. He opened up my life in a way that no one else has been able to do. That part of me is now shut down. My husband is not willing to share me with friends that are men, and because of that there is a part of me my husband will never know. That part of me that was connected to my old friend was the most authentic part of me.

One phrase from Liza sticks with me long after I leave Ohio and her simmering despair, and that is the description of her lost relationship as one of "pure love." Discussions and dissent over pure love that is spiritual and not physical, or *amor platonicus*, have played out for centuries, inspired by the writings in Plato's text *Symposium*, dated circa 385–380 B.C. This friendship dance between a man and woman who are not married can only work if it is openly celebrated and not hidden for fear of triggering spousal ire. Chuck appreciates my men friends nearly as much as I do, because they add to me, which is more for him.

It takes a village indeed. D. H. Lawrence knew this—wow, did he know—as is clear from this writing: ". . . no form of love is wrong, so long as it *is* love, and you yourself *honour* what you are doing. Love has an extraordinary variety of forms! And that is all that there is in life, it seems to me.—But I grant you, if you deny the *variety* of love you deny love altogether. If you try to specialise love into one set of accepted feelings, you wound the very soul of love. Love *must* be multiform, else it is just tyranny, just death."

When Chuck wants silence and no Iris, he is downright chipper when he hears me talking on the phone to Tom Ferraro, whom I worked with in my twenties in Washington, D.C., when we were both at United Press International. He is a Best Boyfriend Forever who is paternal and brotherly and handsome to boot—and he laughs at all my jokes. My adoration for Tom is so vast I fixed him up with my sultry Polish girlfriend Maureen. This matchmaking turned Tom into a first-time husband at the age of fifty-two, and a first-time father when Maureen delivered eleven-pound Hank into the world.

We should all be able to have what Carole King and James Taylor have had for almost forty years—a soul friendship that culminated in their summer 2010 "Troubadour Reunion," featuring King on piano and Taylor on guitar. In the June 3, 2010, issue of *The New York Times*, Anthony DeCurtis examines the duo's relationship. Taylor tells DeCurtis that he was in the balcony at the Troubadour in Los Angeles in 1970 when he first heard "You've Got a Friend." Taylor thought: "She's written it. That's 'The Star Spangled Banner' right there." After years as a backstage songwriter who let others get famous on her hits like "Up On The Roof," King finally stepped out as a soloist, encouraged by Taylor.

One of her trademark songs, "Tapestry," addresses the quest for enduring friendship, emblematic of her bond with Taylor, which was abiding and not romantic. "They never fell out and never broke up," wrote DeCurtis. "Most significantly—and highly uncharacteristically for those freewheeling times—they were never lovers, so there was no complicated personal history to resolve. If the tour can be said to have a message, it's that not everything has to end—or end badly."

This is the quintessential male pal, someone who boosts your talents, boosts your ego, and never leaves your life in "winter, spring, summer, or fall," as Carole King sings in "You've Got a Friend."

Tom never fails to brighten my day when it is dark, regaling me with stories of an era when I was a carefree girl-reporter, memories I never want to lose. By remembering who I was, he reminds me of who I still am. "At times our own light goes out and is rekindled by a spark from another person" is a line from Albert Schweitzer that reminds us of the gifts that are ours in a true friend.

You would expect two balladeers like Carole King and James Taylor to find their ways toward each other. How about this one, though? The left-leaning feminist justice Ruth Bader Ginsburg and the conservative justice Antonin Scalia are best buddies off the Supreme Court bench, routinely celebrating New Year's Eve together with their spouses at Ginsburg's Watergate apartment. Though she disagrees with him on more than half of the cases that come before the court, Ginsburg has said that he makes her laugh, and Scalia has said he likes her intelligence. There is a great picture of the two justices together, Scalia in front, Ginsburg behind him, riding an elephant in India on a judicial exchange that took place in 1994.

We find pieces in other people that we are missing in ourselves. Who knows? Maybe their inexplicable bond, which started in the early 1980s when they were both D.C. Circuit Court judges, fortified both of their long marriages. Ginsburg's husband of fifty-six years and father of her son and daughter died in 2010; Scalia has been with his wife, with whom he has nine children, for fifty-one years.

Along with men friends, my girl circle is also an indefatigable spark that ignites a flame within when the light is going out. These girlfriends are soft, and they are unconditionally reassuring. They settle me down. Yet men provide a tension that sharpens parts of me that need more edge. As a foreign species, our repartees are unfamiliarly jarring, rousing me as a woman beyond her wife-mother role.

Any friend who enforces and contributes to our vision of our finest selves should be allowed to enter and stay in our lives. After all, if we meet current life expectancies for women by dodging cancer and coronary disease, many of us could be married for fifty-plus years.

I am talking to a fifty-nine-year-old actress named Lana, who has deep-set eyes rimmed with kohl pencil and high cheekbones. Her chestnut brown hair falls straight to the chin line. She is very thin and very theatrical, and has remained very tight with two straight male actors she met in the 1970s when they were in experimental theater groups together. Married for thirty years to a man "a generation older than me," she calls these old friends "the touchstones to my raw, real self."

LANA

These two men are my history holders: They knew me long before I met my husband; they know me from a life that few people I know now could imagine me existing in. It was the early seventies, and we were all part of this radical experimental theater at its sharpest cutting edge in New York City.

One of my guy friends is from Philly and the other is from London; one is a photographer and one is an art director. I married someone who is culturally opposite and experientially different; he's from Brooklyn and I'm from Milwaukee. Rick and Lawrence were part of my dowry, and my husband has accepted that. They have been part of our lives since the wedding, and my husband has become their friends, too. I need these other men in my life.

I think it's rare for your husband to be your best friend, though a lot of people think he should be. In the constellation of my life, my husband has the unique position of being the pole star, the one with whom I navigate life. But alongside him in this constellation of mine are my friends, men and women whose different lights help me see in new ways and energize me in new directions.

A husband is your costar and a rock in your life. But if you're a multidimensional person, you need a lot of different colors on your palette, men friends and women friends with whom you can soar. Then you bring all that energy you are getting from the world back into the nest. So whatever I get from Rick and Lawrence I am also offering to my primal relationships with my husband and family. This is the true meaning of friends with benefits: You are getting something much deeper than sex.

Each time I leave one of these men friends, I feel validated and energized in a way no one else does for me. As we age we lose our idealism; we get lazy about our aspirations. A lot of compromise and daily noise that goes on in a long marriage tends to muffle your dreams. You are thinking, "I really should make pancakes for my husband and not go out and take a walk and look at the sky and laugh with friends who knew me when."

Sustaining friendships over time keeps you honest. They are reminders of mistakes you have made, excuses you have given yourself. These real friends don't mince words to get you back on track again. There is always a degree of sexual electricity in friendship, whether it be with men or women. People you choose to spend time with—there is something pleasing about their physicality to you. It doesn't mean you want to sleep with them. It just means you are drawn to them.

And these two guys happen to be very nice-looking.

In the end, to stay married, it takes a tribal effort, it takes a lot of people in your life. You need an inner circle beyond your family. Most women have these little tribes or they bury themselves in a 24/7 work environment, and that's how they stay married. I don't know anyone who would look forward to retiring alone to a beach house with their husband. If they do, they have big fantasies. It takes a lot of people to help you keep going full-throttle forward in life.

IX
Believe-It-or-Not Marriages

"Even when I hated my husband the most I still held
on to a little bit of love."
—BETH

MY SEVENTEEN-YEAR-OLD SON Jack pokes his head into my office to ask for ten dollars to go for tacos with friends in downtown Annapolis. He walks in to get the cash, and I suck in my breath: He is tall and floppy-haired and stunning, just like his father, and he's wearing the sweater that Chuck wore on a wintry night exactly twenty-five years ago this month. I tell Jack the story of that red and green pullover, warning him that he has inherited a potent lucky charm that may be a magnet for love. Jack groans, rolls his eyes, and huffs, "It's just a sweater, Mom."

It's not just a sweater, Jack, I answer silently as the door slams and he's off to see the girls who call our house and are drawn to his banjo playing and James Dean pout. My imagination zooms on fast-forward to the time when that sweater may be the pivotal object that lures some woman to become his wife.

Will he choose wisely? God, I hope so. I know so much, too much, about the impact of good choices and bad choices in marriage. I hope the woman he picks in turn picks him and doesn't mess with his heart. I hope he understands by example that a long marriage takes guts, humility, and constant work from living with parents who love deeply, squabble, and always make up. This message is hard to convey to Generation iPad, which flicks on a new image when they are not instantly gratified. I hope that he and his brothers stand apart from the popular culture that accepts and expects divorce to be part of the human growth cycle.

I've heard just about every story imaginable on how to play to win at the game of love, some of them unbelievable. This chapter features three of those seemingly miraculous marriages, relationships that have little else in common except that they are long-lasting and that when I heard about them they elicited this response: "I can't believe you are still married." The first is the story of Beth, the wife of a man who was withdrawn and downright cruel for most of their marriage, withholding sex, withholding any trace of affection, and regularly coming home drunk.

With small children and without a salary of her own, Beth stayed in her marriage because, as she put it, "Even when I hated my husband the most I still held on to a little bit of love." This is one of my favorite stories in the book, because it is a testament to what I know to be true: Even if there is only a splinter of love remaining on the part of one of the spouses, that marriage has hope. Even if a husband is a despicable jerk like the one you are about to meet, miracles do happen.

It ain't over till it's over.

Life never came easy for Ed and Beth, who met in their early twenties and have been married for twenty-eight years. In their blue-collar Midwestern hometown, no one's life is very easy, and good girls often marry bad boys. She has big blond hair and big brown eyes and wears blue jeans with a maroon hooded sweatshirt. I met her at a wedding shower for a mutual friend, and she was overweight and glum, two parts of Beth that were about to change. Most wives would have said, "the hell with you," early on in the marriage. But Beth is not like most wives.

BETH

I met Ed when I was twenty-one; we both worked the second shift at the phone company. He had big muscles and did a lot of drinking, a lot of drugs. Unfortunately for me, it was lust at first sight. At the time I was dating this preppy guy who was going to law school, a guy headed for wealth and success. But I didn't feel like my real self around Mr. Law School.

So I started to pursue Ed, and although we were way different—I'm not a drunk or a druggie—one thing we had going was that we were hot for each other from the get-go. But this guy had no idea how to treat a woman. He had never had a serious girlfriend. In his world, girls were just something to have fun with and send home in a taxicab. He went to an all-boys high school, so he never learned how to get along with the opposite sex. And there wasn't a lot of love demonstrated in his family: I have never in my nearly thirty years of knowing them seen his parents hug or kiss.

We were married for three months when I got pregnant. He wasn't ready to be a father and I wasn't ready to be a mother, but we had a son by our first anniversary. That baby was so wonderful I wanted another one right away, but my husband couldn't handle that, he was such a child himself. He was on three softball teams and went out to bars and watched sports and drank beer almost every night with his buddies. Here's the kind of irresponsible guy he was: I throw a thirtieth birthday party for him, there's fifty people in our living room, and he shows up three hours late, drunker than a skunk. He was a prick from day one in our marriage and he stayed a prick for a good eighteen years.

We didn't go on dates; we'd go to bars. Then on the way home we'd have these arguments and he'd do things like throw my purse out the car window, and leave me on the side of the street. I'm not kidding—a real prick. He's a really smart guy but he didn't even make it through the community college because he was too busy playing cards, doing drugs, and drinking. My mother detested him from the beginning, and maybe just to spite her I married him anyway, even though I knew I was marrying into trouble.

Turns out she was a right: By our tenth anniversary we had four children, and he was never around, and when he did come home he was shitfaced. Most nights he'd come home completely drunk after work, and I'd be petrified that one of those nights he'd either kill himself or end up in jail because of a drunken driving incident.

He was never violent with me, but he was verbally abusive, calling me really mean names. So for twenty years I lived with a guy who said nothing nice to me. I got no compliments at all. I was craving just to hear something like, "You look nice," or "Dinner was good," but I'm telling you—nothing. He just played sports and watched sports and drank. I tried real hard to keep the kids away when he was behaving really poorly, and I didn't say bad things about him behind his back. He was their father, after all.

Looking back at this awful time when he was so mean and rotten, we both see now that it's because he grew up with very low self-esteem. He was a prick as a way of protecting himself from being hurt. He put this big tough shell around himself so that if I walked away he wouldn't be devastated. He was a control freak with me, and I started to fight back.

Like if I wanted to go out with some of my girl-friends, that would just freak him out; he didn't want me going anywhere without him at night. Because one time

I was out and some of his friends saw me and called him and said, "Hey, we saw your pretty wife out on the town. Don't you have any control over her?" Well, he hit the ceiling on that one, calling me all sort of vulgar names. I yelled back at him and said, "I've got news for you, buddy. You don't have control over me." And that became the argument we had a million times.

Even though there were a lot of bad fights, we continued to make love. Well, it wasn't making love at that point; it was just sex. Then it got to the point where there was no sex at all. And this went on for years. I slept in the same bed with this man and never crossed the midline of our mattress. There was just so much anger. I swear to God, I would cry in bed at night. I would cry in the shower. I would cry at the grocery store, because I felt like I was trapped. But I tried to put on a happy face for the kids. I had quit my job to take care of them, and we were dependent on my husband's salary.

What was I going to do? Unbelievable, I know, that I didn't kick him out of the house. But he gave our family a roof over our heads, that's why I didn't try to divorce him. I thought that if things stay like this I'd leave once the children went to college. Divorcing him while the kids were still so young meant I'd be a single mother who would have to work full time. I didn't want to leave my kids in day care, and I didn't want the kids to be raised in a divorced family. I was stuck.

Oh, how I hated him, and I told him a number of times how much I hated him. This went on literally for eighteen years of our marriage. For eighteen years I was lonely. For four years we had no sex. I had no one to turn to. I certainly couldn't complain to my mother because she would have said, "I told you so."

Then I decided he had insulted me long enough and it was time to stick his nose in his own crap. I got tough. One night we were having dinner at his parents' house and everything started to make sense to me. I realized that it was his upbringing that wrecked him. It was a Thanksgiving dinner, and Ed's father was talking to his mother like I have never heard a man talk to a woman before. And not one of his siblings or relatives at the table was even flinching. He was ordering her around, saying, "Move this," "Do this," and nasty things under his breath. I was mortified for her. When I got Ed alone at night I said to him, "Am I the only person in that room who knows this is wrong? The way your father talks to your mother is horrible!"

Ed didn't yell back, he was dead silent, and he said he had no clue how wrong it was. It's all he ever knew. Ed had never been around an actual loving relationship. My family is very huggy and kissy; we fight like bandits but it blows over and we're all over each other with "I love you" apologies. So from that day on, I took it upon myself to be his professor in a class that could be called "How to Love Your Wife." This man had to be taught everything: how to talk nice to a woman. How to care for your family. How to be responsible. It's taken me several years but he's very good at those things now.

Right before that Thanksgiving I had decided to start making my own money in case I couldn't take his shit anymore and ended up leaving. I heard about an opening at the local library and got the job. The kids were in school all day, and getting out of the house was the best thing that ever happened for me and, really, for our marriage. I started to take better care of myself, and started to care about how I looked. If you're living with someone who is mentally battering you all the time, your self-esteem goes way down. Not having any sex, I wasn't feeling any desire to dress sexy. During our years of hell I packed on forty pounds and didn't wear makeup.

I didn't care about myself; the only things I cared about were my kids.

I got to 180 pounds, the biggest I'd ever been, and my girlfriends talked me into going into Weight Watchers. With my job getting me away from the refrigerator and my husband's better behavior, the weight started peeling off.

When I lost my first ten pounds Ed even bought me a bouquet of roses, the first time he ever got me flowers. He had been at the same lousy job for thirty-five years, and he had just started a new job making more money and getting more respect. So he was starting to feel good about himself, too. He stopped being an asshole, frankly.

Then one night, he had been away on a business trip and I picked him up at the airport. We got stuck in a snowstorm, so we pulled into a motel for the night. We got in bed and in a second we were all over each other: We had sex for the first time in four years! I have no explanation. It was like, bingo! I tell you, I cried almost during the whole lovemaking, it was so emotional for me. I was so relieved that we had found our way back together again. At first, it was rough getting used to each other again physically but since that time our sex life has gotten better and better and better. And I just turned fifty-one. For you young wives out there living in misery, if you still love the guy, call him on his shit and there is hope!

As we went through this making-up period, I got to tell him that all those years he was saying mean things to me it was like stabbing me in the heart. He said he was mean because he didn't trust me. I said, "If you could see my heart you would see you can trust me, Ed." He started understanding that my going out with girlfriends was not a threat to him or to our marriage; it was that I needed to get away from his abuse and from the children that I was basically raising alone.

It's incredible the changes in him. As he gets more money and respect on his job, he has started to feel better about himself. He has started reading books about how to deal with people better and how to be a better husband. Ed is learning how to love, and I'm not afraid of him at all anymore. I tell it like it is. I say, "Ed, I noticed over the years that the minute we get around your family you get sucked into their anger and you revert to acting like this terrible person. We are going to your parents' house tonight; please be your new, wonderful self. Don't turn into your father."

I didn't give up on my husband because deep down I knew there was someone good in there. So I pushed him until he woke up. I said to him, "You keep acting this way and you are going to end up an old and lonely man because you are an asshole to everyone, and no one wants to be around an asshole. Your kids are going to stop talking to you. I'm going to leave you. So you better change."

After all those years of hell he finally trusted me enough to ditch his tough-guy shell and be vulnerable. Every day he is just turning into a nicer guy. It is a miracle, but it didn't happen overnight. We are empty nesters now, and I have never been happier. I don't want to go out with my girlfriends as often. I want to be home with Ed sharing a bottle of wine. I can't tell you the last time we had a bad argument. Oh sure he gets snippy, but we've not again had an all-out war.

Yes, I'm a magician—I turned this guy totally around. Midlife sex is way better than anything. We text about sex. We talk about sex. My kids would frigging die if they could see some of our texts. But, hey, we gotta make up for lost time. This has been so good for my kids to watch the turnaround in our marriage. They saw the bad part and now they see the repair. My kids are in their twenties, and they'll be marrying soon. They will remember in hard times, "Well, my mom and dad worked it out; I need to work hard, too." I hope my kids never have to go through what I went through, but they got to see even in the worst of situations, a marriage can still be forever. Yeah, my journey in marriage is a journey most people in their right mind would have quit long ago.

When I talk to psychologists and divorce lawyers, I ask them what the breaking points are that make it impossible to stay married. The majority of them agree that a long relationship requires these three elements: trust, respect, and intimacy, emotional and physical. These fundamental traits that form the spine of a robust marriage were all missing for Beth, yet she pulled off a miracle. If she were my good friend and told me about her husband while Ed was at his worst, I would have told her to leave the big bully, and might have even staged an intervention. However, I got the story at the happy ending.

No wife should have to put up with what Beth endured. If hers is your story, get help. This marriage transformation is a rare exception to what researchers studying long-term marital satisfaction have found: Early marital happiness is one of the best predictors of later marital satisfaction. Beth started off miserable and didn't make her way out of the black hole until she was nearing menopause. She's a tough woman, and a lucky woman that Ed saw the light before his rancor turned physical.

This next story, of a forty-year-old woman in an arranged marriage, has two of the essentials, trust and respect, but the missing piece is physical intimacy. Her Bengali Indian immigrant parents raised their family in Queens, where Falisha now lives with her husband and their three young children. She herself considers the success of her marriage to be "unbelievable."

Falisha means "happiness," fitting for this forty-year-old wife who entered what she calls a "miracle marriage" with Muhammad, arranged by her father seventeen years ago. She felt "not one ounce of doubt" on her wedding day at an Indian restaurant in Manhattan owned by a family friend as she walked toward her groom in a red veil and a red sari embossed with gold beads.

Falisha is large of frame yet only five feet two, with delicate features and lustrous black hair, dressed today in a navy blue suit, her professional uniform as a CPA. Listening to Falisha speak about her traditional arranged marriage, it is clear that her relationship has little to do with miracles and everything to do with grit and surrender. Surrendering in marriage means humbly yielding to a power larger than your selfish desires. In Falisha's case, it means dwelling on what is positive in her marriage and not obsessing about what is lacking.

FALISHA

My college friends thought I was totally insane to marry a stranger. They thought I was making the biggest mistake of my life. Now when I look at those closest friends, they are in what we call "love marriages" with men they picked. And none of them are in love, really. They are having big problems with their husbands. After seventeen years, I am still in love with the man my father found for me. My life is not bliss all the time, but compared to many of my friends, it's like a fairy tale.

When I was twenty-two years old, my father decided it was time to start the arranged marriage process for me. I was living with my family in Queens, and my uncle came to visit us. My father was telling my uncle that I was about to finish college and asked him if he knew anyone suitable for me. My uncle said, "I have a friend; he's a doctor, and he's trying to finish his medical examination and he would be a good candidate for your daughter." My father said, "Give me his personal information and we'll think about it."

In our tradition, all the bio-data on the potential match is usually presented in writing: his background; the background on parents, grandparents, uncles, aunts; what professions they are all in; what degrees they have; where they live.

After my father reviewed the information, he invited my prospective match to lunch. My father did not tell me he had made this invitation. But one day he says, "Do you think it's the right time to meet someone?" First I said, "No. I'm not ready now. I want to finish college and I want to look for a job." My father said, "Well, then at least let me start looking. I have found someone I would like you to meet." I agreed that sounded fair.

My uncle's friend came over to our home; I wasn't at home that day. My father spoke to him and he liked his personality and his background. Both his parents had passed away and he came from a good family. My father found him to be a nice young fellow; he spoke well, and he was well educated. My father described him to me as decent looking, about five feet seven, medium-dark skin, with a head full of hair, and, according to my father, "he seems like a good match for you." Then my father said, "We have a little problem. You need to meet him immediately. He is thirty years old and he is ready to get married right away."

We are trained in our culture to listen to our elders, so I wasn't going to fight him. I am very passive when it comes to following their wishes. So of course I said, "I'll meet him." Silently I was very upset that day as we waited for him to come to our home for lunch, thinking, "How could my parents want to fix me up with someone so old?" I was only twenty-two, and thirty seemed like an old man. But I had to respect my parents' wishes.

I was wearing my traditional clothing of Bangladesh, and he was in a business suit. At lunch I didn't speak to him at all, but I did get to see him. The arranged marriage process is that you usually meet more than one prospect and the women do not sit at the same table. All the men are at one table, which was my dad, my uncle, and my soon-to-be-husband. My mother was serving and clearing the food, and I was helping. That's how it is; the women wait on the men.

I am hearing them talking about politics, and about their families. As I'm serving, I'm looking at the visitor, the way his hands move, the expressions on his face, and I'm listening to the way he talks. Keep in mind how impossible it seems for a young girl to just look at a person for a day or a month and think, "This should be my husband." But in my country, they have been doing this arranged marriage process from generation to generation, and there are very few divorces.

To be honest, I didn't feel anything when I saw the man I would soon marry. It's kind of strange. When I spoke to my aunts, they felt something like this is going to be my husband. I was numb. The only interaction I had with him was when he came into the house, and my father introduced me: "This is our daughter." Then we bowed to each other in our tradition, and we spoke only for a minute or so, very casually, like, "What do you study? When do you finish school?"—that kind of thing.

That evening my dad said, "What do you think?" I said that he seems like a nice person. My dad asked, "Do you want another sitting? We can give him your phone number," and I agreed that would be fine.

From the beginning, my husband later told me he was attracted to me. Once my father gave him permission to talk to me, he started calling all the time. He was very aggressive in pursuing me. I wouldn't say I was falling in love. I was flattered. I liked the idea of getting all this attention. I liked the idea that I could talk to a man and my father wasn't getting upset. Because in my culture an unmarried woman is not even allowed to have close male friendships; you can work with men, of course. Outside of work and school you can't socialize with men. You cannot be personal. You cannot go on dates.

We are taught that no matter what, the rule is that when you are not married you do not have personal relationships with other men. If you do happen to have romantic feelings for a man, you have to keep it *halal,* which means keep it kosher, no physical contact. Enjoy a movie. Enjoy a nice conversation. But always think in the end of the husband you will someday have, and you may have no premarital sex. I have Bengali friends who have broken these rules; I am someone who cannot disobey my parents or the rules of my tradition.

I agreed to go to lunch with Muhammad about a month after he first came to our home. We had been speaking by telephone twice a day, and each time we spent about an hour on the phone. I was feeling comfortable about meeting him. It was a short lunch, forty-five minutes, and I left feeling it was nice to have all this attention. I cannot tell you how this happened, but we got married two weeks after that lunch. On my wedding day, I already felt like I did fall in love with him. This is not something I can explain to you. After a two-week courtship I felt like this was a person I had known my whole life.

All the attention Muhammad had shown me, all the phone calls, his manners with my family, his respect for our Bengali tradition—I felt like I was so special and said "yes" instantly when he gave me his proposal for marriage. I felt like he would be a good husband. This sounds unbelievable, I know, but in such a short time I had already fallen in love. My father was surprised because this was only my first candidate, and he said, "Falisha, you do not have to go through with this, there can be other meetings with other men." My brother is going through this arranged marriage process now, and he has already spoken to five girls and he has not been attracted to any of them.

When my husband and I talk about it now, he says for him it was love at first sight. I say for me it was love at two weeks. Both of us just laugh: We don't understand how it went so quickly. Love is like this; something just clicks.

In India, a lot of people have big weddings, and the bride gets much elaborate clothing and gold jewelry as a dowry. I'm a simple person: I wore only two gold bangles and a necklace, and nice long earrings with my red wedding sari. We got married at a small Indian restaurant in New York City owned by my father's friend with about eighty guests.

Even after seventeen years I think my husband is a perfect match for me. I don't have any doubts. When I first met him I didn't feel anything, but after I got to know him I fell in love. As a traditional Bengali woman, maybe the love was even deeper because I knew I was making my parents so happy. You do not really know someone, even if you date five years, until you live with them; that's when the true person comes out. I love the true person.

People always ask me, "How could you marry a stranger?" I didn't marry a stranger; after two weeks of courting he felt like family. It was the way we connected because of our shared traditional values, the way he listened, the way he came into my house with proper manners and intelligent conversation. The day he proposed I had no hesitation.

I have many Bengali friends and relatives in the States and in India who are crying on their wedding days because they do not feel this sure about their arranged marriages, and they have no idea what they are getting into. The day I got married was the happiest day of my life.

Maybe I am abnormal but my husband and I don't get into big fights. We trust each other because we know we both are loyal to the rules of our culture: Drinking and drugs are prohibited. He doesn't cheat. We know what to expect of each other, and what not to expect. Oh, maybe once a month we'll get into a little argument about our son, who is fifteen, or our daughter, who is ten.

I am a traditional Bengali, but like most modern American women I have a profession. I have something beyond my marriage that keeps me going. I'm in an arranged marriage, but there is nothing arranged when it comes to what I want to do with my extra time. My husband is 100-percent supportive that I'm making extra money as an accountant. He doesn't ask how I spend my income. My credit card bills are my bills to pay. From day one, he has given me my space. I have girlfriends who are always complaining that their husbands are trying to control how they spend their money, how they spend their time, and don't want them working.

In a good marriage you cannot be possessive; when you try to control something you cannot control it for long. Some days I iron his shirts; when I'm busy with the children and trying to get to work, he irons my shirts. Yes, my husband irons! Although I do act passively at times in my marriage, it has served me well; I get what I want because instead of yelling when I don't agree with him, I listen quietly and try to see his side, then I gently persuade him to change his mind.

My younger sister says, "How do you tolerate all this? The man should not be the king of your life!" I tell her you never get everything in life, and I have more than most people have. Don't think I didn't have a choice in this marriage. He was not forced on me. My father picked him to be introduced to me, but he was my choice and I choose this life we have. Why would I want another life?

My husband has a good income. I am making money. We have beautiful children. What else can I ask for? I am lucky that I didn't have to waste a lot of years looking for a husband. He came to me right away.

Look, my husband has annoying habits like every husband; the worst thing is something most wives would probably consider a good thing. I'm at least thirty pounds overweight right now, but he doesn't say, "Falisha, you are too big. You need to lose weight." He doesn't believe in using negative words. I want him to throw me an insult once in a while that would shake me up. Most husbands would say, "Honey, you are getting fat!" Meanwhile he goes to the gym. He is thin and in good shape. I am busy with my work, and a CPA sits all day; I can't take time off for the gym. When I complain to him about my weight, he says calmly, "Don't worry. No one is perfect." Every tax season I gain ten pounds, and he still doesn't say anything.

So I'm not going to lie to you and say I'm floating on cloud nine all the time. It's not perfect. What I'm saying is that what I have here today is good enough for me. Our marriage is balanced. We are like a fine-tuned machine; he knows what to do in this relationship and I know what to do and we can rely on each other to do it. We are raising children together. We don't have time to

fight. Many people get divorced because they are looking for the impossible dream. Marriage is not a dream. I
don't have unreal expectations.

There are things I wish were better, and I am working on making them better.

I remember when we first got married we lived in
a little studio apartment, and even if we were in an
arranged marriage, our sex life was very nice. It was like
we were two people who were one. I conceived our first
child after only five months. For the past few years, my
husband doesn't make any effort to be sexually active.
He's forty-seven now; maybe it's his age? He tried
Viagra, but it made him feel sick and I don't want him to
take it anymore. I accept this is a period of marriage we
are going through. I would like for us to talk to a psychologist about this but he thinks it's too personal. He
does talk to me about it, and he is trying to be more
sexual. He is very cuddling with me. Who knows,
maybe if I lose weight this will change.

My husband tells me, "You are not going to get
everything in life, Falisha," and even if I miss sex, it is
something I can live without. The most important thing
for me in marriage is friendship. Though I do hope our
sex life changes; sex is important to me. I will work with
my husband on this issue, with patience. But if sex doesn't
return to our marriage I will not tear my hair out. I still
consider my marriage to be a success. My story is good
overall. I don't expect the whole world to be mine. As
many Indian women become more Westernized and
ambitious, they do expect the whole world to be theirs.
I am hearing more stories of arranged marriages that
didn't turn out so well. This is making me reevaluate the
arranged marriage process for the next generation.

Even if their mother is satisfied with her life, I don't
want it on my conscience that we arranged a marriage

for our children and it didn't work out. Our culture can be so strict and can be very tough on young people.

I want to give my children the best of the American life. I cannot imagine arranging their marriages. I want them to find their own spouses, and if they fail it's because of their own choices and not mine. When they come of dating age, I will make sure though that they understand the values of our culture: Take it slow. Don't get physical too fast. Get to know the person very well first so you can understand what kind of future he or she can give you. I will tell them that it is wiser to choose someone of our culture so they will have more in common. I will tell them to be realistic and not to imagine that marriage is a fantasy ride.

There is no manual for a happy marriage, but there are a few things to follow that I believe improve your chances. I will tell my daughter to never depend on her husband for everything. As a woman you have to take responsibility for your own happiness. I am overweight, so I'm the one who has to start exercising more and eating less. My husband can't do that for me. You have to give yourself the power.

I will encourage my daughter to have a job and tell her that work gives a woman power. I like it that when I wanted a grandfather clock, and it happened to cost two thousand dollars, I went out and bought it with my own money. I didn't have to ask my husband's permission. I will tell her that sometimes you have to be passive and don't fight your husband's wishes; I'm passive and I get most of what I want.

God has been very good to me. I don't have it all, but I have a little bit of everything. I see a lot of people fighting with their spouses because they aren't getting enough material gifts or emotional strokes and I say, "Why do you expect so much from someone? Look to yourself." For me, it's the simple things that make me happy. Last night I said to my husband, "Let's go take a walk in Central Park." He said, "Okay, if that's what you want." So we put the kids in the car, dropped them off with my parents, who live twenty minutes from us, and we took a nice walk together in the park. This is love. This is enough for me. If you expect too much your heart gets broken.

Divorce rates in India, where 95 percent of marriages are still arranged, are among the lowest in the world: About eleven of every one thousand marriages fail. "It's because we learn to be patient from our elders, or maybe it's just in our genes," says Falisha. While divorces remain rare in the villages, breakups are on the rise in the urban areas, where the well-educated wives that Falisha describes live. The average life expectancy in India is also more than a decade lower than in the United States, so perhaps couples there figure out even more urgently what most American veterans of marriage also realize when times get tough: Life is short. Family is family. Let's keep the expansive quilt of our lives intact, an elaborate and hard-earned history woven through joy and pain and perseverance. No new lover could bring me this.

I love Falisha's comeback to wives who blame their unhappiness on their husbands: "Why do you expect so much from someone? Look to yourself."

Of all the marriage stories I assembled for this book, Pat and Phil Denniston's comes the closest to perfection. They have it all: trust, respect, intimacy, friendship, and humor—*and* they are partners in a multi-million-dollar business, based in Encinitas, California. Their company, Work Loss Data Institute, publishes evidence-based treatment guidelines for workers' compensation conditions and return-to-work guidelines for illness and injury. They earned a spot in the "Believe-It-or-Not" chapter because it is unimaginable to be with a spouse all day and all night and be as effervescent as they are.

I met them at a cocktail party for Stanford alumnae outside of San Diego, and was drawn to them immediately, their silhouettes shrouded in the rosy hue of sunset against the mountains, her small body curled into his tall body, locked in each other's gaze. I tell them my husband is in Maryland, and I'm in California on a writer's retreat working on this book that touts separate passions and individual pursuits as restorative for old marriages.

Pat looks at me solemnly and says, "We are rarely apart, 24/7."

The Dennistons have been working at adjacent desks since they met in the mid-1970s as colleagues at IBM in New York City. They are both in their early sixties and gorgeous. She has swooping Farrah Fawcett hair, great curves, and flawless skin; he is blond and trim and scholarly, augmented by wire-rim glasses.

Their constant overlap of schedules and experiences sounds oppressive—even impossible—to me. Yet for the Dennistons, married thirty-six years and parents of four children in their twenties, this is what marriage means: togetherness without distractions, one marriage, one life. Unlike the majority of the wives in this book, who credit their own passions as the savior of their marriages, Pat wants what Phil wants, and vice versa.

As Pat talks about some of her marriage-boosting rituals, such as primping for their evening cocktail hour, I am thinking of how I appear when Chuck arrives home after work, in sweatpants that bag at the butt, like a loaded diaper. Their 24/7 unit is an oddity in contemporary marriage, yet their central survival secret is really the backbone of all long marriages, and that is: Think about each other, more or at least as much, as you think about yourself. I've included the rare voice of a husband in this section because when one Denniston speaks, he or she enhances the other's thoughts.

PAT

The danger of developing separate lives is that you can end up going off in your separate directions, like the

Gores. That's the opposite of us; we share the same life at home, and we have the same life at work. Our whole marriage is about unity and commitment. An important factor that has made us so solid is that we surround ourselves with other committed couples. We don't have any close friends who are divorced.

PHIL

One of our rules is not to let your ego get in the way. We could never work together this long if it was always, "Oh that was my idea, not yours." Same in marriage; it has to be an "our idea" approach. When marriages become more about "me" and less about "us," that relationship is doomed. We are business partners and marriage partners, and in order to succeed in both enterprises, you can't try to take the credit all the time, which discredits the other person.

PAT

We really are best friends. So it's not like I even have an urge to call up a girlfriend to go out on the town. In the thirty-six years that we've been married, I have never met a girlfriend for a drink. I meet my sister-in-law occasionally for a cup of coffee, but I would never go out for a drink without Phil. I remember one time very early in our marriage; we were living in New York City and we had no children yet. I met a girlfriend and her sister for a movie and dinner. And that night was a disaster. When I came home, Phil and I were not on the same schedule, the same wavelength, the same anything. I really never did it again, and Phil is not someone who ever goes out drinking with the guys. Phil and I pretty much follow the same schedule every day, from the time we wake up to the time we go to bed.

My parents were about to celebrate their fiftieth anniversary when my Dad passed away. Phil's parents are going to be celebrating their sixty-fifth anniversary. This is the way we've grown up, this is what we know about marriage, this is how we operate—as one. We stick together through thick and thin.

PHIL

We are not ones to sit around and overanalyze our marriage like too many people seem to do in California, where the divorce rate is so high. I don't ask myself every day, "Am I happy in this relationship?" I am married. I have four children, one grandchild, and another on the way. We don't focus on individual happiness. We focus on getting through our responsibilities.

PAT

We do take a short break from each other right after work. Phil likes to surf when he can, and he goes to the health club three times a week. I rarely join him at the club. To tell you the truth, I don't want him to see me sweating. I like to keep a little bit of mystery in our marriage. I love it when Phil goes out surfing because I can see him out there from the window doing his own thing, and I'll be in the house doing my own thing. I may put on the Jane Fonda video, or just relax and read. Then I put on makeup and get myself together. I want to look nice when Phil comes home. Like every couple, we do need some of our own space. We just don't need to get it through other people.

We have cocktails every night; we call it our "festivities." We have cheese and crackers and we both drink scotch and sodas. Just the two of us. We call it festivities because when Phil walks in the door, it's time for festivity. I'm sure our relationship sounds very old-fashioned in this age when many husbands and wives take trips alone to opposite sides of the world. I am proud to be old-fashioned because these old rules in marriage work. I tell my daughters and other young women, "Don't forget why you got married in the first place. You married for love, and keeping love alive takes work. Before your husband comes home, remember to powder your nose, freshen your lipstick, brush your hair, perk yourself up." My mother, who was married nearly fifty years, gave me the same advice.

Believe me, this isn't only about trying to look attractive to your husband. When I look my best, I feel better all around. I'm very old-fashioned in other ways, too. I do all the grocery shopping and most of the cooking, except Phil does the barbecuing. Phil handles the bar. It's just the way I grew up. The men prepare the drinks. I would never pour my own drink.

PHIL

I know a lot of men go out with the guys to bars, and it's just not something I do. I just enjoy Pat's company more than going out with some guys and drinking and watching a football. During our festivities, we get great ideas together, business ideas and family ideas. I learn from Pat all the time, and she learns from me. There is nothing stale about our relationship even though it is old.

I remember our first date, back in 1972. We had a full day of meetings at IBM, and we were riding back to the office on the subway. And I said to her, "Have you had dinner yet?" And Pat said, "I've been with you all day. When would I have had dinner?" We went to an Irish pub and that was that. Our first date is emblematic of the rest of our marriage: We are together all day then we are together all night. This is the third business we have built together, and we really do quite well together as a professional team.

A lot of business partnerships between spouses don't work out because one of you is trying to take most of the credit for a success, or blame the other for a failure. Same goes for marriages that don't work out. You just can't think that way. Marriage is a team effort. Your reward is not stroking your own ego; your reward is building a successful company and a successful family. I'm sure there are plenty of times that Pat thinks my ideas are wrong. She doesn't engage in a power struggle; we talk things out together.

PAT

But in many ways it's still a man's world in business, and I have to navigate that. We find that some of our clients may value Phil's opinion over mine. This was most apparent when our first company was acquired by a good-old-boy network of bosses. They wanted us both to stay on board in a management capacity, but they set it up so that we were supposed to jump through the same hoops in a competitive capacity. If our marriage was ever going to fall apart, that was the time. It was no longer our business, so we didn't feel united; we were each being well paid to essentially beat out the other guy.

Really what the new company was trying to do was to squeeze me out. They figured that if I quit because of an intolerable work situation, they wouldn't have to pay a second salary. It made me so angry that they didn't value my professional contribution. This was the crisis point in our marriage. The kids will never forget this. One night when Phil came home—this was like twenty-five years ago—I was so mad I threw a kitchen stool and screamed, "I'm a person, too." The stool didn't hit anyone, but the kids scattered in different directions and went into hiding.

PHIL

We laugh about it now, but we both learned a good lesson from that experience: We will never again go crashing into each other as opponents just to please some corporate giant. Why in the world would we let any outside force compromise us or destroy us? We also learned that we never want to work for anybody else again. We need to be our own bosses. We need to value each other as much or more than we value ourselves, and this takes patience.

PAT

My younger brother Joey has taught us so much about patience, and about love. He has Down syndrome, and he lives nearby with my mother. Joey is so full of pure love. He can't do a lot of other things that people can do, but this man has a way of communicating that makes you understand the true meaning of love. It's about appreciating the best in each human being. He shows us every day by example that you can have everything in this world—money, travel, new clothes—but none of that is really what fills you up as a human being. Love is what fills you up, and you have to patiently nurture that love, every day.

I was raised Catholic and we always went to Mass on Sundays. My mother used to say to us at church that we were allowed to make three wishes to God. And always one of my wishes from the time I was a child was,

"Please God, make Joey normal, make him perfect."
Well, I wished this for years and of course there was
never a miracle that Joey was suddenly transformed. One
night I was praying to God for Joey—I must have been
in my early forties—and I got hit like a thunderbolt; it
was like this warmth suddenly surrounded me. I knew it
was coming from God. And I heard a voice in my head
that said, "Joey already is perfect; I've answered your
prayers by giving you him. Joey is the best example of
love you will ever find. I haven't let you down." I've
never forgotten that: Having Joey makes my love for
Phil stronger every day.

PHIL

Clearly there's a lot of love in our family, but I think our
longevity is about more than just love. Keeping your
commitment is huge. Everybody we've seen who has a
broken marriage, nobody ends up in a better state. The
kids are messed up. The husband and wife go their own
ways and don't end up happier because they are still stuck
with a very complicated family situation. So you work
through your ups and downs, you stay true to your
responsibilities. The divorce culture is really about losing
sight of the meaning of commitment. When things get
rough, people just pull out. If they aren't instantly happy
they look for happiness in someone else. When you focus
on making someone else happy, that's the real well of
happiness for both of you in a marriage.

PAT

But if your marriage is solely about trying to keep a
commitment, then the relationship becomes lifeless and
loveless and creates resentment. If, however, the focus is

on what the commitment has brought to you, as a person, and to one another, it is a joy! For example, I used to keep a mental list of all of the things I hadn't experienced until Phil and I became a couple. I led a sheltered life, so the list was extensive, from little things like snorkeling and riding a motorcycle and spending a night on the beach to bigger things like buying a co-op in New York City, being a guest on a talk show, and going to Europe. This list goes on and on. Maybe I would have done many of these things eventually without Phil or with someone else. But I didn't. The composite of the exact things in the order and time they were done, with the man they were done with, is who I am today, and who Phil is, as well. That's what makes our commitment an evolving adventure.

Pat walks me to the door and her brown eyes are glistening as she thanks me for helping her remember the blessing of her marriage. Phil is standing in the kitchen, waving and smiling. They are a great couple, no question, exemplary, inspiring—and a little threatening. How could any of us wives who mix our own dirty martinis and have splotches of olive juice on our raggy T-shirts when our husbands come home ever measure up to Pat, who doesn't let Phil see her sweaty because it isn't sexy? Thankfully, working together, playing together, and staying together is not the norm, so don't berate yourself for being a lousy wife. Besides, Pat did hurl a stool at her husband once! She's one of us!

I admire the Dennistons' incomparable bond, and their story shows how varied we are as women in our basic needs. My marriage and the majority of others I studied thrive because of our multiple tracks. We may not want to emulate their marriage, but Pat and Phil offer universal strategies that all of us who wish to stay married should hold on to, the first being that touch-ups with makeup really do help.

I notice that when I apply a little lipstick and swap out my droopy sweatpants for the tight jeans, my "I'm home, dear" hug from Chuck is harder, and his hand lingers a little longer on my butt. A more crucial takeaway from the Dennistons is one that has been the drumbeat of all my writing on relationships: Surrendering to marriage means victory, not defeat. Surrender means yielding to a commitment and a purpose larger than me, me, and me.

Obviously, no one wants to stay in a marriage in which yielding to a partner means your own growth is stunted. Long marriages happen when both partners are growing, as individuals and as a couple. In Tara Parker-Pope's article on the "me" marriage, which characterizes the roots of a "sustainable marriage," and which ran December 31, 2010, in *The New York Times*, she writes: "For centuries, marriage was viewed as an economic and social institution, and the emotional and intellectual needs of the spouses were secondary to the survival of the marriage itself. But in modern relationships, people are looking for a partnership, and they want partners who make their lives more interesting."

Trouble starts when you become more interesting than the person who sleeps next to you every night. Indeed, much of the wifely discontent that I heard stemmed from this disparity of what one woman called "lack of inspiration" in her husband. I told her something along the lines of what Falisha says: "Perhaps you are expecting too much; look for something new to do, or resurrect an old hobby."

While writing *Surrendering to Marriage* I remember feeling very derisive about the book *The Adventure of Being a Wife* because of its frivolous title and how its author, Ruth Peale, chose to use the cover byline "Mrs. Norman Vincent Peale." As a married journalist who never changed her name, I couldn't fathom how another writer could sign her personal expression with her husband's moniker. Today I thumb through this 1971 book again and read a paragraph, I surprisingly find to be sharp advice: "Look around you and decide how many of the best marriages you know are ones where a wife in a deep sense actually knows her husband better than he knows himself," writes Peale. "[She] knows what pleases him. Knows what upsets him. Knows what makes him laugh or makes him angry. Knows when he needs encouragement. Knows when he's too charged up about something and needs to be held back. Knows, in other words, exactly what makes him tick."

On this one, I surrender to Peale and her take on the adventure of being a wife. By nudging our husbands to open up so we can know them better we are helping them know themselves better. Girlfriends do this with each other all the time. And working tirelessly to pry open the clam is remarkably transforming in a marriage, as shown in Beth's believe-it-or-not miracle.

X

Lessons from the Golden Girls

"Young people look at us, married for seventy years,
and ask for advice. I tell them you must have love,
you must have respect, and you must have
a sense of self."

—THELMA POST

I AM TALKING TO *The Washington Post*'s education reporter, Valerie Strauss, a friend of thirty years, a wife of twenty years. We are clucking over the marital carnage in the nation's capital, where we both work, a transient town of power couples who can be entwined over breakfast at the Jefferson Hotel and stealth kissing with someone more powerful they meet at the Italian embassy that night. We congratulate each other that we've made it this long, and nearly in the same breath we share one of our central secrets.

"My husband is the love of my life, but my girlfriends are my soul mates that fill all the other parts of me, and keep me going," Valerie says.

"I love my husband, but I'd die without my girlfriends." I am her echo. Indeed, as much as I cherish Chuck and my best boyfriends, my female soul circle is a mirror and a guide, loving me even when I'm acting like a creep. As the lone woman in a house of five men, I would wither emotionally without these loyal women. It was crushing to hear Shelley's story of how a "best girl-friend" betrayed her by sleeping with her husband, that she was stung by a villain among us. All the rest of the long-married wives I interviewed agree that girlfriends affirm our sense of mission and identity in ways a husband can never do.

April Merenda is the president and cofounder of Gutsy Women Travel, a New York–based company that offers interna-tional tours for women traveling alone or with a pack of girl-friends. Many of her clients are ages midlife through their eighties, women who are reuniting with girlhood pals, mothers escaping with daughters. April, fifty-seven, pinpoints what drives gutsy women to gather in same-sex packs and get the hell out of town: "You spend your whole life as a woman in many roles; you are the caretaker who is giving to everyone else and worrying about everyone else," she begins. "There comes a point that your family circle no longer includes children and you wake up one day and it hits you, 'My project is now to work on me.'

"So you go to Sedona or the Amalfi Coast or Morocco with your sorority sisters or your mother or your girlfriends from eighth grade, and for that one week you are the center of the universe. The common denominator of all my women on these trips is that you get a chance to work on yourself, and to further develop that part of your personality that gets lost when you are pouring your energy into everyone around you.

"Women bring out the best in other women."

Indeed, brave matriarchs throughout the generations link us to our truth as women and to the depth of our potential. A long hug from a girlfriend can make a heavyweight problem feel like dust. By remaining attached to a faithful sisterhood, even those of us whose mothers have passed away will always feel mothered and fussed over.

One of my mom's closest friends, Eileen Cohn, lost her

husband, Sidney, after thirty years of marriage. At the age of eighty-three, Eileen has ice-blonde hair and long red nails and still teaches in an elementary school in Evanston, Illinois, a job she has held for forty-five years. Eileen credits engagement in work she loves and her "Grammar School Girls" with breathing life in her when she was widowed at the young age of fifty-three.

"I've had the same close circle of friends for seventy-five years," says Eileen. "We have lunch. We go to dinner. We go to plays. It's the women who are there for each other to fall back on in the end.

"We know everything about each other; they knew Sidney so well. These were my bridesmaids. And their memories of my husband bring him back to life. We're all still relatively healthy, and you should see us together—we still look excellent! We get our hair done and we dress with style. We all still drive. And when I'm not out with the girls? One of my secrets in living well this long is Dewars.

"I've had a scotch every night of my adult life."

My own friends of forty-plus years, Terry, Debbie, Simone, and Ellyn, live in Colorado, Florida, Illinois, and California. They are eternal soul sisters who knew my parents and my bad boyfriends, and watched me marry a good husband. Sadly they are not a car drive away like Eileen's old pals. Yet in our eighteen years in Annapolis I have conjured up a neighborhood gang of ageless women I can't wait to grow younger with—we drink red wine, not scotch.

Every other Wednesday night, after the family is fed and the dishwasher is whirring, I giddily prep for dinner at Les Folies, a French restaurant where my table of girlfriends, ages fifty-two to seventy, hold court in the center of the restaurant. Envisioning the giant fried oysters and my *bonjour* embrace from the owner, Alain, a hard-bodied Frenchman who races cars as a hobby, I swoop on mascara and loudly sing "You Make Me Feel Like a Natural Woman" (which Aretha Franklin made famous but Carole King wrote). With each stanza and each flick of the wand, I shed years and stress and transform into another animal: unbridled, un-mom, un-wife. I am struck that this generic female bonding ritual commonly called "girls' night out" is far more than a mere outing with the girls.

Our conversations are my lifeline. We anguish over empty nests and deceased parents and bad pap smears. We rejoice over movies like *It's Complicated*, in which an aging divorcée (Meryl Streep) sleeps with her bullish ex-husband (Alec Baldwin), who dumped her for a younger woman. Alec wants her back, and Meryl dumps him for a sensitive white-haired suitor (Steve Martin).

We like the woman to win.

In the absence of this steadfast circle, I could never have been married for twenty-three years. My sons and husband have minimal body fat and zero tolerance for gossip. My girlfriends have bellies and hips and neuroses and can talk, talk, talk. We feel like queens as we're fussed over by Eric the waiter, a cuddly, studly gay man. We bare it all and fall apart and put each other back together again. In each other's company, we always feel beautiful and brilliant and thin, no matter how many mounds of pommes frites we are shoving into our mouths.

In my journey across the country interviewing wives, I found so many astounding women that I wish could be part of our Wednesday club. While they live hundreds, even thousands, of miles from my own kitchen, they have become my kitchen cabinet of wisdom on marital survival, on sex after seventy, and on forging onward after widowhood.

These golden girls are filled with delectable secrets and shrewd advice. Through a balance of humor, humility, acuity, and persistence, the bodacious older babes portrayed in this chapter were able to steer their marriages on a long-distance ride. As I write these last pages, every cell in my body is saturated with marriage statistics and stories, and I can honestly say nothing would shock me. The most bizarre example of what a wife is putting up with comes from a Connecticut woman with a bisexual husband. He started having an affair with the male chaplain of the church they were going to for marriage counseling. Her husband, father of her four teenagers, is now in a program for sex addicts, since he has been a repeat philanderer with both men and women. This tortured wife refuses to divorce him because of her faith: "We take the vows to stay with our spouses through sickness and through death," she told me. "If your husband was in a car accident and ended up in a wheelchair, would you leave him? My husband is a sick man, and my promise to God is to stand by him."

Sagas like this reinforce my conclusion that so much about long love remains incomprehensible. There are, however, a couple of facts I know as clearly as I know my kids' birthdays. While researchers have proven that brain chemistry and pheromones affect romantic attraction, there is no science to the art of staying married. Couples stay together because they slug it out, move forward, the years pile on, and thirty-five and fifty and seventy years later they are still sitting side by side at the opera in the seats they've had since 1966.

The real secret to staying married is not to get divorced. How do you accomplish what can seem impossible? Golden girl wives have made it this far because they have created fulfilling lives outside of their marriages, and theirs is the best secret of all. This is corroborated by my sister Fran Krasnow, one of the leading family lawyers in Chicago, who specializes in divorce cases.

Married for twenty-seven years and the mother of four children, my slightly older sister has more to say on avoiding divorce.

FRAN

Women definitely need to be engaged in something they are excited about beyond their marriages and families. Sociologists and psychologists believe that money is one of the most important issues that people fight about in relationships. Perhaps it is, but that is not necessarily true for the cases that I see. I think fundamentally people can grow apart if they are not both developing as individuals.

When each spouse is leading a fulfilling life, chances are better that they will continue to grow as a married couple.

I'm a big proponent of work.

While, realistically, in this job market the opportunities are not always there, I believe that everyone needs an outlet from which they derive direct self-satisfaction. Not only the pride and happiness we feel as parents or as spouses, but satisfaction which comes solely from you— not from the accomplishments of someone else. This is not necessarily limited to paying jobs, but we all become more interesting when we're focused on something other than our personal daily routines.

The happiest marriages are ones where both partners are deriving their sense of self-worth from both their family as well as their outside "work"—whether it be as a museum docent or as a neurosurgeon.

Other classic rules on how to stay married forever threaded throughout this book are hammered home by the stories that follow, from Dena, Libby, Marilyn, and Thelma. Their hard-earned insights epitomize the central message of *The Secret Lives of Wives*: Wives who don't rely on their husbands for happiness end up having the happiest marriages.

After thirty-six years of living together and the birth of two children, now ages thirty and twenty-seven, Dena and Raymond decided to finally get married; their wedding took place in Las Vegas in 2008. Dena even took his last name, what she calls "a major step for a sixty-year-old staunch feminist." Her relationship with Raymond started with the slow burn of friends-only, instead of bonfire love that gets too hot too fast then peters out. An imposing African American woman in a black turtleneck sweater dress, with closely shorn hair and four-inch gold hoop earrings, Dena stands up from her desk at a Virginia university, where she works in Admissions, and shows me a photograph of Raymond and their two children. She says her marriage, her parents' long marriage, and her siblings' long marriages defy the stereotype that "black men can't commit." Here's more from Dena, inching toward her senior years, and a recent bride.

DENA

Raymond was always more about me than he was about himself. Hardly the absent black husband you read about as typical, and there are plenty more like Raymond you don't read about. This was a man who came over to my apartment and cooked dinner for me on one of our first dates. All this time together, he was never caught up in his own ego. He cared about me. We came together as friends, and I'd say that's still the basis of our relationship; it's not a hot love affair. It's a true friendship.

When I met Raymond, it felt like I had known him forever. Soon we moved in together, and it wasn't like we made a choice not to get married, it just never really happened. One of the biggest reasons we didn't get married, by the way, was financial. Raymond had a small building business and was having some money problems and I had a steady salary, so I figured, "Let him do his own taxes and I'll do my taxes." I had worked so hard for my job title and my own income I really didn't want to combine that part of our lives. You know, I'm a child of the sixties and the women's revolution, and I was proud to stand on my own financially. I didn't want anyone else messing me up.

Most people at my work and our neighbors just assumed we were married; they referred to Raymond as my husband. I felt married, too, although Raymond kept pushing me to make it official. I have three engagement rings. When I first got pregnant, he asked me to marry him, and I said yes. He bought me a ring. We just never got around to it somehow. Then on my fiftieth birthday he asked me to marry him; again, I said yes. Same thing: We moved on and forgot to plan a wedding. Then, at my father's funeral, here I am sixty years old, and my mother, who is very upset and in emotional turmoil over his death, blurts out, out of the blue, "Dena, when are you going to marry that man? It's just not right living together like you've been doing. That man wants to marry you and you are denying him." I said, "Mom, if it will make you happy, I will marry Raymond."

So my mother put my feet to the fire. No matter how old you are, sometimes you've just got to listen to your mother. So that's when I got my third and last wedding ring. We got married a few months ago in Las Vegas, with about fifteen family members there. We would have preferred for the ceremony to be quick and just the two of us, but our relatives started immediately making plane reservations. They were like, "Oh no, we're not missing this! We've been waiting too long."

So now I've got a new last name after sixty years. The hard part for me is to let go of some of the control of the family finances. Everything we owned was in my name; the family insurance, the mortgage. We even had my last name under our door knocker. After we got married, Raymond started checking about refinancing our home and everybody he was talking to was calling him by my last name with "mister" in front of it. He told me this had been happening for years and years, and he was tired of people thinking I was the boss and he was Mr. Dena.

He said, "Why do you insist on being the only person in this house with a different last name?" I said,

"Okay, I'll take your name." Just like I cowered to my mother, I cowered to him. You've got to do that once in a while if you want to stay together. And it feels good to be married and a missus; I can't complain. It feels more like we're one family, a real family. Before it was like, "Okay, I could actually walk away from him at any time." But now there's this permanent sort of bond, a legal bond, a bond with God.

My relationship with Raymond has flowed naturally and has been very consistent. I have a nice man who is not selfish at all. He comes home when he says he's coming home. This isn't what many white people would think of when they consider a typical black family. My mother and father had a long marriage. There are black men who are good and there are black men who aren't so good, just like there are good and bad white husbands. Making a marriage isn't about race; I think a lot of it is about the examples around you. My siblings and the people closest to me are all in committed relationships.

Our son and daughter are not married yet, but they both want to have a tight family like they've been raised in. I'd like my children to find black spouses because then they don't have to worry about any cultural differences. The world is changing, definitely, and there are more and more mixed-race couples. But you don't know what those families of those couples are saying behind their backs. People still have prejudices, even if they don't admit it. Sometimes they don't even know they are prejudiced until their son or daughter brings someone of a different color home.

I have always felt very comfortable with Raymond and with his family. It feels just right; it feels like he's my other half. We have our romantic times, but it's this comfort level that has made me want to stay with him.

We don't walk around lovey-dovey and hugging and kissing and holding hands. Our thing together has always been more of a feeling of best friendship.

I'm a big churchgoer, and I just have a lot of faith that what goes on in our lives is some of our doing but mostly it's in the hands of God. Without that faith, things would fall apart for me. I do a lot of praying—when there's money problems or little arguments, I ask God to "please help me." I talk to God like He is sitting right there with me. I thank God all the time for Raymond. When I was in my twenties, I was thin and just gorgeous. And I used to date a lot of men who were gorgeous, black and white. And too many of these gorgeous men were assholes.

Raymond is a gentleman who respects me for exactly who I am. We have even learned how to fight well together. In the beginning, we used to have ugly fights. We would say hurtful things to each other. He would throw things once in a while, never aimed at me, but he would just whip things across the room. One time he threw a brass vase and it bounced off the counter and shattered the glass in our kitchen window. I shouted at him, "You need to stop these tantrums. You could have killed our baby." That was the last time he threw anything; he was almost crying with his apology.

Lately, his work has been real steady and we're making about equal salaries now. I will always work, though. I know how important it is for a woman to earn her own money. I love my mother, but I don't want to get old like she has. My father was the boss and the breadwinner, and now my mother's problem is she feels helpless after he died. She had no idea how to pay the bills, or how to call repair people to get things fixed around the house. I can't repair a toilet, but I certainly know how to call a plumber.

> If I outlive Raymond, I'll miss him like crazy, but I'll be okay on my own. I know how to manage the house. I have a good income. I can't imagine I'll marry again. I've dated more bad men than good ones, and I will know I had the best, that there's no topping Raymond.

Many older wives echoed Dena's sentiment that they knew when they found a keeper because of all the scamps that came before them. They also share her feelings of self-fulfillment gained from the workplace and have settled into marriages that are more best friendships at this point than steamy. Others confess that their unions stayed very hot for a very long time. While Dena's marriage has been erected on friendship, Libby Zurkow says that great sex, at least once a week, was a primary component of her fifty-eight years with George, who died in December 2006. Libby does have this crucial trait in common with Dena: She had a profession throughout their marriage and didn't stop working after George's death. At the age of eighty-six, Libby is one of the top residential real estate brokers in her home state of Delaware.

A 1946 graduate of Wellesley College, she was tapped in the mid-1950s to do a weekly segment called "Wise Buying" on the NBC *Home* show, hosted by Arlene Francis and Hugh Downs and later combined into the *Today* show. This gig required commuting between her home in Wilmington and Manhattan three days a week. When the opportunity came to continue with the show, Libby and her dentist husband George had two young children. While he was a big supporter of her professional dreams, he didn't want their children to be raised with a commuting mother. So he put a stop to her national TV career even before it started.

Here is more from Libby, a siren of an octogenarian in black high heels and a black short skirt that shows off her toned legs. She drives herself in a steel gray 2010 Cadillac DTS and simply "ignores all my wrinkles" while she concentrates on closing real estate deals.

LIBBY

Perhaps the story would have turned out differently and I'd still be on TV, if it weren't for George. But after our oldest child, four at the time, curled up to him and said, "Now Mommy is gone so much, you have to be Mommy and Daddy for us," George came up to New York on the next train and he said: "I'm not going to see a perfectly good marriage go bad and the children grow up without a mommy around. I'm telling you right now. I'm going to divorce you and I'm going to marry Jeanie if you take this full-time New York job!" When I looked in his eyes I knew he was dead serious. Jeanie was an intelligent and attractive woman a few years younger than me who lived in town and who absolutely adored him.

It was really a hard decision for me. I was twenty-nine with two kids under the age of five at home, yet I still wanted to fulfill my professional dream. This was long before this era when most moms worked outside the home. But I deeply loved George; he was a great guy and a wonderful lover so I walked away from this once-in-a-lifetime opportunity. A third child was born soon after.

George and I never lost the magic of our physical attraction for each other. All George's friends used to say to him, "You are the guy whose wife really likes sex." To the end of his life at ninety-one, it was still magical, and this business that every woman over the age of seventy doesn't lubricate is nonsense: We never needed K-Y jelly. I guess people today would call us sex addicts because we made love so often and thought about it every day. Not only was he technically a great lover, but he was funny in bed! His humor spilled over to every part of his life. He was brilliant. He was very handsome. He was a scratch handicap golfer. He was a leader in the community, and a dedicated dentist.

I was twenty-four when we were married. He was thirty-four, and since he was older I always trusted his judgment. Some of George's good friends were what they called "having a little fun on the side." In fact, they often shared their secrets and frustrations about sex with me! George and I were totally monogamous; because our sex life was so magical we never wanted to do anything that might spoil it. My kids tell me now they knew what was going on. They say, "All our friends' parents took them on adventures on Sunday afternoon; you and Daddy closed the door at one P.M. on Sundays and didn't come out until four."

Once the children were in school all day, I went back to school to get a master's in consumer marketing and ended up heading a college program there in real estate development. I have been in real estate now for more than forty years, and I have always thought it is absolutely essential for a wife to have her own profession beyond the country club. A career helps women stay centered, and it makes us more interesting to our husbands. I would often bring home crazy stories about my experiences in the real estate world, and George would do the same about the medical community. Our dinner table conversation was quite riotous. I had become a very successful professional woman well before the official women's liberation movement, and to a lot of people I seemed like a freak. Since George was financially successful, people couldn't understand why I wanted to work. George understood, and I understood: A wife has emotional needs and intellectual needs that her husband and children can't meet.

My husband's friends would sometimes confide in me; I was like one of the guys. One of his best friends would tell me, "My marriage is dull. My wife had so many ambitions when I married her and she hasn't done anything with her life. She hasn't grown outside the home." I'm not telling you this so people will think I'm so much better; I'm sharing vital information about how to have a long marriage. A woman needs her own life! I always felt like my own person. I always had something new to bring to the relationship.

It certainly has helped me get along as a widow. I have just kept going; having my own work and my own life kept me strong during George's final illness. He had heart problems then he got prostate cancer. It wasn't the diseases that got him; his cancer treatment was an experimental radiation, which in the end killed him. It burned his entire lower bowel area. So the last few months of his life were difficult. In October 2005 our children gave us a 170th birthday party for 150 of our best friends. The number came because George turned ninety and I turned eighty.

We were both very comfortable talking about death. We knew George didn't want to die in a hospital. So, as his heart was giving out and he was so sick, George left the hospital and came home with me. The night he died we ate three dozen oysters; we both love oysters. We had a glorious last night together. He woke up in the morning and said, "I don't feel well," and he collapsed and died in my arms.

I was married for fifty-eight years to a wonderful lover and a wonderful man, and I was delighted to find I didn't fall apart when he died. I think it was because of the way we had conducted our marriage. At George's suggestion, we always lived our lives on a five-year plan;

we'd figure out where we wanted to be in the next five years and we would usually accomplish what we had set out to do. While he was so sick, George sat me down and he said, "Libby, what are you going to do after I die?" I said, "George, I really don't know." He said, "I want you to promise me two things: You will go back to full-time real estate and you will go back to golf because you are very good at both of them." As we got older I had switched to part-time at my office, and while George and I used to golf at least once a week, I had let that slide, too. Well, I did both, and while my real estate career has really taken off, my golf game stinks!

I have to be honest. Soon after George died, I hit the ground running in residential real estate. Most agents my age had long ago quit because they weren't good on computers. But back in 1982, when my younger daughter was going to graduate school, she was starting to learn about how to work on the new personal computers. I said to myself, "Hell, I'm going to learn, too." So we learned together, and now I know how to create spreadsheets and analyze properties as well as any of my younger colleagues. I even have my own interactive Web site that brings me a lot of my new business from around the world.

I'm Libby alone now, and although I am eighty-six, it feels like fifty-six. I don't have anything in common with older people who only talk about what they ate at their last meal or complain about their aches. My youthful spirit and my successful marriage came because, with George's support, I was always true to myself, and because, of course, we always had great sex!

I have introduced you to women decades younger than Libby who have no passion in their marriages and have turned to other men to fan their embers. Libby is testament to the fact that if you have passion early on, chances are good you can return to that crackle as you age. Many wives I interviewed start marriages as close friends without physical compatibility, hoping that lust may build with each passing anniversary.

When younger women at around the ten-year mark in marriage write me letters along the lines of, "I married my best friend and sex was never that great. Now, I'm not attracted to him at all. Will sex get better?" I tell them I'm not a therapist and sounds like they should see one. But I do offer my journalistic take on what wives and husbands have told me over thirty years: Sexual chemistry can be felt right from the start, and if you don't have it, it's tough to invent. I also tell those who solicit my advice that good sex can go a long way in marriage; when trouble arises, which it always does, an afternoon romp can cure most anything.

Libby's bawdy testimonials about the joys of senior sex leave me very curious about how other older women feel about their own sexuality. Are they doing it? What lies ahead for me?

Data from the University of Chicago's National Social Life, Health and Aging Project published in the *New England Journal of Medicine* (August 23, 2007) showed that many men and women remain sexually active well into their seventies and eighties, participating in vaginal intercourse, oral sex, and masturbation. Heralded as the first comprehensive national survey of senior sex in the United States, conclusions were based on intensive face-to-face interviews with 3,005 adults ages fifty-seven to eighty-five between July 2005 and March 2006. More than half of the respondents reported having sex at least two to three times per month; 23 percent reported having sex once a week or more. About half of the men and women interviewed under age seventy-five engaged in oral sex in the previous twelve months.

The study found that older women were less likely to be sexually active because they often outlive their partners, and the most common reason for sexual inactivity among both men and women was the male partner's physical health problems. With the rise of older women now hitching with younger men, the percentage today of older women with bustling sex lives will likely be higher.

Eager for specific stories beyond the statistics, I take my questions again to sex and relationship therapist Marilyn Charwat, who, from her base in the Boca Raton–Palm Beach area, is surrounded by spry, sexy senior wives, of which she is one. A willowy woman of an indeterminate age with black Cher hair, Marilyn teaches sex workshops for seniors at the local community center. She sells state-of-the-art sex toys at these seminars, which have titles such as "What Your Mother Never Told You about Sex."

Here's Marilyn's take on the subject based on four decades in practice with clients who are mostly women, ages forty through ninety. Some of her perceptions stem from her own marriage of thirty years to a man she calls "not my first husband, but definitely the best relationship of my life." Marilyn floors me when she says she just turned seventy-seven years old; she is edgier and more progressive than most thirty-year-olds I know.

MARILYN

This concept of an "old lady" is really a stereotype that doesn't exist anymore. Women my age and older are staying fit and are sexually alive! One patient I'm seeing right now is married to a lovely guy of seventy-eight who gives her a very nice life financially. He is okay in the sack, not great, and she is at the moment having an affair with a young bartender who has worked her parties and is great in the sack. She loves sex; her husband loves her but doesn't love sex. How does she try to make her husband more sexual? How can she leave a great sex partner? She is trying to reconcile those feelings in therapy.

Another woman in one of my classes is seventy-nine; she looks amazing and recently discovered vibrators. This has helped her immensely to rediscover the joys of sex and its energizing benefits. Sex in our later years can be amazing; I have so many women in my practice who are my age and who have been reawakened to sex late in the game. Their problem often is that their men can't perform like they used to, so they become open to experimenting with vibrators and attending tantric sex workshops with their partners. This, along with Viagra, in many cases can really pick up an old marriage.

I tell women the golden years should be our best years. I go to the gym every day and do the elliptical machine and lift weights. I know every vibrator and sex toy on the market, and I teach other women how to take advantage of them. Women need to keep having orgasms; it's good exercise: like the Kegel, it lifts and tightens the floor of the pelvis and it can help you from depending on Depends.

All women should use these tools; women should have an orgasm once a day. Just like you wake up and brush your teeth and eat your breakfast and exercise, use your vibrator and have an orgasm. It takes thirty seconds. The more orgasms you have the easier it is to have them, and it keeps your sexual parts more youthful. Vibrators also release you from any kind of tyranny in relationships. There is nothing like a hard penis in sex, but 65 percent of all women do not have orgasms during intercourse. Unless the husband knows the clitoris is king, having an orgasm can be very tricky, and vibrators become a wonderful supplement. A favorite among the women is the tiny Silver Bullet vibrator: It fits in your purse and can go anywhere! Just don't use it while you're driving.

The beauty of a vibrator is that you're in charge and orgasms give you whole-body relaxation. A vibrator also allows you to have a secret life, which everybody should have.

For many older women, the marriage has gone on for so many years without sex and sex just isn't important. They have developed other areas of their lives that satisfy them: girlfriend groups, travel, new hobbies. They don't miss sex anymore. So you may have an eighty-year-old woman who is walking around sexually neutral, and when her eighty-year-old husband suddenly wakes up sexually with Viagra, this can pose a clashing of desires. But I can tell you I see many men who are still quite potent even in their eighties, without a boost from drugs.

What would surprise people is that women in their eighties and even nineties are just like the forty-year-olds as far as their interest in self-discovery and in deep intimate relationships. They are just young people in old bodies. Older women may look a little shriveled, but they are vital human beings. Old bodies can slow you down, but your ideas keep you going. Figuring out how to embrace aging and not lament the loss of youth is a big reason older women land on my couch. I am seeing a woman right now who just lost her husband to a thirty-five-year-old woman, and this is particularly disturbing since she never thought they had a problem. I stress with my clients to stay very attentive to each other in their relationships. We are all vulnerable to letting communication fallout lead to a broken marriage.

Sex at the age of seventy-seven is very good, but it's very different than it is at fifty. In younger years, most women report their orgasms come quicker. At seventy-seven it takes more work; you may have to imagine a more vibrant fantasy, and perhaps warm up with a vibrator. In our seventies and older, the orgasm can be just as intense, though, and even run longer and deeper. Fantasies are necessary—I hear that all the time; it's really the secret of great sex at any age.

Over the course of forty years, I've dealt with every issue and problem that could arise in a marriage, from falling in love with lovers to falling out of love with spouses. Particularly in recent years, I've counseled women who are leaving husbands for other women. I am not here to pass moral judgment; my job is to help people move through the stages of their lives. It's foolish for us to judge other people's sex lives.

And don't believe what you read about little old ladies. At one of my recent sex workshops for seniors the most vibrators we sold were to women between seventy and ninety-four. The oldest customer told me she had never used one and it was "high time to liberate myself!"

I love Marilyn's candor and nonchalance, and the rejuvenating alternatives she offers women as they age. Feeling sexually alive does squash nagging feelings about the gullies forming in our necks, and the lip lines that are filling with lipstick more often, like we noticed as kids on the faces of our grandmothers.

That said, the Silver Bullet may be a vehicle toward multiorgasmic pleasures, but there is no silver bullet that can lead to a long-haul marriage. Feeling liberated, however, certainly helps.

The liberation comes in fleeting bursts with a vibrator; it can last for seventy years, like the next story, when liberation comes from what we all ultimately seek in our marriages beyond sex: friendship, trust, and respect. Thelma Post just celebrated her ninetieth birthday and has been married for seventy years—this in Hollywood, where the term "disposable marriage" was birthed. Thelma's husband, Ted Post, directed many episodes of old TV series including *Gunsmoke*, *The Twilight Zone*, and *Peyton Place*. He is also the director of *Beneath the Planet of the Apes* and *Go Tell the*

Spartans with Burt Lancaster, as well as two Clint Eastwood movies.

Dressed in all black from Chicos, her naturally brown hair spliced with silver, Thelma is seated on an apricot floral couch in their Los Angeles condominium. She first saw her husband when she was two and he was four at her father's Brooklyn grocery store. Ted remembers his first glance at his future bride; Thelma does not. "She had the most beautiful blue eyes, just brilliant," said Ted.

Thelma with the sparkling blue eyes recounts a remarkable love story that started when she was fifteen.

THELMA

We lived in Brooklyn, and this was the height of the Depression, and every Easter young kids would go into the East Side of New York City and apply for summer jobs at the resorts in the Catskills to work as waitresses, busboys, musicians. We called it the Borscht Belt, and it had these grand hotels like Grossinger's and cheaper little places where families set up camp in one or two rooms with their young kids, and the husbands came and went on the weekends. I applied for a waitress job at a hotel and the guy said, "Okay, you're hired. You'll come out in the middle of June." It was a little place in the mountains, and I had never been out to the country.

When the owner met me, he took one look at me and said, "Why did you hire her? She's too young; she looks too fragile to be a waitress. Stick her in the children's dining room." The other waitresses were older and bigger, and I thought, "Oh my God; what have I gotten myself into?"

This was seventy-five years ago, but I remember going to sit by myself in the lounge, and suddenly in comes a young man in white ducks and a white shirt with lightning black hair. He was very handsome. I thought, "Hmm, things are picking up around here." He was one of the busboys, and we chatted for a moment. We exchanged names, and he said, "I know you. I know your parents. Your father has a grocery store. I live two blocks from the store and your father delivers eggs to my mother and we go to your store all the time."

Teddy was only seventeen, but he seemed so manly and mature. I thought to myself, "My God, what a fabulous stroke of luck." I felt a beginning of a romance already, even before the guests had arrived. Soon he left his job where I was working and got a better job at a fancier hotel nearby as a teaboy, which was someone who served high tea in the afternoon to the ladies. We were together most nights. I don't mean overnight, of course! But it's as if from the first moment we met we were already boyfriend and girlfriend. He taught me how to dance. I was very much in love right from the beginning.

We just had a lot in common. He was Jewish and intelligent and we both could keep up with each other. Neither of us ever had bourgeois values. I never believed in makeup and still don't. Even with my husband working in Hollywood all these years, I never did go through a period of caring about cosmetic and couture fashions. Teddy doesn't care about it either; he doesn't want it for me. Who wants to kiss a face with grease all over it? I do use lipstick, but I never dyed my hair or anything. I always felt comfortable with myself just as I am.

After that summer I saw him during the year when I went to Brooklyn College. Teddy was starting to find his way into the field of drama. He tried a little acting but soon saw that wasn't for him and became interested in directing. I was absolutely thrilled about this man who was so attractive and who was someone who had a vision of what he wanted to do in his life. Just before I was twenty-one years old we got married. We were going around and around with it, then one day Teddy said with a smile: "I'll die if you don't marry me." We had a very modest little wedding, then moved into my parents' house, where I grew up, into a room that had a private entrance. Both my children were born in that house.

We struggled in those years before Teddy achieved some success, but those early years were wonderful. Even though we were newlyweds living with my parents, I always felt my life was good. I was in love with my husband, and that was enough. I loved the fact that my husband had a dream, and to be married to someone driven and enthusiastic who had put his wife into that dream, it was just fantastic. I loved that he wanted me to take this journey with him.

And here we are seventy years later. I've been in this living room when Burt Lancaster was sitting across from me. We have been part of the exciting scene of Hollywood, but we always tried to march to our own tune. I mean, celebrity to me does not mean Marilyn Monroe; celebrity to me means Albert Einstein. That's how I grew up, and that's how I raised my two children. When we moved from the East Coast we deliberately chose Beverly Hills, because it had the best school system. I wanted my son and daughter to have our values, not what I called "maid values." I never had a live-in maid; I just didn't believe in it. Who wants someone other than family in your house all the time? I certainly didn't grow up with it.

I had the most wonderful mother, so intelligent, and my father, he had a fantastic sense of humor. They both came from Russia. My dad had this grocery store and my mother would help him out. She was a teacher in Russia, and she and my father were childhood sweethearts. He came to America first, then he sent for her. They stayed married until she died, then my father lived with us for many years. I had a good example of what a marriage should be.

As soon as we got to California, Teddy worked diligently and he worked constantly. I brought up the children; that was my part of the deal. I made it a point though to never stop expanding my own horizons; I was president of the women's group at the University of Judaism in Los Angeles, and to this day I take classes in literature. I could have done anything I wanted; Teddy never held me back. But my choice was that I wanted to raise my children; that was a wonderful, important investment for me.

Anything I've done in my marriage, Teddy was always there to help me, to do, to go, to be. Our marriage was never about submission for me; as a woman and as a wife you want to keep your own identity. That's another secret to why we lasted so long; Teddy really has been the wind behind my wings.

I'm not saying the journey through life is smooth. I've had a lot of illnesses, including two kinds of cancers, breast and colon. This will tell you something important about the man I am married to. When I had my breast cancer, we were having this big debate, should I just take out the tumor, should I take off the breast. Teddy said, "You know, Thelma, it's the enemy. Let's get rid of it!" And I thought, "Good. I'll lose a few pounds just like that." I mean, when you get that kind of support from your husband in critical situations, what's more endearing than that? Growing up the way we did, we both know what to value and what not to value; what's important and what's not important.

He's always been a good partner because his life, even though he has gotten very famous, has never been about him, it's about me and our family. Teddy doesn't go out to bars and drink. He's not a poker player. His family is everything to him. When our children turned sixteen, we didn't go out and buy them cars like their friends got. We spent our money on the *Encyclopedia Britannica*. We both knew that we wanted to teach our children that hard work and education mattered more than anything.

We always kept a low profile. Teddy is an excellent director, but we weren't high fliers. I sure have met a lot of interesting people, though. After my mother died and my father moved in with us, we kept a kosher home. Chuck Connors was at our house one night at a party, and he drank a little too much and was getting tipsy. So Chuck goes into the kitchen and puts his head under the faucet to run some cold water, and my father sees him and says, "What are you doing? You can't do that here; this is a kosher home."

Now that we've gotten older we don't go out that much. Teddy and I can stay in our condominium alone for days at a time, just sitting and doing our thing, and we don't get in each other's way. We come together and eat, we come together and laugh, we come together when we're sad. You know, we just live, and this is the way it has been since I was fifteen. Young people look at us, married for seventy years, and ask me for advice. I tell them you must have love, you must have respect, and you must have a sense of self. Even if you are giving in to the other person, you never can lose yourself.

I know how lucky we are to have each other this long. It's been ten years since my colon cancer, and who knows what will come next? I am happy to have my husband, and I have made some wonderful friends over the years. We talk about our children and our grandchildren. We wonder what kind of world they are inheriting. I worry about that a lot. It's almost a physical pain. You know when you are old and most of your friends have died, you do think about the world you will leave behind.

I tell my son and my daughter that when someone you love dies, at the moment it is unbearable, but in the long run, knowing she or he has had a good life, you can manage that loss. If you have not had a good life with your spouse, you will never be at this place of peace that I am at now.

As I leave the Posts, I am thinking of the wives and husbands I know who have been together for decades, and how when one dies the other falls quickly. Then there are widows like my Aunt Gloria, my father's sister, who embarked on a second act at the age of seventy-nine. A year after Uncle Herbie, her husband of fifty-seven years, died, she was fixed up with the charming Borden Mace, an eighty-one-year-old widower who wears snappy sports jackets with silk handkerchiefs in the pockets. To be around them is to feel romantic love as well as best friendship. They hold hands and snuggle, even today, in their ninth year of going steady. Aunt Gloria is now eighty-eight, and she still exudes a girlish glimmer, enhanced by her ninety-year-old live-in boyfriend, Borden.

"It is divine to have started a second life in my eighties," says Aunt Gloria. "Borden is unflappable. He has integrity. He has character. I've had two great men in my life."

Aunt Gloria also worked throughout her marriage, well into her seventies, another crucial age-defying force. She ran a flourishing interior design business from her home for forty years, which she considered "the perfect solution to the work-parenting dilemma," holding office hours from nine A.M. to three P.M. while her two daughters were in school.

When I was a young girl, Aunt Gloria was my idol. She and

Uncle Herbie and my cousins would often visit us in Chicago from their home in Washington, and I would just stare at her, sitting at her feet like a dog. She was almost a full head taller than my rotund uncle, and she had the lanky frame and carriage of Audrey Hepburn. She was quick-witted, and always a hip dresser, lately in spare designs by Eileen Fisher.

And now she has the courtly Borden who sent her flowers every week to woo her. "I found true love in my eighties, and I had a long and good marriage before this," said Aunt Gloria. "Herbie and Borden let me be me. You should be so lucky."

When I am in a period of marital malaise, which generally happens when I want Chuck to talk to me and he's catatonic in his La-Z-Boy watching hockey (a seven-month sport), and the man next door isn't home, I think of Aunt Gloria's words. Chuck has never stood in the way of me being me; in fact, he makes me mightier, this while taking care of our family. He let me go back to summer camp at the age of forty-five without him. He cuts our hedges with a chain saw. He loves me. We are in this for the long, hellish, wondrous haul.

Sometimes I feel like we are war heroes, soldiers who are bruised and disillusioned, yet we persevere, because we said we would on our wedding day and because we know nothing is perfect. My friends who left long marriages to start over with new men certainly do not have perfect lives either. Their second husbands are no longer hubba-hubba heartthrobs; they detach into TV screens and burp after meals and pass gas just like their first husbands did.

Yes, I'll keep this flawed marriage of mine. Seeing Chuck in his recliner is as soothing as it is irritating. At least I always know where to find him, which is more than a lot of wives can say about their husbands.

Why get divorced? If I leave Chuck, what would I have to complain about with my girlfriends? It's Wednesday night, and time for girls' night out at Les Folies. Eric the hunky waiter will preen over us, and we will down a couple bottles of wine. I am on the phone calling my neighbor Gail to tell her what time I will pick her up, and through the kitchen window I see that my husband is walking toward me. He has a saw in his hand and mud on his face, and he isn't smiling.

I ask Chuck, "What's the matter?" He says to me, "What do you mean, what's the matter?" I say, "What I mean is you look mad or sad or something, but definitely not happy."

He sighs deeply and says, "I am not happy or unhappy. I just am." Chuck then closes his eyes in a mock trance and lays out his hands, palms up, in Buddhist meditation repose. He stays like that for a minute or so. I hear him tittering to himself as he goes back outside to finish trimming some branches that were left in jagged shards from last night's storm.

"I just am" sticks with me long after Chuck is out the door. I am thinking how my man of few words is usually spot on with his sparse replies, even profound. He really is just as he is, nothing less, nothing more, a blessing when you consider how awful it must be to be married to someone who isn't truly how he seems.

Yes, in this older marriage of mine, I am learning to expect nothing more and nothing less about who my husband is and isn't. Unlike the first decade of marriage, I no longer hold on to the fantasy of who Chuck will someday become. Chuck already is, and will never be someone else. We grate on each other, and it is okay; it sharpens us as individuals. We were the couple Emerson must have imagined when he said of close relationships, "It is better to be a nettle in the side than an echo."

Chuck is walking toward me again, finished with his chore, and I stare hard at the face and form I've seen for nearly a quarter of a century. His hair sits farther back on his forehead; his shoulders are hunched; his gait is shifting to a lumber. Kids and wife and life have weathered this onetime college lacrosse star, and I am caught off guard with an immense love, a protective love, like you love a child.

What hasn't changed since the honeymoon is that Chuck

remains unfailingly self-contained. I will grow old along with this husband who asks little more then to be left the hell alone, and who is relieved to be able to leave me the hell alone. We love and we loathe and we carry on, two people, one couple, four sons, and a rusting red tricycle on our porch waiting to be ridden again by the next generation.

Acknowledgments

FIRST OFF, I'D like to thank Lauren Marino and Bill Shinker, Editorial Director and Publisher of Gotham Books, respectively, who instantly got my book idea, and soon after dispatched me to research, analyze, and vent about long marriages. As my editor, Lauren was brilliant, funny, and incisive, nudging me to "dig deeper" into the raw truth about what sustains intimate relationships. From her prods and advice, I came away with scenarios that were both titillating and prescriptive, an author's dream for her book on how to attain lasting love.

An enormous thank-you to my loyal and loving agent, Gail Ross, for connecting me with Lauren and Bill and with Gotham, an innovative publishing house that felt like home the minute I stepped through its doors. You are a girlfriend and a literary genius, and I am blessed to have you firmly planted alongside me as I pursue the mercurial writer's life. A thank-you also to Howard Yoon, Gail's partner in the Ross Yoon Agency, who offered a wry and sharp male perspective that helped me birth this concept for the book.

Constructing a book requires many levels of masonry, and the mortar these following women provided helped me greatly. My deep appreciation goes to Susan Dalsimer; this marks the fourth book Susan has worked on with me. She is patient and scrupulous and a scholar about women's issues. Thank you also to Anna

Sproul, the Foreign Rights Editor at the Ross Yoon Agency. Single and twenty-five, Anna fed me with a youthful perspective and clippings that enlarged my focus to embrace themes for young women contemplating marriage or crashing from post-honeymoon euphoria.

To John Turco, thank you for letting me retreat to your beachside cottage when I needed the solitude; I got some of my best writing done at your dining room table and some of my best thinking done on the nearby bluff overlooking the Pacific Ocean. I'd also like to thank my wide circle of girlfriends in Annapolis. Your compassion and laughter kept me moving through raising kids and through birthing books: Gail Watkins, Randi Altschuler, Marcy Curland, Jan Flaherty, Max Prevatt, Robin Papadopoulos, Barbara Heussler, Milissa Murray, Maureen Ferraro, Barbara Holch, Missy Attridge, Tammy Beigel, Sonia Feldman, Beth Plavner, Elizabeth Buckman, Ginger Wooldridge, Lee Anderson, Corky Piwoz, Laurie Berman, Patti White, Marina Avram, Fran Catterton, Julie Blamphin, Alex Ngo, and my French *amies*, Moe Hanson, Eileen Cimbolic, and Babette Lashinsky. In our community of rivers and hills near the Chesapeake Bay, this sisterhood sustains me in work and in play.

I am lucky to remain linked to layers of relationships from my childhood in suburban Chicago, and from college. Thank you to these friends who have never left my life, men and women I grew up with who keep me from growing old by indulging me with hilarious stories from our past: Terri Rubin, Debbie Butler, Ellyn Dooley, Simone Gould, Amy Rudnick, Margery Eagan, Sarah Haskell, Cobe Haskell, Jan Miller, John Rasmus, Fran Marshall, Patti Christian, Donna Outlaw, Donna Aikens, and Josette Sheeran. You all look better than you did in your teens, I promise!

To my assistant of more than a decade, Mame Thioune, I offer profound gratitude as well. Mame has been my partner since our children were young, and has given me support and love in running a household in which there is always a friend to offer female camaraderie in a family of one husband, four sons, and two male cats. Mame, you are the best of the best!

My parents are gone, but my sister, Fran, and brother, Greg, are here, and our tight relationship is at the core of who I am. The very vocal pride of my parents was always very important to me as I climbed in my journalism career. Fran and Greg have now taken over as my beloved cheerleaders; I love you both so much, and so do your nephews.

I'm a low-tech journalist who came of age on an IBM Selectric, and I am thrilled to still have on my team high-tech wizard Laura Hollon. Laura has worked with me on all five books, fixing everything from computer and printer freezes to the transcription of tapes. You are a savior!

Cara Bedick, an assistant editor at Gotham, and Jennifer Manguera, literary manager at the Ross Yoon Agency, have also been essential allies in the grueling process of assembling hundreds of pages. Cara, thank you for easing me through track change edits and kindly taking my dozens of phone calls, smoothing out every wrinkle that I faced. Jennifer, you, too, were part of my team of rapid responders, and I could not have navigated this arduous and joyful journey without you. Thank you, thank you for firing away an e-mail or overnight package when I needed a specific nugget of relationship research or a one hundred-page document on long-term marriages.

May I also thank here a handful of wise women and one wise man who shared with me their stories of marital fortitude and commitment that will always be an inspiration: Jim Aldworth, Patty Zimmerman, Jane Howe, Adell Crowe, Bonnie Kyle-Blamphin, Eileen Garbutt, Barbara Sidel, Erin Gay, Ellie Rand, Mervylin Willie-Brausse, and Julia Crowley. I would also like to express my gratitude to filmmakers Mike Flanagan and Courtney Bell, who included me in their "American Marriage" documentary to premiere in 2012. After years of journalistic digging to excavate the history and mysteries of marriage, Mike and Courtney decided to get married themselves, and are now parents of an infant son. They know what I know after my own deep digging on the subject: Despite its flaws, I believe in marriage.

Finally, and most importantly, I'd like to thank my steadfast husband, Chuck Anthony, who makes it possible for me to be a woman and a wife who feels like she has it all—a strong career and a strong family. You gave me the greatest gifts of all, our sons Theodore, Isaac, Jackson, and Zane. They show me each day, in huge and small ways, why working on marriage should be an unrelenting effort, a promise to keep.

And to my late parents, Helene and Theodore Krasnow, wherever you are, a giant thank-you from your second child for staying married. Coming from a home where a mother and father, and a husband and a wife, stuck it out has given me two crucial traits that help me handle relationships *and* handle life—tenacity and optimism. And you thought I'd never settle down!

Finally, I am so grateful for all the generous women who allowed me to air their stories in *The Secret Lives of Wives*. Your startling honesty about husbands and marriages forms the spine and spirit of a book that hopefully will give every reader tenacity and optimism about their own unions.

Bibliography

Ackerman, Diane. *A Natural History of Love*. New York: Vintage Books, 1995.

Brontë, Charlotte. *Jane Eyre*. New York: Signet Classics, 1960.

Eisler, Benita. *O'Keeffe and Stieglitz: An American Romance*. New York: Penguin Books, 1991.

Ephron, Nora. *I Remember Nothing*. New York: Knopf, 2010.

Gottman, John. *The Seven Principles for Making Marriage Work*. New York: Three Rivers Press, 1999.

Greer, Germaine. *The Female Eunuch*. New York: McGraw-Hill, 1971.

Fisher, Helen. *Anatomy of Love*. New York: Fawcett Books, 1992.

Flaubert, Gustave. *Madame Bovary*. New York: W. W. Norton & Company, 2004.

Fromm, Erich. *The Art of Loving*. New York: Harper & Brothers Publishers, 1956.

Jong, Erica. *Fear of Fifty*. New York: HarperCollins, 1994.

———. *What Do Women Want?* New York: Tarcher, 2007.

Krasnow, Iris. *Surrendering to Marriage*. New York: Hyperion, 2001.

Malone, Thomas Patrick, and Patrick Thomas Malone. *The Art of Intimacy*. New York: Prentice Hall, 1987.

Osho. *Love, Freedom, Aloneness: The Koan of Relationships*. New York: St. Martin's, 2001.

Ovid. *The Art of Love and Other Poems.* Cambridge, Mass.: Loeb Classical Library, 1979.

Peale, Mrs. Norman Vincent. *The Adventure of Being a Wife.* New York: Prentice-Hall, 1971.

Tolstoy, Leo. *Anna Karenina.* New York: Modern Library Classics, 2000.

105782